BOOKS BY CHARLES HIGHAM

Theatre and Film

ERROL FLYNN:
The Untold Story
HOLLYWOOD IN THE FORTIES
(with Joel Greenberg)
THE CELLULOID MUSE:
Hollywood Directors Speak
(with Joel Greenberg)
HOLLYWOOD CAMERAMEN
THE FILMS OF ORSON WELLES
HOLLYWOOD AT SUNSET
ZIEGFELD
CECIL B. DeMILLE:
A Biography
THE ART OF THE AMERICAN FILM
AVA
KATE:
The Life of Katharine Hepburn
CHARLES LAUGHTON:
An Intimate Biography
THE ADVENTURES OF CONAN DOYLE:
The Life of the Creator of Sherlock Holmes
MARLENE:
The Life of Marlene Dietrich
CELEBRITY CIRCUS

Poetry

A DISTANT STAR
SPRING AND DEATH
THE EARTHBOUND
NOONDAY COUNTRY
THE VOYAGE TO BRINDISI

Anthologies

THEY CAME TO AUSTRALIA
(with Alan Brissenden)
AUSTRALIANS ABROAD
(with Michael Wilding)
PENGUIN AUSTRALIAN WRITING TODAY

STAR

The Autobiography

HAL WALLIS and CHARLES HIGHAM

with a foreword by KATHARINE HEPBURN

MAKER

of Hal Wallis

MACMILLAN PUBLISHING CO., INC.

New York

Macmillan Publishing Co., Inc.
866 Third Avenue, New York, N.Y. 10022
Collier Macmillan Canada, Ltd.

Library of Congress Cataloging in Publication Data
Wallis, Hal B., 1899–
Starmaker
1. Wallis, Hal B., 1899–   2. Moving-picture
producers and directors—United States—Biography.
I. Higham, Charles, joint author. II. Title.
PN1998.A3W2554   1980   791.43'0233'0924   80–14983
ISBN 0–02–623170–0

Designed by Antler & Baldwin, Inc.
10 9 8 7 6 5 4 3 2 1
Printed in the United States of America

FOREWORD
by Katharine Hepburn

Hal Wallis has been in—and when I say in, I mean IN THE WHIRLING MIDDLE of—the motion picture business since he was a kid in the early 1920s. He got into it when it was a friendly, wild, adventuresome business. Anyone in it was expected certainly to know at least a little bit about everything. Photography —cutting—set dressing—money—personalities—clothes—scripts—excitement—music—tears—laughter—slapstick—selling—buying—creating—making a profit—and not taking a loss.

He caught the pass and zigged and zagged down the field carrying himself and everything he touched to glory. Fleet of action, quick in judgment, happy to take the wildest chance if it just happened to hit him right. Romantic in his love of the business. Never afraid to act on his own hunch about a story or about a person. Ready for any new idea.

Never wedded to the past, although the past for him was made of gold.

A real eye for the different. Never afraid of being wrong. *Does it interest me?* Yes. *Do it! Try it! Why not!* Power—progress—passion —he built himself a career of granite.

He is a delight to know, to work for. No bunk. Of course granite can take you by surprise if you bump into it. But then you can lean on it too and it won't crumple. I bumped into it once. I had done a movie with Hal—*The Rainmaker*. It was a wonderful experience and we all had a wonderful time. He was stimulating and imaginative and fun to work for, and had a capacity for enjoying the experience which was enriching. So he handed me another script. A wonderful script by a brilliant writer.

Oh, yes, I said—great. But I won't do it for the same salary that I got for *Rainmaker*. I want ——————, and I named a figure considerably in excess of what he had given me before.

Silence.

Had he heard me? Yes, he had. Silence.

Well, that was the last I ever heard of that project. The very last I heard. I'd hit the rock. Head on. And it didn't give. Granite doesn't give. An inch.

And he was right. And I was wrong. And I wasn't dumb enough to do that again, you can bet. And of course I secretly had great admiration for his cool. He simply never mentioned it. And never has—although I worked for him again when I did *Rooster Cogburn* with John Wayne.

We're great friends now. Real friends. Thick-and-thin friends. You know, there's something very satisfactory about a stone wall. It supports you. It's dependable. And he does and he is. He's just there. Simple—strong—straight. And that's a good thing to say about a man —especially a Show Man.

HERE'S LOOKING AT YOU, HAL

The letter was characteristically terse, spare, and to the point. There was something Hal Wallis wanted to talk with me about. Would I please contact his office?

Visions of a major script contract floated in my mind. The mention of Hal Wallis conjured up gutsy Warner melodramas of the 1930s, with Bogie and Cagney and Blondell and Glenda Farrell, smoky bars and streets wet with recent rain, gunshots and fedora hats with turned-down brims, sleazy encounters in roadside diners late at night. The name Wallis also made me think of Bette Davis in unbridled women's pictures, Max Steiner's throbbing sub-Brahms melodies accompanying her pop-eyed frenzy as she pumped somebody full of bullets or flung herself recklessly onto a ballroom floor to shock New Orleans society. I remembered the big thirties biographies, with Muni as Pasteur, Zola, Juarez; the somber confrontations of *King's Row*; above all, of course, Bogie and Bergman in *Casablanca*, conducting their tortured love affair in a studio North Africa, while Steiner throbbed away and lines like: "Are those cannons pounding or is it my heart beating?" were spoken. And when no one else dared, Wallis attacked chain gangs, Nazis, the Ku Klux Klan, the Mob.

Warner pictures were always my favorites. Cynical and disillusioned from the first, I could never swallow the saccharine concoctions doled out by MGM with Garson and Pidgeon, chins high and eyes shining, discovering radium, or the sub-Lubitsch high-life comedies of Paramount in the late forties, or Zanuck's pious excursions into religion and mysticism in *The Keys of the Kingdom* and *The Razor's Edge*. Warners told it like it was.

The Warner brothers and Hal Wallis, their resident genius, gave us a view of life that was acrid, unsentimental, witty, and straight from the shoulder. I always felt that one man must have dominated the studio from the first, that the Warner pictures, no matter who directed them, who wrote them, were stamped with the same tough signature. That signature was Hal Wallis's.

So, when he wrote and asked me to come by, I felt like John Garfield or Jeffrey Lynn or Robert Cummings in a Wallis picture, shiny-eyed at the Big Break. I found his office high up in an impersonal building overlooking the arid stretch of Sunset Boulevard. We were in the midst of a Gothic thunderstorm, and I was working on a Gothic subject: the melodrama that was the life of Errol Flynn—a story that rivaled a Wallis movie, with its feverish elements of espionage, manslaughter, late-night confrontations, and sleazy sex.

I found a remarkable man that stormy afternoon. I knew at once I'd been right all along: Wallis *was* the Warner style. He was quite unlike any other executive I had ever met. I had once encountered Selznick, Goldwyn, and Disney all on the same day; they had granted me the last interviews before their deaths. When I told that to MGM bigwig Joe Cohn he ordered me, "Just turn around and leave my house as fast as you can!" Selznick, a bundle of schmaltzy, high-powered clichés; Goldwyn, like a latter-day Pharaoh, screaming at a subordinate through a public address system the size of Grand Central's; and Disney, morbidly self-pitying because brother Roy wouldn't let him be an artist—all were depressing in different ways. Wallis wasn't. He was just as I wanted him to be: hard, disillusioned, witty, and as smart as his pictures were.

We hit it off from first base. I had been a hopeless pupil at school, slept during church services, skipped college at sixteen to work my way on board ship from Britain to Australia, taught myself everything, trusted nobody, and, despite a rather scholarly British look, had steel in my soul. I was a graduate of the Warner, or I should say, the Wallis School of Life. I knew the best way to live was with humor and no bunk. I knew life was a comedy of errors and if you took it too seriously you were finished. I knew you could only succeed by not taking crap from anybody. I knew good writing came from telling a story at a crackerjack pace, with active verbs and slam-bang adjectives, with fun and excitement and love of the whole bloody action of life.

So I wasn't talking to a big producer. I was talking to my teacher, my guru, my rabbi. Even when I learned he had no script in mind for me, I took it on the chin. And then came sequence two. He wanted me to work with him on his memoirs . . .

I saw the critics yowling. HIGHAM TURNS GHOST WRITER. HE'S ALL WASHED UP. The titles leaped out of the newsprint at me the way Don Siegel's montage titles used to do in Wallis melodramas. So what the hell. It would be the pupil relating the master's story in his own words. They could be mine.

And then I knew, as we talked, that it wouldn't be a ghost job at all. Since Wallis was my aesthetic godfather, I would be living another life vicariously, a life that had changed my own. And I could indulge in my favorite pastime—spading through the rich pay dirt of old studio files. The Warner files were available, thousands of them, at USC. I would be in the wild position of telling Wallis, my mentor, two or three things that even he had forgotten.

Thus began the happiest professional association of my life. OK, scream sycophant if you will. Frankly, my dear critics, I don't give a damn. I'm telling it to you straight, buster, Wallis is swell. I never knew a guy that gutsy. Who could cut stories to the bone, slam across a judgment, lethal or kind, or sum up a guy the way he can.

Our minds meshed. And he wasn't like Warner Baxter in *Forty-Second Street,* driving me with a whip. Or like Robinson in *Little Caesar,* strutting about giving orders in a black homburg. Or, thank Yahweh, like Claude Rains in *King's Row,* talking sage aphorisms to a tremulous Robert Cummings with the look of a superannuated screech owl.

No way. Hal Wallis turned out to be patient, polite, measured, calm. Like me, he enjoyed good food, good conversation, paintings; hated parties; enjoyed quietude; and despised lies. He exists without pretense.

Lunches and dinners at his houses in Palm Springs, Trancas Beach, and Holmby Hills, served and cooked exquisitely by his Chinese servants, were experiences even Bette Davis or George Brent in their most luxurious forties movie melos couldn't hope to match. Martha Hyer Wallis would join us: a beautiful, civilized, adorable woman. Garfield, Bogie, Cagney, you never had it so good. And I didn't even have to listen to Max Steiner, very loud, fighting our long and golden discussions of past and present.

OK, Charlie, you're getting soft. Cut the schmaltz and get on with the action. I heard you, Hal. And here it is: the book itself. Lights. Camera. Get it moving. We did it in a year, not a day over schedule and not a dollar over budget. *Shalom.* Enjoy.

CHARLES HIGHAM

CHAPTER 1

The Early Years

I was born in Chicago near the beginning of the century. My parents, both of whom were Jewish, came from Europe in the flood of immigration at that time; Father was Russian and Mother was Polish. We were quite orthodox as a family and went to temple regularly.

Mother was a beautiful woman, one of nature's aristocrats, with chestnut hair, blue eyes, fair skin, and a sweet expression. She was a superb cook, and our simple walk-up apartment was a center for the neighborhood children who wanted to sample her pies. They were in such demand that they became the talk of our part of town.

We had very little money, but Mother managed to feed us well. As a result, my sisters, Minna and Juel, and I grew up strong and healthy children. Unfortunately, Mother did not enjoy good health. She had tuberculosis, and the severe Chicago winters were hard on her. Her family was her whole life; she had no other interests. It was a constant struggle for her to keep us alive.

Father worked as a tailor, but he was a gambler. What little he earned he gambled away. Our furniture was heavily mortgaged, and often it was removed because the payments had not been made.

Those were the days when clothes were hand-stitched, and a sewing machine was the ultimate luxury. Father's life was that of the sweatshop, and he wasn't a happy man. He loved us children, but he seemed distant and preoccupied. After he was promoted to manager of alterations in the tailoring department of Gimbel Brothers, we enjoyed better times, but he still couldn't resist gambling away his earnings.

We lived in cold-water flats in run-down neighborhoods in Chicago and, for a time, in Milwaukee. By 1917, just before America entered the war, we lived on Thirteenth Street and Independence Boulevard in Chicago in a building with twenty-four other tenants. In the winter we did not have adequate heating and huddled around the stove to keep warm. In the long, humid summer months we slept out on the steps at night.

As I grew older, lack of privacy became a problem. Because our apartment was too small, I did not have a room to myself and had to sleep on the living-room couch.

My sisters ribbed me a lot. I was the only boy, the youngest, and they teased me quite unmercifully, though in good spirits.

I was, of course, my mother's favorite.

The best part of my life then was the life of the street with my young and growing male friends. We formed lasting friendships. One of those friends, Al Cohn, calls every birthday to congratulate me. He founded the Universal Battery Company in Chicago, and is now living comfortably in retirement in Arizona.

Most of us did well in business. Young Katz, who lived upstairs, became half of the famous theater team, Balaban and Katz. Other friends were Jack Saper, Mike Rosenberg, Ben Liss, Jack Arvey, and Hy Feldman.

I was tough and able to hold my own in street fights. We quarreled and fought the way kids do, but I didn't come out too badly. Though I was never very athletic, I played softball and enjoyed it.

When my father sent me to the neighborhood saloon for beer, I would stand outside until someone offered to take my bucket in and fill it for me. One time I went in myself. On the counter was a hole in which patrons put cigars to have the ends sliced off by pressure. I was very curious, put my finger in, and sliced off the end of it. The pain was nothing compared with the punishment inflicted on my bottom when I got home.

I started kindergarten at the age of six, graduated from McClaren Grammar School, and then went to McKinley High for one year. At the end of that year I had to go to work. The family was destitute, and there was no way for me to continue my studies.

I was fourteen years old.

At this time Father left us, and never came back. Years later, we heard he had died in Canada. After the shock of his departure, Mother realized it was for the best; we settled down to a lifetime without him.

Times were hard: even my sisters had to work. Minna, who was to become one of the most powerful agents in Hollywood, never went to high school. She got a job as a clerk in a department store. So did Juel.

I became an office boy for Cobe and McKinnon, a large real estate company in the First National Bank Building on Dearborn and Monroe streets in downtown Chicago. I answered an ad in the paper and got the job, for which I earned five dollars a week. The work was dull, but it helped pay the rent. I was a "go-for": I ran errands, filled the water coolers, picked up the mail, and delivered it. At fifteen, I would rather have been doing other things, but I had no alternative—I had to earn.

My days began at six o'clock in the morning. Mother cooked breakfast and packed a box lunch for me; I got to work about eight on a streetcar often stuck in heavy, winter snows. The people at work were impersonal but not unkind. Somebody had done my job before me and someone else would do it just as well after I left. The work meant nothing.

Every week I gave Mother my wages. That twenty dollars meant a great deal to her—to all of us. She, in turn, gave me an allowance so that I could go out with my friends.

We went to various South Side jazz places known as the Black 'n' Tans. We heard the young Louis Armstrong and Earl Hines, and sometimes strolled along Douglas Boulevard and stopped for an ice cream soda with neighborhood girls.

I started dating when I was seventeen, but there could be no real question of romance. I was too young and the responsibility to my family was too great for me to become seriously involved.

On rare occasions friends and I went to the College Inn at the Sherman Hotel. Ben Bernie, the bandleader and violinist, appeared there, and he was great. Sometimes we went to fights, sometimes to the biographs to see the simple movies of the time. I hadn't the beginnings of an idea that one day I'd go into the motion picture industry.

Real entertainment meant vaudeville, the delight of seeing Sophie Tucker, Eddie Foy, and W. C. Fields on the Orpheum circuit. These entertainers were magical, and whenever I could, I went to see them again and again. I worked as an usher without compensation just to get in; I saw the plays that came to Chicago the same way.

We boys went to nightclubs owned by Al Capone, Machine Gun

Jack McGurn, and other gangsters, completely oblivious to the fact that they were the hangouts of criminals. They were in basements, full of smoke, noise, girls, and cabaret routines. We had beer at a nickel a glass, propped up the bar, and watched the entertainment.

Finally, I got a better job. I went to work for a streetcar company on the Near North Side. My salary shot up to a magnificent twelve dollars a week, and I had a courtesy card that enabled me to ride free, a great blessing. I have to admit I foresaw the blessing when I applied for the job.

Later I stepped farther up in the world: I answered an ad for and was given a position as a clerk at the Hughes Electrical Heating Company, which manufactured electric ranges and bake ovens.

The vice-president, a man named Vaughn, advised me to take up stenography if I wanted to get ahead. I did. Putting in sixteen-hour days, I worked in the daytime and attended Gregg Stenographic School at night. Because there was no time to go home between work and school, I ate baked bean dinners at Pixley and Ehlers, or soup at the Automat. It was very hard, but I learned shorthand and typing and graduated as a secretary.

George Hughes, founder of the organization, was very kind to me, as was Walter Fagan, the general sales manager. When Hughes Electrical Heating merged with the mammoth Edison General Electric Company, they sent me out on the road to represent them in four midwestern states: Iowa, Nebraska, Missouri, and Kansas, with headquarters in Omaha.

I will never forget my first trip away from home. I was seventeen at the time and left Chicago in the dead of winter. Walter Fagan drove my mother and sisters to the railroad station to see me off to the wilds of Nebraska. Mother was coughing and ill, and I was determined to make enough money to move her to California.

I arrived in Omaha in a blinding snowstorm. It was five degrees below zero when I got off the train and took a streetcar to the Castle Hotel. My room faced an alley, and I was so homesick I wanted to get the hell out and run all the way back to Chicago.

But I had to go on. And I did.

It was a lonely life, traveling by train through the severe cold of the Midwest. Because I couldn't afford a sleeper, I slept sitting up in the day coach. When there were no passenger trains, I rode in the caboose of freight trains.

4

Hotels were cheap and not too pleasant. I had no friends, my only companions being Horatio Alger stories in early paperbound editions. They nurtured my dreams of fame and fortune.

When I arrived in a town, I contacted dealers interested in buying electrical equipment and talked to the local power and light companies. My job was to persuade them to buy demonstration models with which to introduce electric cooking and heating into the community. I also demonstrated models to domestic science classes in high schools and usually sold twelve to twenty electric hot plates at each school.

I was earning about fifty dollars a week, which was good money in those days, and the company picked up my hotel expenses. One of my favorite hotels was the Harvey House in Hutchinson, Kansas, a rare treat.

After a year on the road I was still homesick, but I was doing fine, and was considered an up-and-coming young salesman. Yet, far from being financially secure, I had only two suits—which I wore on alternate days—and, while traveling, washed my own shirts and underwear.

Eventually I sold so well that the company brought me back to Chicago and made me assistant to the sales manager. It was good to be home again.

Then doctors put my mother into a tuberculosis sanitarium in Naperville, Illinois. Minna, Juel, and I visited her every Sunday: we left the house early in the morning and got home about midnight. The railroad station was a mile and a half from the sanitarium, and we walked both ways. Saving every nickel was important to us. In winter we walked in the snow, unless someone gave us a ride.

We were able to pay for Mother's treatment there for a year, but when doctors advised us that a move to a warmer climate might save her life, the decision was made for us. In 1920 we moved to California.

Minna went west to pave the way for the family, and I was able to transfer from Chicago to company headquarters in Ontario, with southern California as my territory. I covered it in a Model T Ford, from mid-California to the Mexican border.

In those days Palm Canyon Drive in Palm Springs was a two-lane dirt pathway. Dips in it were filled in and covered with planks, so it was called Plank Road. The town was little more than an oasis, and the place to stay was Nellie Coffman's Desert Inn. It was, in fact, the *only* place to stay. Outside of a gas station and the Desert Inn, Palm Springs was desert land. Half of what is the city today could have been bought for a few thousand dollars.

It was wonderful to see sunshine, palm trees, and clean streets after dark and damp Chicago. Mother felt better: she loved California. We all did.

Minna got a job as secretary to a man named Edward Loeb, member of a law firm representing Warner Bros., a newly formed motion picture company from the East Coast. She was very good at her job, and Jack Warner was so impressed with her that he asked her to work for him. That was the beginning of our lives in Hollywood. When Jack became head of Warner Bros., Minna was his right hand and very much a power at the studio, in charge of casting and of many aspects of Jack's work.

Juel, my other sister, got a good job in the office of a large chain of shoe stores.

We had an apartment in a pleasant four-flat building on Western Avenue not far from Warner Bros. Studios at Sunset and Bronson. It was quite nice and certainly more comfortable than what we had known in Chicago.

What we didn't know was that the very well-known Madame Frances was operating a bordello in the same building—a very fancy bordello. One day Minna saw a studio executive in the hall and asked what he was doing there. He laughed and asked, "Well, don't you know who lives here?" We moved soon afterward.

When a man named Gumbiner, who owned several theaters in Los Angeles, asked Minna to help him find someone to manage the Garrick at Eighth and Broadway, she recommended me. She knew I was ambitious and did not intend to work for an electric company the rest of my life. Gumbiner interviewed me and we liked each other very much.

I knew nothing whatsoever about running a theater, and I knew nothing about movies either. I liked them—saw every one made—but I don't know why he thought I'd be good for the job. He took a chance on me. He was that kind of man.

The Garrick Theatre was a small operation; the entire staff was made up of an organist, an usher, a cashier, and myself. I booked the films at the exchanges on Olive Street, and screened and lined up enough pictures to change our program two or three times a week. If one did well at the box office, we held it over an extra day and made a bold announcement to that effect. We booked the pictures we wanted. We weren't tied to a studio and were not governed by the block-booking system that forced other theaters to take films they didn't want.

At night I changed the lobby cards and still photographs, and mounted eight-by-ten glossies on cardboard to set up in frames. I wrote all the publicity for the newspapers, opened and closed the theater, and kept a sharp eye on the customers. Often, I even acted as cashier at the box office. We did moderately well, most of the pictures we ran having played out their commercial life in first-run theaters.

In those days, movies were shown all day, so I was busy from morning until late at night. I seldom got home until midnight, never had a free evening, and had no social life at all.

Lacking any enthusiasm for the job, I did it chiefly for my mother and my sisters. It was lonesome work, and I missed my friends in Chicago. As a salesman I had met interesting people in every walk of life, but I found theater management drab and flat.

The family could see I was bored. Minna knew I didn't like what I was doing, and engineered an introduction to Sam Warner.

Sam Warner was perhaps the most brilliant of the brothers. A marvelous man in every way, his genius produced talkies. It was a tragedy that he did not live to see the innovation he pioneered make film history. Sam interviewed me at the studio on Sunset Boulevard and Bronson for the job of assistant publicity director. He explained that Warner Bros. was a dynamic organization—expanding rapidly. They wanted bright young men fast on their feet. I was hired.

Charley Kurtzman, an aggressive New York type, was publicity director. He wasn't happy with the job, and would be leaving it soon. There were only three of us in the entire department: Kurtzman, myself, and a secretary.

Since my salary was so small, Jack told me I could supplement my income by handling a few outside publicity accounts. I did some work for Dorothy Farnum, a writer, but Harry Warner heard about it and promptly fired me. When I tried to explain to him that Jack had given me permission, he would not listen.

Just as promptly I was hired by Sol Lesser for considerably more money. He was making a series of pictures based on the stories of

Harold Bell Wright, and I became publicity director for Lesser on *The Mine with the Iron Door*.

Ten months after I was fired, Jack asked me to come back to Warners at twice my previous salary. When Kurtzman left a few months later to handle publicity for a chain of theaters in Boston, I found myself in charge of the department.

At the age of twenty, I was publicity director of Warner Bros.!

CHAPTER 2

At Warner Bros.

The formative years of Warner Bros. were very exciting. Changes were taking place in the offices and on the stages—and in me. Hollywood was growing and I was growing with it.

I took great pleasure in what I was doing; I liked my job very much. Without any great ambition to make a name for myself in the industry, I just wanted to become financially independent so that my mother could live in comfort. I remembered the poverty of my childhood, and I never wanted to be poor again.

After Mother's health had much improved, she wanted to be active, so we borrowed money and opened a restaurant for her on Hollywood Boulevard. She did the cooking and served counter lunches to the movie crowd. Charlie Chaplin, George O'Brien, and Valentino could often be seen there at high noon, enjoying a hamburger between scenes. Unfortunately, too many of them signed checks to be paid later, and Mother was too generous. She insisted on using the finest ingredients and charged too little for her food. This kindhearted naïveté cost her the business. After sinking more money into it, we finally gave it up.

Minna continued to work in the industry with me. Juel did not, except for an occasional bit part in pictures. She eventually married a struggling writer named Wally Kline, but the marriage failed. Juel didn't have the kind of life I thought she should have had. She was a joyous, outgoing person; everybody loved her. She died of cancer much too young.

At that time the Warners organization was a tightly knit group. Bennie Zeidman was in charge of production under Jack Warner, Bill Koenig was production manager, Darryl Zanuck was principal writer, and I was publicity director. Because of the closeness of this group, I participated in planning the studio's program: filming the pictures, editing, distributing—all the phases of production. The experience was invaluable.

The financial man of the organization, Harry Warner, was kept busy meeting the weekly payroll. Another brother, Albert, was in charge of sales. Headquartered in New York, they were seldom seen on the Coast.

As publicity director, my job involved making up a press book on each picture. The press book contained stills from the film, informal on-the-set shots of stars (which I personally supervised), posters, an outline of the plot, and biographies of the players. I was also responsible for making the trailers that announced forthcoming productions I wrote the scripts for the trailers and supervised their editing. I worked out the sales approach. Arranging interviews and writing stories that could be planted in the columns was also my responsibility. Fred Applegate, a pleasant, easygoing man, was my assistant.

This was before the days of the gossip column, when stories were simple, bland, and devoid of scandal. The public worshiped the stars, loving them as though they were personal friends. They wanted to hear about their lavish homes, luxurious gardens, parties, automobiles, and clothes. Millions of people who lived frustrating lives could fantasize that they were sharing the existences of their favorite stars: Anna Q. Nilsson, Lenore Ulric, Carmel Myers, Irene Rich, Monte Blue, Florence Vidor, and Marie Prevost.

Seldom were these stars temperamental or difficult. Rather, they were pleasant, fairly unpretentious people who enjoyed tennis, golf, riding (you could still ride through Beverly Hills in those days), and swimming in their own oversized pools.

I took well-known journalists to stars' homes for photographs and light conversation, all done on a social level. Reporters were not vicious then, but were thrilled to meet the stars. Fan magazines were all powerful, led by *Photoplay*. The leading star reporter of the time was Adela Rogers St. Johns. It was a tremendous coup to have Miss St. Johns interview a star: she was a major personality in her own right and could make or break a newcomer.

Another of my jobs was going to Pasadena to meet important performers arriving by train from New York. I had red carpets laid for them to walk on, chauffeured limousines to meet them, and a very large press contingent on hand to record the event. We rented great mansions for our stars, and photographed them in opulent surround-ings. The public was insatiable in its desire to know every detail of their lavish life-styles.

The leading star at Warners was not a human being, but a dog, Rin Tin Tin. We featured him in stories in which he aided the hero and heroine. Unfortunately, he was not heroic in person; he was very bad tempered, and, democratically, bit both stars and extras. (Actually, there were several Rin Tin Tins. He had stand-ins who had stand-ins to double many of the stunts.)

My job was to make the dog star internationally famous, and also to hide his true nature. His trainer, Lee Duncan, was a genial man who was a great help to me in devising publicity for the animal. He had found Rin Tin Tin as a puppy on the Western Front in World War I, left behind by the Germans when they abandoned a dugout. The name *Rin Tin Tin* was the nickname airmen of the time gave the lucky yarn-dolls that hung over their cockpits.

Rin Tin Tin first made his name at a dog show at the Hotel Ambassador in Los Angeles. His picture was in the *Los Angeles Times,* and Jack Warner signed him to a contract. I took him on a sixteen-week tour across the country. Almost human, he was able to pick up a coin with his nose and put it in a cup, jump up and down on a stool, and count up to ten with his paws. I publicized his reper-toire of tricks and even arranged for a biography to be published. Lee Duncan and Rinty, as the dog was known, went to countless hos-pitals and sanitariums, cheering up patients. Duncan even taught him to bark in ragtime—a very popular feat.

Darryl Zanuck got his start writing stories for Rin Tin Tin. He sold Jack Warner the idea of a picture called *Find Your Man* by get-ting down on all fours, scratching, snarling, and running up and down in his self-appointed role as Rinty. Jack laughed so much that he hired him on the spot.

Find Your Man was shot in Klamath Falls, Oregon, in the pine forests near an Indian reservation. I took a team of journalists there by train to watch Rin Tin Tin in action. In his big scene, the dog was shown trying to deliver a note to a judge at the height of a trial. Blocked at the door of the courthouse by a sheriff, Rinty clambered up the roof, slithered down a chimney, ran through the courtroom and delivered his message. In another picture Rin Tin Tin made a similar journey disguised in a beard.

I issued thousands of Rin Tin Tin badges to be worn by young boys. When I announced that he was receiving twelve thousand fan letters a week, it was no exaggeration. A tie-in with Ken-L-Ration Dog Biscuits put his face on their boxes. When radio was born in 1925, he barked a message to his fans from the Warner Bros. radio station, KWBC, later changed to KFWB.

A star on one Rin Tin Tin picture, *The Lighthouse by the Sea*, was a beautiful and sweet-natured actress named Louise Fazenda. She played the daughter of a blind lighthouse keeper who hides her father's infirmity by running the lighthouse herself. Louise was regarded as the "Queen of Comedy" at Warners in those days and occupied star status on the lot. Working together, we became very good friends, and eventually I had the temerity to ask her out for a date. She agreed, and we went to a Chinese restaurant for dinner and then to a movie. A car buff, she had one of the first of the limited number of twelve-cylinder Cadillacs made at that time. On weekends we took long drives into the country for picnic lunches.

An outgoing, warm, friendly person, Louise was extremely kind and charitable, often anonymously helping people in need. Everyone loved her, including me.

Her parents were elderly. Her father had retired when we started courting—as was the pleasant term in those far-off days. I got on with them fairly well, but we didn't really warm up to each other. I don't think her mother approved of me. Louise was a very successful motion picture star and I was a struggling young publicist. They made me well aware of the disparity in our incomes, and life was awkward for a time.

Irene Rich—one of the leading stars on the Warner lot, a great beauty, and a friend of mine to this day—was very close to Louise. She warned her, "I think you're making a big mistake. This boy isn't making enough money. You're rich, you're living well, you like Cadillacs. . . . Hal will never amount to anything. Give him up!"

Fortunately, Louise didn't take her advice. She saw possibilities in my future. We went together for about a year and were married at her home, a duplex on Ninth and Detroit. Her mother came to the wedding despite her doubts. (Her father had died a few months earlier.) A judge married us. My mother and sisters were present, and it was a quiet, lovely wedding.

We lived happily in Louise's house. I couldn't have provided a home as nice as the one she was used to, and neither of us felt any discomfort in the situation. If we were criticized for this arrangement, I'm sure it made no impression on us: we were too fond of each other to care.

Every morning I drove from the house on Ninth Street to the studios at Sunset and Bronson. I drove a second-hand Packard as soon as I was able to afford it.

Los Angeles in the twenties was a much more attractive city than it is today. The streets were lined with shade trees, and you could smell orange blossoms and ocean breezes. Hollywood was a nice little village, clean and sparkling and sunny, and the word "smog" was unknown. People were neighborly; if somebody was sick, their friends dropped in with gifts of fruit or flowers or cups of soup. People left their doors open at night in the hot weather. They went to church or synagogue in large numbers. Even though Hollywood Boulevard had some new office buildings, there were still a great many private residences, only two of which exist today. When automobiles drove off the side streets, they kicked up dust, and children played in the water released from the fire hydrants on summer mornings. There were very few police about, and of course no freeways until many years later. Some of the grocery stores still had windup telephones.

We were healthy people in the golden, unpolluted sunshine of the time. The future looked very bright.

Most of us in the picture business were in our twenties; people often forget today how young we were. Jack Warner was running the studio at the age of twenty-three. I was head of publicity and later head of First National before I was thirty. Most of the stars were under twenty-five.

Everyone played tennis or golf. There were lots of swimming pools at the homes of friends, and in those days, you dropped by whenever you felt like it for an informal dip. Sometimes we went riding in the San Fernando Valley or even in parts of Beverly Hills. Where the great homes are today in Bel Air, there were rolling alfalfa fields with oak trees and horse corrals and little farms. When Westerns were shot out at the Ince ranch at the beach, the crew and lesser cast arrived by red trolley car from downtown. They were met by a horse-drawn tallyho, which rolled and rattled along the beachfront to the ranch.

My office at Warners-Sunset was on the first floor of the big white building immediately to the left of the main entrance.

I saw Jack Warner constantly. Dressed in natty suits or yachting blazers with highly polished patent leather shoes, he always sported a big smile; he had a remarkable set of flashing white teeth. Jack was a dynamo. Nervous, restless, he couldn't sit still a minute. He was like a jumping bean, endlessly interested in everything that was going on. He wanted to be in on every publicity campaign I devised, and often made outrageous suggestions he knew I couldn't carry out. He liked nothing better than telling very bad jokes in a loud voice. I did my best to be a good audience.

At Radio KFWB, which opened in the mid-1920s, Jack was master of ceremonies. He made sure that everybody under contract was presented on the air. The first performer was Leon Zuardo, the famous baritone who sang (slightly out of tune) "When the Red Red Robin Comes Bob Bob Bobbin' Along," a performance followed by deafening applause. I don't think anybody out there knew that Leon Zuardo was none other than Jack Warner, and that the applause came from members of the Warner staff who valued their jobs.

I tolerated all this as best I could. Actually, I was fond of Jack. He was very good to me. He gave me my break, and he was a great administrator. A very skillful man in his dealings with the stars, he straightened out any actor or actress who refused a part or misbehaved. He understood them, knew how to feed their egos.

Jack was a showman who played his hunches. I never saw him read a script, let alone a book. Just from glancing at a title or riffling through a few pages, he could sense whether a property would interest millions of people all over the world. He was usually right.

When we were considering the very large, indeed loaf-sized bestseller, *Anthony Adverse*, for which the author's agents wanted a great deal of money, I felt he should break his usual rule and read the book. I sent it to him with a note of recommendation. After two days had passed, I asked him if he had read it. He said, "Not only haven't I read it, I can't even lift it!" But he bought it just the same.

He had an instinct for casting, too. When an actor turned down a part, he could replace him without an instant's hesitation with someone better suited to the role.

Although he couldn't edit a script, Jack had good ideas for cutting scenes in the editing room. He telephoned me every morning from the toilet, a custom that never varied. When I heard him ask "What's doing?" in that familiar brisk, hard-bitten voice, I knew he was on the Throne, and wanted to know everything that was going on. Our conversation was often terminated by a loud flushing sound. One of his favorite expressions was "Uneasy lies the head that wears a toilet seat." And whenever he read a bad review, he would say, "Don't worry about it: today's newspaper is tomorrow's toilet paper."

My work at the studio continued to be pleasant. Rin Tin Tin's publicity was only part of it. Warners' production schedule increased in the 1920s.

Our leading director was Ernst Lubitsch. He was an authentic genius—rotund, with slicked-down black hair and sharp black eyes. He was never without a cigar in his mouth, and walked with his hands behind his back like a little Napoleon. He made his first success in Europe working for Max Reinhardt—historical pictures like *Madame DuBarry* with Pola Negri, and *Anne Boleyn* with Emil Jannings. Mary Pickford hired him and his assistant, Heinz (later known as Henry) Blanke, to come to Hollywood.

Lubitsch directed a picture with Mary entitled *Rosita,* but was not happy. When Harry Warner heard about it, he decided to sign him and sent Irene Rich to Lubitsch's house. Irene, a great Warners star, rang the doorbell. Lubitsch looked out and was enchanted. Irene said, "Harry Warner is coming in a few minutes to talk to you about an offer." Lubitsch was so captivated by Irene that when Harry arrived, he signed a long-term contract with Warners.

Sometimes Lubitsch stopped shooting in the middle of the afternoon and served coffee to the cast. Jack Warner came down on one occasion and complained. Lubitsch simply invited him to stay for coffee.

He always stopped work at five o'clock, and encouraged his cast to take life easy in the evenings. He felt they would be more relaxed the next day.

When Lubitsch was directing *Lady Windermere's Fan,* from the Oscar Wilde play, Jack Warner told him the horses were running in the wrong direction in a racetrack scene. Lubitsch reminded him that it was a British story; the horses run in the opposite direction there.

Lubitsch became a celebrity in his own right, and I made sure he got lots of publicity. Cooperative with the press, he loved to talk, and his stories were always funny. He gave many radio interviews and appeared at premieres often. It was a pleasure working with him.

In 1926 we opened our new Warner Theatre at Hollywood Boulevard and Wilcox Avenue. Sid Grauman, whose famous Grauman's Chinese Theatre is still a landmark in Hollywood, was very jealous. As our financial backer, Motley Flint of the Security Bank, broke ground with a golden spade, a large black hearse rolled up. A man in mourning got out and carried a sign over to Flint reading, "SUCCESS TO WARNER BROS. SID GRAUMAN." Later that day, Jack sent for a dummy and dressed it up as Grauman, burying it publicly in a plot with a sign reading, "HERE LIES SID GRAUMAN. YOUR HAIR WILL WAVE NO MORE."

While Harry was scouring Europe for talent, and Jack was being funny and running the studio in Hollywood, Sam Warner, my favorite of the brothers, fell head over heels in love. At a party at Victor Watson's (publisher of the *New York Journal-American*), he met a beautiful Follies girl named Lina Basquette and soon after proposed to her. He was a very happy man—but, sad to say, not a well one.

When talking pictures became a burning obsession with him, everyone thought he was crazy. In 1925 Major Nathan Levinson of Western Electric demonstrated talking pictures to Sam. The film showed a man walking to a table, removing a straw hat, placing it on a table, unbuttoning white kid gloves, and putting the gloves in the hat. He spoke a few words, starting with "Good evening." Then he sang to violin and piano accompaniment. The film had been matched to a large, slowly turning disk. Sam was very excited, but Harry, Albert, and Jack were not. They didn't see much future in talkies.

Sam finally talked Harry into looking at a new musical short with sound. Harry liked it and talked to his friend and financier, Waddill Catchings of Goldman, Sachs. Catchings underwrote the four-million-dollar note issue that made it possible to proceed. Western Electric gave us an exclusive license to use Vitaphone, the device that made pictures talk.

I was responsible for issuing the first publicity on Vitaphone. On April 26, 1925, I sent out a release to every newspaper, magazine, and radio station in the country, which read: "Warners will enter a policy of talking pictures. Our researchers show that this is practical and will bring to audiences in every corner of the world the music of the greatest symphony orchestras and the voices of the most popular stars of the operatic, vaudeville, and theatrical fields." A year later, I issued another statement that we would be launching a series of "movie grand opera excerpts which would bring 'The Met to Main Street.' "

In New York, Sam was busy making short subjects with opera stars to demonstrate the new technique. He shot at the old Manhattan Opera House, where the slightest sound—pigeons fluttering on the roof, the rumble of the subway, the sound of distant traffic—jolted the equipment and necessitated a complete revision of the work.

The shorts were sent out to the Coast, and we decided to hit the public with them all at once instead of releasing them individually. We realized the appeal they would have for millions of people in remote areas who had never seen an opera or heard the great stars of the musical stage. In spite of its being the jazz era, there was an avid public waiting for just such entertainment. The group of shorts was shown, as is well known, with our premiere release of John Barrymore in *Don Juan*. The presentation was an instantaneous success.

I traveled to New York to coordinate the promotional campaign with our New York office, and we spent a fortune on advertising. Our opera stars went on radio to discuss bringing art to the cinema—possibly the first talk shows. We tied in with soap companies and automobile manufacturers to present musical medleys with the same performers. Busy day and night on the campaign, lucky to get six hours sleep, I was fired up, as we all were, with the new invention and its possibilities.

Most people in Hollywood thought we were crazy. One who didn't was that fierce competitor William Fox, head of Fox Film Corporation. He and his lieutenant, former police reporter Winfield Sheehan, decided to take us on by printing sound on film while we were still struggling with the more laborious method of sound on disk. Fox made a big splash at the Roxy Theatre in New York with a film of Lindbergh's takeoff from Roosevelt Field. The public cheered when they heard Lindy's voice and the roar of his engine.

But we were way ahead of the game. We had *The Jazz Singer* in production, starring Al Jolson, the greatest entertainer of his day.

Jolie was an amazing man. People said he was cold and heartless beneath the schmaltz of his performances. I knew better. As publicist for *The Jazz Singer,* I had to spend hours with him on interviews. He was a true professional—tireless, considerate to a young man like myself, never temperamental or difficult, totally obsessed with work.

Matching his voice and lip movements was an ordeal. The cameras were in booths so airless the cameramen and their assistants frequently passed out. The work was slow and demanding. There was no air conditioning and little ventilation on sound stages in those days. If a plane flew over or a car horn sounded, whole scenes had to be redone. But I never once heard Jolie complain. He would give a number everything he had—belt it out on his knees, hands working, eyes popping—and then be told by the director, Alan Crosland, that it would have to be repeated. He would get up, unable to wipe his face because of the black makeup, and plunge back into the number as if nothing had happened.

It was exciting to be in charge of the advertising and promotion of this revolutionary picture. But I knew the gamble the Warners were taking. I knew the coffers were dangerously low, and that the loan from Goldman, Sachs, involved putting up their personal property as collateral.

If it hadn't been for Motley Flint, our kind and generous supporter, I doubt if Warners could have survived that difficult period. But we were convinced we would make it. Once more, we spent every cent we could afford on the publicity campaign. I don't think any of us doubted for a moment that the public would love *The Jazz Singer* and that a new era in movies would be born with it.

Sam, happy with his beautiful wife and young daughter, seemed to have the world at his feet. But his health finally failed under the desperate strain of preparing for the premiere. Like that other genius, Irving Thalberg, Sam never took the time to exercise or eat properly. He collapsed three days before the premiere of *The Jazz Singer*. His young heart simply stopped: it was as worn out as an old watch. We had no alternative but to proceed with the opening. We knew Sam would have wanted it that way.

After the first number, the audience sprang to its feet and cheered. Every successive number got a standing ovation, and when Jolie came out on the stage and repeated the hit songs in person, you could hear the crowd roar down several city blocks.

The New York and Los Angeles openings convinced us, as nothing else could, that the gamble had paid off. The future was ours —and we were all under thirty years old.

CHAPTER 3

The Talkie Era

So great was the rush into talkies that one studio wasn't enough for the Warner brothers. Looking for larger fields to conquer, they snapped up First National, a beautiful new studio in Burbank.

The original Warner studio was still located on Sunset Boulevard in Hollywood. The government forbade the merging of physical plants, requiring that the two companies operate separately for a period of years. Now that the Warner brothers controlled First National, they wanted their own man there to oversee operations. I was made studio production manager at First National in Burbank. I was overjoyed, as was Louise, and I will always be grateful to Jack Warner for giving me this step up. I did my best to please him.

When I moved to First National, Colleen Moore, Corinne Griffith, and Colleen's husband, producer John McCormick, were the biggest figures. I liked Colleen enormously: she was vital, adorable, and full of fun. But McCormick was difficult, insisting upon using lavish sets and costumes, and scripts heavy with the Victorian sentiment of the previous decade. I wanted to stop making these perfumed melodramas and film modern, up-to-date stories with which Americans could identify. McCormick and producer Walter Morosco resented this, but Jack Warner sided with me. The old regime was overthrown, and I succeeded Al Rockett.

Warners now had two functioning production organizations: one at Sunset under Darryl Zanuck, and one in Burbank under my supervision. There was friendly rivalry between the two studios; First National was in second place, but determined not to stay there.

We operated independently. Darryl never saw my rushes or my

completed pictures until they were cut, scored, dubbed, and ready for the theaters—nor I his.

Because of the shortage of equipment, First National couldn't make sound pictures at the same time the Sunset studio was shooting them. So we shot all night, hooking up to the recording equipment at Sunset studios by telephone line. Warners would finshing shooting at 6:00, and we would begin shooting at Burbank at 7:00, working until early morning. Our first sound pictures at First National were made in this manner, while technicians were busy installing our own sound system. We had no complaints from crews, actors, or directors. All of them felt they were making motion picture history—and they were.

Hoping for a success like *The Jazz Singer,* we decided to make musicals at First National. We imported the famous Otis Skinner from New York and filmed his elaborate stage show *Kismet,* an Arabian Nights fantasy full of dancing girls, wicked sultans, and handsome young princes. This expensive epic failed to make the impression on movie audiences it made on theater crowds, but the picture did introduce the sweet and beautiful Loretta Young, who has remained a star and friend to this day.

We were more successful with *Sunny,* starring Marilyn Miller, the beautiful blond mistress of Flo Ziegfeld who immortalized the song "Look for the Silver Lining" in *Sally.* She was a reckless girl who once stowed away on an ocean liner because she couldn't bear to leave her Latin lover, Don Alvarado. She so charmed the captain that he took her all the way to France free of charge.

When she arrived in Pasadena, she would not get off the train until we sent a Rolls-Royce to meet her. She insisted on a new wardrobe, including a chinchilla coat, which cost thousands even in those days. Her dressing room had to be completely remodeled with paneled walls, French antiques, and a sunken bathtub fit for Cleopatra.

Marilyn was extremely spoiled and grumbled about having to work nights because it ruined her social life. Jack Warner was fascinated. (Oddly enough, he later married Don Alvarado's wife, Ann.) They had an affair, and quite often Miss Miller proved hard to find because of it.

We had a problem with her voice. On stage, her personal magnetism blinded audiences to her lack of talent. She actually had a very thin voice, and we understood immediately why she had never made a recording. Her contract specified that nobody must dub her.

The sound department did everything but stand on its head to make her sound vocally exciting, but it didn't work. The magic she had on stage, that indefinable charm that made up for her tiny voice and moderate acting talent, utterly vanished on camera.

The next picture in her contract was *Her Majesty, Love,* in which she appeared with W. C. Fields. He drove her crazy by goosing her off camera just before going into dramatic scenes. She jumped and spewed obscenities, surprising from the mouth of so delicate a creature. In one scene Fields infuriated director William Dieterle by improvising bits of business. He threw dishes against the wall and upset the salt and pepper shakers into Marilyn's hair. She stormed off the set. Soon after, her affair with Jack Warner broke up and she went back to New York, telling everyone Hollywood "stank."

Marilyn didn't live long. Because there were no antibiotics in those days, she died of blood poisoning from a gum infection.

William Dieterle was one of my favorite directors. An early talking picture I am still proud of is Dieterle's *The Last Flight.* It starred Richard Barthelmess, one of the few silent stars to survive the transition to sound.

Barthelmess was a nervous, withdrawn man without the virility the public expected in its heroes. But he was a thinking actor who "lived" his scenes and played them with great sincerity and depth of feeling. Because of his fine qualities as an actor and a human being, the public responded to him, and I used him again and again. We were very friendly, and remained so even after his career faded.

The Last Flight was the story of World War I fliers (members of the Lafayette Escadrille) who couldn't adjust to the postwar era. They were healthy young Americans, longing for action, unable to relate to the dullness of ordinary life. They were the lost generation, driven to drink, some to suicide.

The author of the story was a very interesting man named John Monk Saunders, who later married Fay Wray. A handsome ex-flier, young, successful, and a fine writer in the Scott Fitzgerald mold, Saunders, like the people he wrote about, was never completely at ease in civilian life. I was shocked, but truly not surprised, when he hanged himself after years of heavy drinking. He was a brilliant but very unhappy man.

Dawn Patrol, which we made before we made *The Last Flight,* is much better remembered. Barthelmess and the young, dashing Douglas Fairbanks, Jr., were ideally cast as fliers risking their lives in

World War I. I hired Howard Hawks to direct *Dawn Patrol,* and John Monk Saunders wrote a beautiful screenplay, authentic in every detail. His only weakness was a tendency to overwrite. We worked together, trimming and tightening, until we had a lean, workable script.

This picture brought me into contact for the first time with Howard Hughes, who had started shooting his epic *Hell's Angels* two years earlier, in 1927. In whatever he undertook, Hughes was determined to be the best. He raised competitiveness to the level of mania. Before he started his film, he hired people to tour the world, buying up World War I fighter planes. And he offered any amount of money to stunt men and fliers to put these crates into the air.

Our huge success with *The Jazz Singer* swept silent pictures off the map, and *Hell's Angels* had to be reshot with sound. (As everyone knows, Norwegian Greta Nissen, playing an English girl in the story, was replaced by Jean Harlow.) Hughes was furious that we dared make a rival picture. He would call me at two or three in the morning and say, "Hal, Hughes speaking. I hear you're trying to rent those Spads and Camels I want. Now listen. I'm going to buy every goddamn one of them in the country so you can't get your hands on them!" Before I had a chance to reply, he'd hang up.

He snapped up planes the day before we arrived to rent them. We laid out a fortune buying them, sometimes hours before his men arrived with fat checks in their hands. He was determined to stop us, and issued a blanket order to buy every single vintage aircraft available, no matter what its condition. But we still managed to get in ahead of him most of the time.

Hughes made up his mind to steal our script. He bribed a young girl on our staff to get hold of a copy. When she arranged to meet his people in an apartment in Hollywood, we got wind of it and arranged for two detectives to slip into the apartment and hide in the clothes closet. They waited there for hours until Hughes's men arrived. As the girl took the script from a desk drawer and handed it over, our men jumped out from the closet and arrested the culprits for theft.

We took the matter to court. We prepared an injunction preventing Hughes from any further interference with our picture on the basis of restraint of trade and out-of-hand coercion. Not to be outdone, Howard sued us in turn for plagiarism and insisted *Dawn Patrol* be withdrawn from the theaters in which it was playing.

I sat with Jack Warner in Judge Cosgrove's chambers, U.S. District Court, while he ran *Dawn Patrol* and *Hell's Angels*. His judgment was unequivocal. No plagiarism was involved. As it turned out, both pictures did extremely well and probably helped each other.

There was great interest in gangsters at the time. We took note of the fact that *Little Caesar*, a first novel by the young Chicago writer W. R. Burnett, was a runaway best-seller. The story was based loosely on the career of the Italian-American thug Johnny Torrio. Burnett was a midwesterner used to seeing bodies lying in the streets after Chicago gunfights. One night, as he was listening to a radio broadcast of a jazz band in which a friend of his was playing, gangsters killed his friend. He heard the shooting and the death cries over the air. As a result he wrote *Little Caesar:* a bitter, savage portrait of hoodlums in the big city. Twenty-eight and lacking any writing experience, he worked at white heat for four weeks to vent his anger. He sent the book off to the famous Maxwell Perkins at Scribner's. Perkins liked it, but the Scribner's board refused to publish a crime novel. Burnett tossed the book in a trunk and took a job as night manager in his uncle's hotel. A year later he dug out the manuscript and mailed it to the Dial Press, who bought it at once. It was a Literary Guild selection, and Burnett became world famous overnight.

I read the book and was fascinated. It was a powerful story, brilliantly written. Burnett knew these people; the grim mark of the Chicago underworld was stamped on every page. I sent the book over to Jack Warner, and without even reading it, he approved my making it into a film.

I was determined that Burnett should write the script himself, but he refused. Then his wife decided she wanted to see the Southwest. He drove her to Arizona, but it was a hundred degrees at midnight in Phoenix, so they came on to Los Angeles. We had meetings at the studio, but Burnett still wouldn't write the script. My friend Robert Lord did a first draft, but the dialogue was too cultivated. I had it rewritten by Francis Farragoh and it was much better.

Burnett wasn't happy with our picture. He complained that the relationship between Rico, the gangster played by Eddie Robinson, and Joe Masaro, played by Douglas Fairbanks, Jr., was homosexual in our version! No such thing was in our minds. He was also furious that in an Italian story not a single Italian was in the cast. I pointed out that there were no Italian stars suitable for the parts, but Burnett was in no mood to listen. On the set he grumbled that Douglas Fairbanks, Jr., was too elegant to be a gangster and Glenda Farrell too weak to be a moll; they overheard and were ready to slug him. But Burnett had no complaints about Eddie Robinson.

I first saw Eddie in a New York play called *Mr. Samuel.* The play was bad, but he was marvelous, a dynamo whose electricity knocked the audience cold. I went backstage and we discussed a contract. The deal we made with Eddie was on a picture basis rather than a weekly deal, and he had certain approvals. Special material would be created to suit his talents.

I had intended to have Robinson play the small part of Otero in *Little Caesar,* but Eddie was determined to play Rico. He walked into my office one day wearing a homburg, heavy black overcoat, and white evening scarf, a cigar clenched between his teeth. He *was* Rico. He says in his memoirs that we had differences about his playing *Little Caesar.* Not so: I was quickly convinced.

I decided the best director available would be a humorous, determined young man named Mervyn LeRoy. I gave him the script to read and he fell in love with it. (He and my sister Minna pushed hard for a young actor named Clark Gable to play Joe Masaro, but Jack Warner said no, he'd never amount to anything, his ears were too big.) Mervyn did a good job of directing the picture. The performances were excellent and the action sequences fast and exciting. Our sets were authentic: drab and cheerless rooms appropriate for lives lived in the dark. Chicago was suggested by brief glimpses of cold, depressing streets. In the days of the small screen, it was not necessary to go on location to achieve a sense of realism.

Because I was on the set every day, I noticed that Mervyn's joking irritated Eddie, who was extremely intense, "living" his part. I saw to it that the jokes stopped. To run a studio, one had to be not only an executive, but a diplomat.

Little Caesar was an immediate hit. It was the first of a series of true-life crime pictures we made based on newspaper headlines and cases taken from the *Police Gazette.*

My favorite director then and always was the amazing Michael Curtiz. He directed such classics as *The Adventures of Robin Hood, Yankee Doodle Dandy,* and *Casablanca.* Mike was a tall, flamboyant, high-living Hungarian who mangled the English language outrageously. He described Bette Davis as "the flea in the ointment and a no good sexless son of a bitch." Making *The Charge of the Light Brigade,* he not only said the famous "Bring on the empty horses" (bringing horses through without riders), but "If they won't stand still, nail their hooves down." Directing an actor on a yacht about a hundred yards out from the camera on shore, Curtiz called to him, "When you step out on the deck, vink."

The actor, Ricardo Cortez, called back and said, "How can you see me wink from there?"

He said, "I can see you, vink." What he wanted him to do was wave.

Mike and I had our differences, chiefly because he tended to build up scenes unnecessarily. But he was a superb director with an amazing command of lighting, mood, and action. He could handle any kind of picture: melodrama, comedy, Western, historical epic, or love story.

Harry Warner "discovered" Mike. He heard glowing reports of his European film *Moon of Israel* and went to Germany to sign him to a contract. When their boat docked in New York, there was a huge crowd to greet them with flags flying and a brass band. Mike said to Harry Warner, "All this for me, Michael Curtiz?" and Harry said to him, "Sorry, Mike, it's the Fourth of July."

He was a demon for work, and hated to go home at the end of the day. A slave driver, he demanded the utmost from his actors. Never stopping for lunch himself and tending to resent those who did, he paced the floor while everyone was off the sound stage, thinking about what he was going to do when they got back. If an actor blew a line later, he would scream, "You lunch bum!"

Curtiz's wife, writer Bess Meredyth, was Louise's close friend. The Curtizes had a ranch in the San Fernando Valley, and we often rode with them on weekends.

Mike was a member of the polo group at Warners, headed by Darryl Zanuck. I played with them occasionally and kept a horse at his ranch. One day he told me that he had sold all of his ponies. When I asked about mine, he said, "Oh, I sold that too."

We also shot skeet together. As a matter of fact, we were shooting on Mike's ranch the Sunday Pearl Harbor was attacked. George Brent and Ann Sheridan were with us when Curtiz's stepson, John Meredyth Lucas, came tearing out in a car, yelling, "Pearl Harbor is being attacked!" We huddled around the car radio, listening to news reports—our first knowledge of that tragic event.

While Mike was extremely "wild" and high-strung, Bess Meredyth was a shrewd, down-to-earth homebody who stood for no nonsense. She was his anchor in life. Curtiz liked food, and Bess learned to prepare his favorite Hungarian dishes: goulashes and dumplings. On the whole, the Curtizes' marriage was happy. Although there was a lot of gossip, I never knew him to be involved with other women.

But he was restless in other directions. When we went on location, he explored everything in town. He had a thirst for knowledge: he wanted to see the poolrooms, the flophouses, the Chinese sections, the slums—everything strange and exotic and seedy so that he could add to the knowledge that gave his pictures their amazing degree of realism.

In many ways, he was eccentric. The first car he drove in Hollywood was a Packard. He drove it for a year in second gear before he found out there was a third gear in which the car should be run.

One of Mike's peculiar habits was leaving out scenes that were in the script for no better reason than that he didn't like them. I had to watch the daily work very carefully to see that he didn't make arbitrary cuts. Fortunately, I had a good memory and the script was sacred to me. Casey Robinson, one of my favorite writers, recalls that one night at a dinner party a director said to me angrily, "What the hell is this goddamn script anyway? The Holy Bible?" Casey says I replied, "Yes, that's exactly what it is!" I felt that way and I always protected the writer. If Mike cut a scene, I asked him to restore it.

At other times, he added scenes. I remember one of his early silent pictures was *The Third Degree*. I ran some scenes one night and was amazed to discover circus scenes complete with acrobats, clowns, and high-wire walkers, scenes that hadn't been in the script. We hadn't planned for the scenes, and they increased our budget enormously. When I asked Curtiz for an explanation, he said, "I felt something extra was needed." I was surprised to learn recently that we kept the scene in. Having spent so much money, I guess we had no alternative but to do so.

I miss Mike Curtiz badly: his humor, his color, his liveliness, his genius.

I wish he were with me today.

CHAPTER 4

Into the Thirties

We began the thirties with a terrible shock.

I have mentioned Motley Flint, Warners' benefactor during the studio's struggling days. His Wall Street contacts provided funds for the films we made and the gambles we took, like talking pictures. I liked Motley very much: he was a gentleman, a fine man in every way. I'll never forget the day Jack Warner came into my office and told me what had happened to him.

Motley was testifying in the David O. Selznick case: Selznick was suing the Security First National Bank for failing to pay him $250,000 when he tried to withdraw it from his account. When Motley stepped off the witness stand and stopped to talk with David's mother, Mrs. Lewis Selznick, Frank Keaton, an aggrieved real estate man who blamed Motley for his financial losses, jumped up behind Mrs. Selznick and rested a gun on her shoulder. He fired directly into Motley's face, killing him instantly. The judge ran to the killer, demanding the gun. Keaton fled, was apprehended, and sent to jail.

We were grief stricken. And no sooner had we recovered from the shock of this meaningless and terrifying incident than we had another to endure.

We received word from Havana that twenty-two-year-old Lewis Warner, only son of Harry, had been stricken with blood poisoning from infected gums. Jack was unable to leave Hollywood, but Albert and Harry flew from New York to Lewis's bedside in Cuba. They managed to transport the boy to Miami in a chartered plane, and then by ambulance and railroad car to New York. But they were too late. Lewis died of septicemia and double pneumonia on April 5, at Doctors' Hospital in Manhattan.

In November 1930, when the government allowed the companies to merge physically, all Warner production activity moved to the First National Studios in Burbank. The stages at Sunset and Bronson were used occasionally, but the Valley lot was modern and large enough to accommodate our entire film program. Because Darryl Zanuck was the senior executive, he was put in charge of all production at the combined studios. I became a producer and worked independently under Zanuck. I liked Darryl, and we worked well together. He was a good friend and a lively companion.

Zanuck liked to cut his pictures at night. He would run one of his and then run one of mine with me—sometimes our sessions lasted all night. Often I asked him to run my picture first so I could get a few hours' sleep.

But there was trouble in the industry. Because of a sudden fall in profits in the early days of the Depression, the heads of the studios wanted to cut salaries across the board. Darryl, a fighter, battled this decision at Warners and had violent quarrels with Harry over it. But Harry held the purse strings, and Darryl made a mistake in crossing him. One evening, we went to the Brown Derby for dinner before returning to work in the cutting rooms. After a drink and a spirited discussion of the pictures in production, we began an excellent meal. Suddenly, Harry Warner poked his head in the front door and motioned Darryl to come outside. Several diners looked up in astonishment. Hollywood, in those days, was a very small town, and the protagonists in this little scene were instantly recognizable.

Darryl gave me a significant "this is trouble" look, rose from his seat to Harry's command, and disappeared into the street. I could hear voices raised in anger outside. Then the door opened, Darryl reappeared, flushed and irritable, sat down, and ordered another drink.

"What happened?" I asked him.

"The inevitable," he replied. "I'm leaving Warners and I'm not coming back. Joe Schenck offered me a job. I'm going to take it." (At that time, Schenck was the head of Twentieth Studios, which soon after merged with Fox as Twentieth Century-Fox.)

I was concerned that Darryl might be making a mistake. I said, "Don't do anything drastic. Things will cool down. Stay." But I knew from the expression on his face that his mind was made up.

Next day, Jack called and asked me to come to his bungalow, a magnificent second home on the Burbank lot. As I entered the room,

Harry and Jack rose from their chairs to shake my hand. Jack beamed, "Well, Hal, you're 'it.' " It was a very succinct way of saying that I was replacing Zanuck.

In a way, it made up for that morning when, just after the two companies had merged, I came to the studio and found a workman taking my name off the door as Executive in Charge of Production. Now it went back on and it stayed there for nine years.

I can't say that Louise and I rushed out to celebrate. Actually, the increase in salary meant more to us than the honor involved. I was aware of the enormous work load facing me. Between Warners and First National, I would be in charge of forty or sixty features a year. I knew I would have little social life, yet I loved making pictures and could think of no better future for myself. I was young and happily married, my creative juices were flowing—I was on top of the world.

Darryl Zanuck went on to a brilliant career at Fox and never looked back. Nor did I.

My first decision as head of production was to place the emphasis in our pictures on contemporary subjects, although I felt there should be room for historical films in our program, too. While I enjoyed the lavish escapist pictures made by Paramount and MGM, I wanted to tell the truth on the screen. Even a musical, I felt, could comment effectively on contemporary life.

I told my art directors I wanted the rooms our characters lived in to look like real rooms, their clothes to be subdued and correct for their income. If they were working people, I didn't want them dressed expensively and living in costly houses. I would show them in small bungalows or cold-water walk-ups, and have them move in replicas of the real world: automats and cafeterias, buses and street-cars, cheap bars and flophouses. After all, we were in the Depression. I wanted the public to see life on the screen as they lived it. The research department, under Herman Lissauer, was instructed to have photographs taken of the interiors of countless low-income dwellings so that we could duplicate exact dimensions and furnishings. I found a gifted Polish artist named Anton Grot, and an Austrian, Carl Jules Weyl, to reproduce these interiors.

My cameramen were told to utilize correct lighting sources. If a room was lit by a bare bulb, I wanted the source of light on the set to seem to come from that bulb. If it was at night, I wanted sketchy lighting, a rich contrast of light and shade, natural in a room lit by small lamps. I hated the floodlit look Louis B. Mayer insisted upon at MGM to show off his glamorous sets. People in real life moved in shadows, through pools of light, through sudden shifts of lighting. Sol Polito and Tony Gaudio, Arthur. Edeson, Ernie Haller, and James Wong Howe understood what I wanted and supplied countless brilliant ideas of their own.

I kept with me most of the people I had worked with at First National. Bill Koenig, my gifted studio manager for many years, was known as being very tightfisted with the dollar, which was his job. He cut corners and saved money wherever he could, but at the same time was a likable man and a very efficient operator. Director Roy Del Ruth, known for his bizarre sense of humor, attended Koenig's funeral. As Koenig's casket was being wheeled to the hearse from the chapel, Del Ruth said, "Koenig is liable to sit up and say, 'Lay off two of these men. . . . This thing is on wheels and we don't need six men.' "

Roy Obringer was the head of the legal department. His work in dealing with the countless suits and contractual problems remained amazingly thorough and adroit over a period of more than twenty years. He worked in tandem with our shrewd lawyers, Preston and Files, in downtown Los Angeles.

We began to build very big stars in those days. Undoubtedly, the biggest was the great John Barrymore, whose career began in the 1920s.

Jack, I feel, has been badly wronged by history. He wasn't the flamboyant person he has been painted; it was a role he played. Behind the rakish hats, astrakhan collars, and long cigarette holders he was as insecure and scared as many great actors are. Enormous demands are placed upon them by the public: they are expected to be brilliant and dazzling at all times. Fear drives many of them to drink, as it did Barrymore. He was a courtly gentleman when sober —old-fashioned, stately.

But he was as impish as a child, and loved to shock with four-letter words. A typical approach would be, "My dear Wallis, how very pleasant to see you. Now is there anything you can do about these f —— costumes they've dreamed up?" He had a sly, wry sense of humor, and a great knack of flattering his way out of trouble. But when he drank too much, he was uncontrollable.

One of his silent pictures was *The Sea Beast*, directed by Millard Webb, who also enjoyed the bottle. This was a version of *Moby Dick* in which Jack played Captain Ahab, the ship's master obsessed with the Great White Whale.

We built a set near San Pedro to harbor our replica of the whaling boat *Pequod*. On either side of the *Pequod,* we set up large metal tanks filled with hundreds of gallons of water so that we could simulate the wash of huge waves over the decks.

One night, Bill Koenig called me and told me both Jack and Millard Webb were dead drunk and getting into a fight. He told me he didn't want to go down there, but knew he must. When he arrived, Millard and Jack beckoned him to come up on deck, then ran off, triggered the water tanks, and swept Koenig overboard. It's surprising he wasn't drowned.

Jack hated the wooden leg he had to wear. His own leg was bent at the knee and strapped behind him, which was painful and kept his blood from circulating. It was little wonder he yelled and swore at the wardrobe and makeup men.

One day, he was caught in the rush of water from the tanks himself and broke two ribs. Our men had to carry him by rope and pulley to a small boat and row him ashore. They laid him on a stretcher. As they lifted it, a shaft snapped and he fell groaning onto the dock.

In one scene, he had to plunge a harpoon into the side of a mechanical whale made by the prop department. A special sac had been arranged that would burst when he punctured it and drench him in blood. Instead of attacking the whale from the side, Jack jumped drunkenly onto its back and stood on top of it. The waves washed over the whale, spilling him into the sea. Though drenched to the skin, he climbed back again and the sac burst, covering him with red paint.

In spite of all the troubles we had, I was sorry when we lost Jack to Metro. He was colorful and fun.

We started making musicals again in 1932. Zanuck had had a big hit with *Forty-Second Street,* and I followed it with a series of backstage stories.

Our reigning genius of the musical genre was the amazing Busby Berkeley. When I first met him, he was in his late thirties. His parents were actors, members of the well-known Frawley Repertory Company. They were a brilliant but unstable family. Busby's

31

brother George became a drug addict and was found dead on a park bench in New York.

Busby was a sharp-faced man with a large nose, a prominent chin with a dimple in the middle of it, a high forehead with balding hair, and a small, wiry inexhaustible body. A high-strung, nervous prankster who drank more than was good for him, with little or no training as a choreographer, he bluffed his way to success. What he did have was an amazing visual sense. The dance routines he worked out for the Shuberts and for Sam Goldwyn revolutionized musical comedy. He was simply inspired.

I remember attending Berkeley's wedding to Merna Kennedy, a former Chaplin star. Jack Warner was the best man, and everyone at the studio was there. There was lots of champagne, and Buzz consumed more than his share. The marriage didn't last long. He made eight pictures in two years, and had no time for home life.

Along with his great talent, Berkeley had a stubborn, somewhat obnoxious personality. He knew how important his contribution was to the musical pictures we made, and enjoyed the power it gave him. He deliberately designed and coordinated the numbers so that when he finished shooting, it was only a matter of splicing the shots together. There was nothing left to cut, not a single frame, and no angles whatsoever, except those he dictated should be on the screen. He literally cut his scenes in the camera. He thus became a power unto himself, and there was nothing whatsoever we could do about it.

Musicals were fantastically expensive—often there were a hundred girls on the stage at once. In order to select them, Buzz would audition as many as one thousand. He was brutal in winnowing them down, but once he had made the selection, based on glamour, dancing ability, and sex appeal, he won the admiration and adoration of the girls (and had affairs with a few as well). He worked tirelessly through endless rehearsals. We kept a constant check on him because of the time and money he spent. We worked out each number in detail in advance, although Berkeley later claimed he improvised them all.

The preparation for these pictures was difficult and exhausting. The story was often simply an excuse for the musical numbers. Satirists still joke about Warner Baxter saying to Ruby Keeler in *Forty-Second Street*, "Go out on that stage a nobody and you'll come back a star!" That script dealt with the situation of a hard-driving producer putting on a show so that we would have an excuse to have the show itself.

Of course, the moment Busby Berkeley took over, we left reality far behind. The scenes he created could never have taken place on the stage of any theater. The dimensions would have been far too small for his configurations of giant jigsaw puzzles made of human figures, living water lilies, snow crystals, or luminous violins.

Once our writers had worked out the run-of-the-mill plots filled with wisecracks, sugar daddies, ambitious chorus girls, desperate producers, young kids crooning to each other in parks or on ferries—the songs would be put together by the marvelous team of Harry Warren and Al Dubin. They would come to see me and Jack Warner, and play and sing the tunes that became world famous: "By a Waterfall," "Shadow Waltz," "We're in the Money," "Honeymoon Hotel," "Remember My Forgotten Man," "I Only Have Eyes for You," and above all, "The Lullaby of Broadway." We arranged the stories so that each number flowed naturally from the dialogue. The only influence I can claim over the lyrics was that I asked for contemporary comment. Thus, in "Remember My Forgotten Man," we made very telling points for the men who had served their country in World War I and were now unable to get work.

The first musical in which I was involved as head of the studio was *Gold Diggers of 1933*, directed by my old friend Mervyn LeRoy. Mervyn and I sat down with writers Erwin Gelsey and James Seymour and devised a plot in which we could give ample play to Busby Berkeley's inventive genius. He didn't disappoint us. He came up with the idea of wiring the girls with violins and neon tubes—sixty in all, dancing on a great curving staircase with batteries controlling each violin.

It was a very difficult sequence, and we began shooting early in the morning. As I came onto the sound stage, I heard a rumbling. Then the entire structure swayed alarmingly and began to move and shake; the noise was terrifying. It was an earthquake, and as I looked up at the great staircase, it began to slip and slide and the girls wound up in a tangle of violins and neon tubing. Some crashed to the studio floor and clung desperately to the steps. At the same time, there was a short circuit, and the lights went out. All you could see were a few violins glowing in the dark. The stagehands opened the sliding stage doors, and we yelled to the girls to get off the platforms and make their way outside. Fortunately, no one was seriously injured, and we continued shooting as soon as the set had been repaired.

Audiences loved *Gold Diggers of 1933*. It was a great success, and we rushed into production several more pictures along the same lines. We had no idea that they would be regarded as classics one day. It was more a matter of giving Busby Berkeley his head.

Footlight Parade dealt with the struggle between talkies and live theater. It was the story of a Broadway producer who, finding it hard to compete with the new medium, finally concocted shows of amazing invention and variety. In reality, nobody on Broadway could possibly have duplicated the sequences we showed, like "By a Waterfall" or "Shanghai Lil."

We shot the bankroll on *Wonder Bar* with a tremendous cast: Jolson, Kay Francis, Dolores Del Rio, Ricardo Cortez, Dick Powell, and my wife Louise, who played Mrs. Pratt. The huge set of a London nightclub was so expensive, I was forced to caution Berkeley. When I told him he couldn't have more than a hundred dancers (a fantastic extravagance at the time), he groaned with disappointment—then went on to make the hundred look like a thousand with the use of mirrors. Somehow, he managed to hide the cameras in a mirrored room.

One of Berkeley's biggest numbers was "Lullaby of Broadway" in *Gold Diggers of 1935*. The opening shot of Winifred Shaw's face growing larger and larger until it filled the screen was achieved very simply with black velvet and white makeup. Amazing.

Buzz became a director, but he tended to direct all scenes as though they were musical numbers, circling and circling the players. I was particularly aggravated by his handling of *Garden of the Moon* in 1938. Jack was so annoyed by his direction of this picture that he fired him.

Berkeley was impossible to deal with during the entire production. He hated the title song and wanted it dropped, played all scenes in medium shots and refused to shoot close-ups, wouldn't move the camera, and failed to give direction to the young and inexperienced John Payne. He had the crazy idea of casting Edward G. Robinson in a singing and dancing role. Pat O'Brien was as reliable as ever as the hero, but Buzz was unhappy with him. Margaret Lindsay had so little rapport with him that she lacked her usual spark and flash. Berkeley shot very little film each day, used muddy photography that looked like underexposed negative, and dressed the cast unbecomingly. I lost count of the memoranda I sent to him, but they had no effect. Eventually, of course, we had to let him go.

Our worst experience with Berkeley came in the mid-thirties, when he got drunk at a party, drove into the wrong lane, and crashed head-on into another car, killing three people. His own car burst into flames, and he was lucky to survive. He was also lucky that attorney Jerry Giesler handled his case. Giesler convinced the jury Berkeley was innocent, and Buzz was acquitted. The tragedy appeared to have no effect on him, however, and he was much his same self when he came back to work.

Despite the difficulties we had with him, Busby Berkeley was undoubtedly responsible for the great success of our musicals. He was a genius. We missed him when he left Warner Bros., but the day of elaborate musical presentations was over.

He worked at Metro later with great success, but as his career declined, he drank heavily and at one stage cut his throat and wrists. For years, he was down and out. He had a brief comeback with Doris Day's *Romance on the High Seas* and *Take Me Out to the Ball Game,* but he died in a small house, in reduced circumstances. I remember seeing him occasionally in Palm Desert, not far from my home today. He seemed lost.

Most of our musical stars of the thirties played themselves on the screen. Acting ability was not as important as personality.

Dick Powell was our leading juvenile. A cheerful, crew-cut youngster, as outgoing and fast-talking as the roles he played in pictures, he was the typical boy next door, without a hint of temperament—never a problem. He came in, sang, acted expertly, and went home. During *Hollywood Hotel,* he was in especially high spirits because (although married) he was having an affair with Joan Blondell.

Joan Blondell, too, played herself in pictures. She was cute, warm, sexy, and sweet. Audiences loved her big eyes and Cupid's-bow mouth.

There was a big problem with *Hollywood Hotel.* The Campbell Soup people, who sponsored Louella Parsons's radio show of the same name, sued us for using the title without authorization, as did the owners of the Hollywood Hotel. They held us over a barrel for weeks until we settled by giving Campbell Soup's boss two sixteen-millimeter copies of the picture and the Hollywood Hotel a new pair of revolving doors. Louella Parsons got a mink coat. Jack Warner was furious. He sent me a telegram from New York: "Parsons will be Parsons and there are no people like soup people!" It didn't help, but I had to laugh.

Al Jolson and Ruby Keeler's romance was the talk of the thirties. Al, the complete extrovert, fell madly in love with introvert Ruby. It was very much the attraction of opposites. She was extremely shy and sensitive, and the marriage didn't have a chance. Because he wanted to be out with his pals, and she wanted to be home with him, their breakup was inevitable.

Music was a very important part of the pictures we made in the thirties. My tastes ran to classical themes and strong orchestral scores.

When I first thought of bringing Max Reinhardt's famous production of *A Midsummer Night's Dream* to the screen, it was important to me to preserve the music of Mendelssohn. Reinhardt's conductor and arranger was a roly-poly opera composer named Erich Wolfgang Korngold, an imposing name for an imposing and quite enchanting human being. He came to Hollywood to supervise the score of *Dream,* and we became very good friends.

I used him again on *Captain Blood* with Errol Flynn. His rousing music caught the spirit and tempo of the pirate days magnificently. He did *The Prince and the Pauper* and *Another Dawn,* then returned to Vienna to work on his opera *Kathrin.* He was arranging its premiere when I cabled him to come back to California to do the score for *The Adventures of Robin Hood.*

While Korngold was in Hollywood, he heard that the Nazis were in Vienna and had seized his home. He could not reach his family, and it was days before he heard they had made their way over the border into Switzerland. They soon joined him in Hollywood, where they remained the rest of their lives. Korngold's misfortune became our good fortune. He stayed on to do memorable work for us.

Our other great composer was Max Steiner. He had been at RKO and Selznick, but I persuaded him to come to Warners, and he worked for us for many years.

Steiner was as much a part of Warner pictures as our stock company. A tiny, fast-talking, hypersensitive gnome with great wit and a strong streak of schmaltz, he received visitors at his home on Sundays in white pajamas, smoking a large cigar, with rich strains of his latest score as background music. The only time I saw him ill-tempered was when I suggested bringing in an outside composer to help him. Although his work load was heavy, Max wanted to do everything himself. Had he been able, I think he would have composed music for every picture we made: close to one thousand in the period in which he was employed. He was impassioned, wholehearted in everything. And it showed in his work.

His only problem was that he never wanted the screen to be silent. When his music became intrusive, I edited and eliminated and took out large chunks of music that had already been recorded.

If there was time, Max played themes for my consideration on the piano in my office. He hummed and moved his tiny body up and down the keyboard with tremendous energy. I always looked forward to these sessions. Steiner and I decided whether it should be a heavy score or a light score. I suggested, at times, that only a piano or a solo violin accompany a scene. I liked solo instruments for effect.

Often, he wrote the entire score without our first hearing anything but the theme. He always composed on the finished print of a film. When we had a rough cut, he ran it on a moviola in the music department. On the scoring stage, twenty to fifty musicians played under Steiner's direction.

Korngold had a different approach. His scores were virtually symphonies. I was impressed with his genius from the time I first met him at Reinhardt's castle near Salzburg in 1934. He played the piano for us there one evening—unforgettable music of concert quality.

Korngold's work was on an operatic level; Max Steiner was expert in commercial program music. They were both indispensable to the success of our pictures in the thirties.*

* Higham's Note: Pictures for which, incidentally, Mr. Wallis was awarded the Irving Thalberg Award by the Academy of Motion Picture Arts and Sciences for general excellence of production.

CHAPTER 5

Stars and Directors of the Depression Years

In the thirties, we made fifty pictures a year, and I worked around the clock. There were always four pictures shooting, four or more in script preparation, and four or more in editing. I was involved in every phase of each film.

I had to be at work very early in the morning. To be closer to the studio, Louise and I decided to move to the San Fernando Valley. Incredible as it may seem today, we bought sixty acres of rolling land on Woodman Avenue for $30,000. Beyond our property was grassland as far as Encino and Woodland Hills; the country dotted with small chicken farms and fruit and nut orchards. The air was clean and clear, full of the scent of mimosa and honeysuckle. Every weekend after work we went out in the Packard, sat on our lot, and planned our dream house. We wanted an English-style down-home American farm, and we got it.

Our pine-paneled living-room walls surrounded an open hearth. We bought an antique fireplace and fittings from an English manor house, and our oak dining room was a copy of the famous Bell Tavern in England. We collected period furniture, polished brassware, and English china, and combined them with comfortable chintz-covered chairs and leather sofas. The exterior was of white brick, with a pool and a stable of riding horses. We put in electric gates. The house was 150 feet back from the main street up a private road, an almost impossible luxury today.

We arranged a small cottage for Louise's mother to live in. I had lost mine; Mother died in 1934. Though I felt her loss more than I want to say, I was grateful that she had lived to see her family successful and happy. She was as proud of us as we were of her. She was our inspiration: the bedrock of our lives.

Louise and I planted orchards of walnut and apricot trees and set up a grape arbor near our home. We bought other lots. One was a large piece out in Encino, also sixty acres, and another, our best investment, was a corner of Ventura and Sepulveda boulevards. We bought twenty acres of open land there for a mere $10,000—beautiful scenery then, today the busiest area in the Valley.

When business boomed, we built a Thriftimart on one of our lots and leased it to that famous chain. It gave us an escalating income, and we still retained ownership of the land. Our sixty acres in Encino was an orange grove. We made a deal with Sunkist to harvest the crops, marketed the oranges, and made quite a profit. On our own ranch, we dried apricots, laid them out, and sold them through a marketing organization.

Louise and I built our fortune together—developing and increasing our incomes by putting the land to use, growing quality produce. Today it is almost impossible to deal in real estate in Los Angeles. The initial investment is so heavy and the interest rates so high, the average person can't afford to invest because the risk is too great. But in the 1920s and 1930s, a young couple starting out could ensure their future this way.

We lived within our means, and invested every cent we could save in land. You *could* save in those days—as much as a quarter of your income. Neither of us liked to live "high" or go to parties; we weren't extravagant. We entertained small groups of friends for dinner and went to their homes but, by choice, lived far outside the social whirl of Hollywood. Quiet people, we liked each other's company, and enjoyed our undemanding, subdued relationship.

My sister Minna was busy making a name for herself as an agent. I was delighted with her success. She knew everyone. Garbo was one of her closest friends. Two of the top agents in Hollywood, Myron Selznick and Leland Hayward, financed her first year in business.

Clark Gable was one of Minna's earliest clients. She saw him playing Killer Mears in *The Last Mile* at the Belasco Theatre in Los Angeles, and knew at once he had star quality. His first interview was for a part in a Western. When the casting director asked if he could ride a horse, Minna answered for him. "Of course he can," she said. "You can tell just by looking at him." As it turned out, he couldn't.

But Minna took him to Griffith Park for lessons, and in two weeks Clark was a horseman.

Though people criticized Gable's jug ears, Minna swept aside such complaints. He was described as a human sugar bowl, a barn with the doors open, and a bat's face stuck on a restless body. Even at the height of his career, Jack Warner never called him anything but "the guy with the big ears." But Minna made Clark a great star—fought for better stories for him, bigger costars, more publicity, everything. And he remained her friend always. If anything troubled him, he came to Minna. She was like his big sister.

Many of the stars felt that way. They loved Minna, and when they had problems, they called upon her for help. When she was sick, her house in Beverly Hills was filled with flowers. The famous of the world sat in her living room.

My days at Warners began with script conferences. I worked with writers on work in progress, and checked finished pages very carefully. I conferred with cameramen and scenic designers to set the style and tone of a picture, discussed costume sketches with Orry-Kelly, went over scores with composers I have mentioned, and worked closely with Jack Warner to solve any and all production problems.

The studio installed projection equipment in my home, and every night after dinner I ran eight or ten reels of rushes (film shot the day before by the companies in production). For two hours I reviewed isolated scenes from melodramas, comedies, Westerns, and musicals. I dictated my notes (on performance, direction, lighting, script, etc.) into a dictaphone, and they were transcribed by my secretary in the morning and passed over to the various departments and people involved. When the picture was finished and cut, I ran it again for final polishing before the first preview, usually held in Huntington Park or Pasadena.

Max Reinhardt's production of *A Midsummer Night's Dream* at the Hollywood Bowl created a sensation in the mid-1930s. I believed it would transfer excitingly to the screen even though *The Taming of the Shrew*, Mary Pickford and Douglas Fairbanks's Shakespearean experiment, was a disaster. This picture made film history with the classic credit line, "Script by William Shakespeare, Additional Dialogue by Samuel Taylor."

I think Jack Warner felt as though a brick had fallen on his head when I announced my intention, but with great foresight he quickly approved the project. Our stock company would lend itself ideally to the undertaking: we could fit them into the leading roles and borrow Mickey Rooney from MGM to play Puck. We hoped *A Midsummer Night's Dream* would appeal to children as well as adults.

We all agreed that only Reinhardt could produce the picture for the screen. He had turned the Hollywood Bowl into an enchanted vale with illuminated trees, shimmering cobwebs, and torchlight processions—created a gossamer world, untouched by reality, pure cinema. Reinhardt's name on our picture would guarantee important international attention. The most famous European entrepreneur of his time, he lived and dressed as flamboyantly as a prince of the realm. Young actors and actresses flocked to his classes; his theaters in Germany and Austria were enormous and decorated by the finest artists. His productions were the most spectacular seen outside of Russia in the twentieth century.

Reindhardt met with me at the studio for preliminary discussions, and later I went to Austria to see him. Leopoldskron, his castle near Salzburg, was overpowering: four stories high in acres of groomed gardens and walks. Henry Blanke and I had three wonderful visits there, and I will never forget our conferences in his beautiful salon. We sat under thirty-foot ceilings on hand-embroidered chairs, discussing plans for the production. The castle had a marble staircase from the hall into the upper quarters. There were several dining rooms, and we dined in a different one each night. One was known as the Venetian Room, another the Porcelain Room, and so on.

In front of Leopoldskron there was a large terrace bordering the lake, and adjoining it an outdoor garden where Reinhardt staged plays in the grand manner. On the long summer evenings we dined on the terrace by candlelight, and performances were staged for us. The very large staff of servants wore period livery with white gloves. We felt we were taking part in an opera, or being entertained by royalty of the seventeenth or eighteenth century.

Reinhardt himself was a striking-looking man. With his rugged features, dark hair, brooding eyes, and impressive figure, he was a handsome and commanding presence. He was extremely warm to us, cordial and hospitable. Although a martinet in the theater, he was utterly charming and relaxed at home.

Eager and excited about working in Hollywood, he never

stopped talking about it. He dreamed of becoming a famous film personage, and was very pleased that we chose William Dieterle to direct the picture. They spoke the same language, literally and figuratively, and from the beginning, he and Dieterle worked intimately together. Reinhardt visualized everything in sketches drawn up for him by our art director, Anton Grot, and Dieterle set up the cameras accordingly. Hal Mohr, a most accomplished cameraman, did a fine job of lighting the production.

Making *A Midsummer Night's Dream* began with a major problem. Reinhardt had instructed Anton Grot to build a fairy forest that extended over two sound stages. Even he couldn't bring an entire forest indoors, so the trees were made of burlap dipped in plaster of paris. But he did insist on real leaves. We sent an army of men to strip leaves from the trees of Sherwood Forest and pile them in trucks. They were then driven to the paint shops at Burbank to be sprayed silver. We also dug up great quantities of moss to carpet the vale, but it was pulpy underfoot and the players got caught in it. It had to be watered down daily. Eventually, nature lovers caught our people stripping Sherwood Forest and complained so bitterly we had to find replacement leaves elsewhere.

The night I ran the first day's rushes of the forest sequence, I couldn't see the trees at all. The screen was completely dark! I realized that there had not been room to hang sufficient lights because Reinhardt had demanded that the trees be as tall as the rooftops of the sound stages. Without proper lighting, the images were reduced to zero. Hal Mohr explained that he had promised Dieterle and Reinhardt that he would do his best to light the scenes indirectly. He had feared the worst, and certainly had achieved it. Mohr said to me, "I need a weekend to change the set. Will you let me cut off the tops of the trees? We'll work all through Saturday and Sunday nights. We'll sleep in shifts, two hours at a time." I told him to go ahead.

He was as good as his word. By Monday, he had shaved the tops of the trees, removed branches, and done marvelous things to improve the images. Mohr sprayed the trees with aluminum paint and orange shellac: orange, being an impenetrable color, photographed black. He covered the trees with cobwebs and tiny metal particles that reflected the light. The effect was lovely.

Mickey Rooney was another problem. He went tobogganing at Big Bear and broke his leg, so we had to shoot him on a tricycle moving back and forth behind bushes. You couldn't see the tricycle, only Mickey flying by as a somewhat robust fairy. Other times, he had to be hoisted on wires, which couldn't have been very comfortable.

James Cagney was Bottom, playing the part with great energy. He was particularly good in the scene of the ass's head.

Victor Jory was an impressive Oberon.

Voice coaches worked with all of the actors to help eliminate their American accents. Incredibly, some of the players followed their usual custom of ad-libbing. When they found they couldn't ad-lib Shakespeare, they were greatly disappointed.

A Midsummer Night's Dream wasn't a blockbuster. It didn't make records at the box office, but it was reasonably successful and earned us unlimited prestige.

Sadly, Reinhardt never worked in pictures again, as it was too difficult to find anything suited to his talents. When, as a Jew, he could no longer function in Hitler's Germany, he was reduced to running a drama school in Hollywood while his wife played housekeepers and maids in obscure horror movies. It was the fall of a colossus. After his death, there was an auction of his personal effects, and I bought several pieces as mementos of the wonderful times we had spent at Leopoldskron Castle with this remarkable man.

Another fascinating personality involved with Warners was the multimillionaire newspaper publisher, William Randolph Hearst. As everyone knows, his mistress was Marion Davies, a good-natured blond girl against whom I never heard a bad word—unheard of in Hollywood. She was Hearst's whole life, and he was dedicated to making her a major motion picture star.

Marion was talented, but she lacked a really distinctive personality: star quality. And the vehicles Hearst chose failed to show her to advantage.

She had a long-term contract with MGM. Hearst was a major shareholder there and he argued constantly with Louis B. Mayer about his plans for her. Marion was very anxious to play Marie Antoinette, but Irving Thalberg was determined that his wife, Norma Shearer, should play the role. Mayer took Hearst's side, and finally succeeded in persuading Thalberg. Mayer told Hearst that if he put up the entire cost of production, Marion could have the part. Insulted, Hearst refused, called us immediately, and made a deal with Warner Bros. We agreed to back Cosmopolitan Pictures, the Hearst production company, and give Marion full approval of her films.

However, Miss Davies wanted to live at one studio while working at another. She refused to leave her bungalow at MGM, a two-story building that included an office for Mr. Hearst, a dressing room for Miss Davies, a dining room, a kitchen, and a bedroom. She said she would be housed in no other structure. Culver City was a very considerable distance from Burbank, so Hearst had a problem. It took him about a day to find a solution.

A large work team systematically sliced the bungalow into three parts. Each part was then put on wheels and drawn by truck through the streets of Los Angeles. The procession could travel only five miles an hour because of the weight of the structure. At one point a third of the building fell off onto Sunset Boulevard and lay on its side for several hours before it was replaced on the wheeled metal base. Crowds gathered and explored portions of the rooms before police arrived and cleared them out. One person was discovered sitting on the toilet which lay sideways on the now horizontal wall.

In order to admit the building to our studio, we had to cut through an entire wall surrounding our sound stages. Marion followed in her limousine, weeping copiously. It was quite clear that she felt leaving MGM for Warners was like leaving Park Avenue for Hoboken.

Piece by piece, the bungalow was reconstructed as men worked night and day, narrowly avoiding putting it together in the wrong order. The furniture was brought over from MGM, and soon the house was the showplace of the studio. We all went to have a look at it.

I liked Marion very much personally, but she was a headache from the beginning: she complained about everything. Jack Warner added two lavish rooms to her quarters and gave her a silver Rolls-Royce, but it still wasn't enough.

After her sister jumped to her death from the window of Good Samaritan Hospital, Marion took to drink, and was unable to report for work until noon each day. We began her first picture, *Page Miss Glory*, with considerable misgivings. To make matters worse, Marion fell in love with her costar, Dick Powell. He was a promising juvenile, while Hearst was one of the most powerful men in the country. We persuaded Dick to cool his ardor.

After *Page Miss Glory*, we made *Hearts Divided* with Marion. Neither picture did very well. Marion continued drinking, and behind her laughter and gaiety she was a very tragic figure.

Because I produced the Davies pictures, Hearst often invited Louise and me to San Simeon, his magnificent ranch in central California. We flew up in his private biplane and were met by a uniformed chauffeur who drove us up the winding road to the castle. Hearst was not present to greet us. But the butler, housekeeper, and other uniformed servants made sure we were comfortable, whisked away our bags, and guided us to our guesthouse. Louise pointed out with delight that the bathroom taps, towel rails, and basin stoppers were made of gold. The walls of the villa were hung with Goyas, each one worth a fortune.

Soon, Hearst appeared and we met and mingled with guests such as Gable and Lombard and Cooper and Marlene and Myrna Loy. We often saw Harlow and William Powell strolling casually about the grounds. At night, there would be thirty guests at the dining table, and after dinner we had the choice of seeing a recent picture or playing billiards or pool. There were certain restrictions, surprising in view of Marion's weakness for the bottle: Hearst frowned on drinking. He reluctantly permitted his guests to have one cocktail before dinner, but never served wine at the table. If a star drank too much, he was told that a car was at the door to take him to the airplane, his bags packed and in the trunk.

Despite the fact that every Hearst paper gave Marion's pictures rave reviews (the critics valued their jobs), the public remained indifferent. When we made *Ever Since Eve*, we realized we were in real trouble. The best thing about this picture was that my wife, Louise, had one of her finest comic roles in it, playing a publisher with women's lib ideas. But Marion was showing the effects of drinking, overeating, and late hours. She was forty-one, and it showed. *Ever Since Eve* was her last picture with us, and the end of her career. As much as we all loved her, we were relieved—because her pictures were losing money, and Harry Warner was screaming.

Fortunately, most of our other stars did well. At the top of the list was Edward G. Robinson, who had made such a great success for us in *Little Caesar*. Eddie fascinated me. Quite different from the tough gangsters he portrayed, he was cultivated, sensitive, and good-natured. His profound knowledge and appreciation of art resulted in one of the finest private painting collections in the world.

After *Little Caesar*, we needed a strong follow-up for Robinson. My favorite writer, Robert Lord, and his associate, Byron Morgan, convinced me to buy *Five Star Final*, a play by Louis Weitzenkorn.

It was a powerful drama—a true story of a newspaperman who revived a buried murder case and exposed the murderess. I remembered a fine Belasco actress named Frances Starr, whom Ina Claire had parodied in the Ziegfeld Follies. I brought her back for the part of the accused woman, and she turned out to be marvelous.

One concern I had in *Five Star Final* was to make sure that the newspaper office was authentic. Members of our staff in New York had sketches made of the interiors of two newspaper offices so that our dimensions were exactly correct. We even duplicated the neon lighting in the ceilings by having exceptionally bright arc lights blazing down from the top of the studio sound stage.

Eddie Robinson loved the part of the dishonest editor, Randall, who changed character in mid-career, and decided to devote himself to telling the truth in his paper. With his strong sense of justice, Eddie told me he regarded the part as one of the most important of his career. The whole picture revolved around him, and when he had a part he believed in, there was nobody quite like him. I went down on the set day after day to watch him work. Eddie's attack, his vigor, his electric energy, made you forget he was a small and ugly man. He was a towering figure in pictures—a great star.

Eddie was justly disappointed with the pictures that followed *Five Star Final,* but we couldn't produce movies of that caliber at the rate of five or six a year. He also had marital problems, which were patched up when his wife, Gladys, gave birth, but that son was a changeling, a child who, at the age of seven, attempted to drown his own mother. Fortunately, he didn't succeed, but he did many equally dreadful things later in life, and was in and out of jail until his death.

Eddie was never happy in Hollywood. Like so many theater people, his heart belonged to the theater and he went back to New York whenever he could. He never turned down a script, though he grumbled loudly if he didn't like a particular property. Yet I must add that no matter what he thought of a picture, he worked hard and never gave anything less than a very fine performance.

We finally found another property worthy of Eddie: *I Loved a Woman,* a bitter attack on the evils of the meat industry in Chicago. Eddie came in to discuss it with me, and we made a number of changes in the dialogue. All of his suggestions were intelligent and to the point.

He and his costar in *I Loved a Woman*, Kay Francis, were oddly matched. Kay was so tall that we had to put Eddie on a box in some scenes to bring him level with her and, understandably, he was humiliated. Irritable and self-conscious, he argued with Kay frequently. But he was a gentleman, and years later, when he wrote his memoirs, gave credit to her fine acting.

One of our best pictures with Eddie Robinson was *Bullets or Ballots,* the story of Johnny Broderick, a well-known New York detective. During the filming of that picture, Eddie faced charges of fathering an illegitimate child, but the case turned out to be a hoax. Eddie was helped considerably by the fact that he was not a Don Juan in appearance. Few people could imagine him in a romantic liaison, and the matter was laughed out of court.

We costarred Eddie with Bette Davis in *Kid Galahad*. After the first day's work, he said to me, "This Davis girl. She's hopeless. She's an amateur. She's totally out of place in this picture." I assured him that she would give a fine performance, but he did not warm to her, nor she to him. Neither recognized the other's talent.

Eddie begged me to take him out of gangster roles, and was greatly relieved when I offered him *Confessions of a Nazi Spy* and *Dr. Ehrlich's Magic Bullet*. In the 1940s, we starred him in *A Dispatch from Reuter's* and *The Sea Wolf*. He was very good as Reuter, the newspaper genius, and powerful as Wolf Larsen, Jack London's terrifying sea captain who cruelly punished his crew.

On *Manpower* we had problems initially because Eddie was temperamentally unable to cope with Marlene Dietrich, whom he found cold and haughty. But he grew to respect her, and discovered to his delight that she was a great lover of Impressionist paintings. As shooting progressed, he and George Raft both fell in love with Marlene. They fought over her at the studio one day, a real fight complete with punches. He and Raft loathed each other, and I refereed their bitter battles. I think Eddie's hatred of Raft had something to do with his leaving our studio in the early forties.

George Raft was—is—an extraordinary individual, who came to us in the late 1930s after a successful career at Paramount. We needed another strong leading man for our gangster pictures, as Eddie Robinson and James Cagney were always threatening to walk out. The moment we signed Raft, we were swamped with angry mail, demanding to know why we were hiring a hoodlum and a racketeer.

I knew nothing of Raft's private life and was astonished by charges that he had connections with the underworld. He assured us from the beginning that he did not.

Our association with Raft was a constant battle from start to finish. Hypersensitive to public accusations of underworld connections, he flatly refused to play the heavy in any film. This was ridiculous, because his greatest role had been the slow-smiling, coin-tossing hoodlum in *Scarface*. Time and time again we offered him gangster parts, and time and time again he turned them down. He was on suspension without salary most of the time.

No sooner had Raft joined us than he asked for loan-outs to other producers. He insisted upon doing *The House Across the Bay* for Walter Wanger. We were surprised to discover that in it he would play a tough, low-life type, exactly the kind of character he refused to play for us. Wanger begged Jack Warner to release him, but Jack refused. Raft sent him a series of telegrams from New York, saying he couldn't digest his food, his future would be ruined if he didn't play this part, etc., etc. Wanger said he would go out of business if he couldn't get Raft. Jack and I let him go for the one picture.

In *Manpower* he and Eddie Robinson played telephone linemen. In one scene Raft was to hold Eddie in a belt from the top of a telephone pole, but the belt was to slip out of his hand and Eddie would fall to his death. Raft stormed into Jack's office and said he would not play the scene as written. "If the belt slips from my hand, that makes me the heavy," he said.

Jack looked at him in astonishment. "How can you help it if the belt slips out of your hand?" he asked.

George looked nonplussed. "Maybe the belt could break," he said. Jack shrugged, and accepted the idea. Eddie maintained that George was afraid people might think he was a weakling if he let a man slip from his grasp. He may have been right.

Raft made lots of noise about wanting to be loaned out to Universal for *The Flame of New Orleans,* but we didn't let him go for that one. He was very annoyed, and we realized why: Marlene was to costar with him.

George finally sank his own career when he turned down two tremendous parts: Sam Spade in *The Maltese Falcon,* and the gangster in *High Sierra.* Humphrey Bogart stepped into George's shoes in both these pictures and became a very big star. Audiences loved him, and of all the Warner stars, he has the greatest following today.

People like his lack of sentimentality, his honest and healthy cynicism. He was one of the great artists of the screen.

Bogie made several false starts in Hollywood, and returned to Broadway in 1935 for a role in *The Petrified Forest*. As Duke Mantee, the unhappy gangster who holds a group of people hostage in an Arizona café, he was totally convincing. We signed him to re-create the role on the screen. Bogart was just as good in the movie version as he was on the stage. And he was also superb as the disillusioned private eye in *The Maltese Falcon*.

Although people have written that offscreen Bogart was a soft and gentle man, I never found him so. He was as much the tough guy at home, in his dressing room, or in my office as he was on the sound stage. He drove a hard bargain, and every time he made a picture, he wanted an increase in salary. The moment the day's work was over, he drove home, and seldom mingled with the other players. I knew him best in the years before he met Betty Bacall.

He was married at the time to tough, hard-drinking Mayo Methot, who appeared in some of our pictures. Their fights were legendary. At one party she threw a highball at him, at another she punched him in the nose, and one evening at his house, she stabbed him with a knife—fortunately, the tip broke off and his life was saved. There was no particular reason for these onslaughts: they were based on unfounded jealousies. I believe Bogie enjoyed the fights. He always wanted to seem as tough as possible. One night he met a man at a party who chewed glass in a circus, and Bogie smashed glasses and began to chew the pieces. His mouth was full of blood before he gave up.

Bogie was always short of money. The studio files on him are full of requests by his agent, Sam Jaffe, for more money. His divorce from Mary Philips came only a few days before his marriage to Methot. What little earnings he had saved were split in half with his ex-wife.

We had major problems with James Cagney, who became our house rebel. He fought endlessly over everything throughout the thirties.

Famous because of the grapefruit scene in *Public Enemy,* Cagney built his reputation in such pictures as *Blonde Crazy, The Crowd Roars,* and *Picture Snatcher.*

He and I never became friends. He was cold to me, and I wasn't particularly fond of him. Nevertheless, he was very talented, and few could equal his energy and drive. He was particularly good in *G-Men,* made at the time J. Edgar Hoover's FBI was first attracting worldwide attention for its attacks on crime.

Perhaps Cagney's best acting of the 1930s was with the Dead End Kids in *Angels with Dirty Faces,* the picture in which he pretended to be afraid on the way to the electric chair in order to discourage the Dead End Kids from following his example. In his memoirs Cagney says he played the part with deliberate ambiguity so that the viewer could decide whether he was faking or was genuinely afraid. The script's directions were very specific on this point, and I believe the audience understood it perfectly.

People often forget that Cagney was an expert dancer long before he became an actor. Also an extremely sensitive, high-strung performer with a passionate involvement in his work, he was often seized by stage fright. One studio report indicates that he even threw up before playing a particularly difficult scene. He wasn't as tough as he seemed to be—only nervous and very obstinate.

Our biggest female star was Bette Davis. I had great respect for Bette's judgment and she for mine. My relationship with her through the years has been a good one, and I value her friendship very much. She came to Warners from Universal, where she played frumpy little girls at the request of George Arliss, who used her in our picture *The Man Who Played God.* We took over her contract, and she became the queen of the lot.

Bette had a remarkable New England strength of will and a self-assurance that some people found formidable. She had definite likes and dislikes in the choice of material for her films and was inevitably right. She was a perfectionist, and gave fantastic performances.

She wasn't easy. We had a rule that actresses and actors must not improvise on the set, but she frequently asked for rewrites and got them. We tried to give her the best writers available. Bette and Jack were usually at odds. He was quick to put her on suspension if she balked at doing a specific property. Her creative discussions were with me. Jack "wielded the club" if he thought she got out of line.

Bette had a number of minor health problems. She had sinus trouble and laryngitis, and frequently lost her voice. She also had delicate white skin that freckled and burned badly in the sun.

Her love affair with William Wyler, one of the best directors, was the talk of the studio. We borrowed him from Goldwyn to direct her in *Jezebel* and *The Letter.* She left her husband, Ham Nelson, for him, but these two powerful temperaments overpowered each other, and the relationship collapsed. I do believe the emotional tension between them added an extra quality to the pictures they made together: the air hummed with feeling from first frame to last.

Wyler had a mania for endless takes, and on *The Letter,* it became an obsession. The first scene called for shots of a plantation in Malaya. Coolies lie in their hammocks, and the moon filters through trees. A cockatoo flutters on a fence. Rubber drips from a tree. Suddenly, we hear shots. Bette appears on the veranda of her bungalow, firing at a man in a white tuxedo. After emptying the revolver in his body, she turns and walks back into the house.

The scene involved a long traveling shot from the trees to the house. It was a simple setup, and could easily have been done in two or three takes, but Wyler insisted on shooting thirty-three. Bette kept running out of ammunition, the extra playing the shot man kept brushing his tuxedo free of dust, and the white cockatoo had to be taken out and brought back again and again so that it would respond to the sound of the bullets. Everyone grew weary, especially Bette, who by the last take was so exhausted she could hardly raise the gun.

Jack Warner and I were furious. When we demanded to know why Wyler was wasting so much time, he had no explanation. I think he simply enjoyed the scene so much he wanted to spend two days doing it over and over.

Finally, I took all the cut footage home and looked at it. I sat up all night watching the thirty-three takes, then made a selection of one of them. When the picture was completed, I ran it for Wyler and asked him if he was pleased with the opening scene. He said, "Yes. Now you see the value of doing it thirty-three times."

"I'm sorry to inform you," I replied, "that I used the first take."

Bette reached the peak of her career under Wyler's direction. Her love for him and her profound admiration show on the screen.

Errol Flynn was her exact opposite. Whereas Bette lived entirely for work and was restless during vacations, Errol quite obviously had no interest in filmmaking and couldn't wait to get away from the studio.

We first heard of him through my good friend, Irving Asher, head of production at Warners' Teddington Studios near London. He had used him in a picture called *Murder at Monte Carlo,* and thought he was great.

Irving sent Errol's film to Jack Warner and recommended we sign him. Jack obviously never saw the test, as he replied to Irving's cables "No, she stinks." I wired Irving: "Will abide by Svengali Asher's judgment, send Flynn over." Irving and his lovely wife, Laura (La Plante) bought Errol a new suit and put him on the boat with a Warners contract in his pocket. At that time we were forming a stock company, signing new talent to six-month contracts, with options covering a period of seven years. Flynn was more than happy to sign, and his starting salary was $125 per week.

Shortly after his arrival, we were shooting a picture called *The Case of the Curious Bride* and needed a corpse to lie on a table in one scene. Since we had Flynn under contract with nothing else for him to do, we decided to use him for the body. This was his first work in an American picture.

When Lloyd Pantages, the well-known columnist, introduced Errol to Minna, she sensed his potential immediately. She took one look at this six-foot, one-hundred-and-seventy-pound athlete and knew he would be a star. She signed him as a client, and urged me to give him a break.

Soon after this, Robert Donat announced he could not come to Hollywood to star in *Captain Blood* because the climate might aggravate his asthma. We were desperate for a leading man to replace him. Our sets were built; the picture was in production. (Irving Asher later told us Donat burst into tears in his office and told him the real reason he wouldn't do the picture was because he couldn't bear to leave the girl with whom he was living. Asher suggested bringing her along, but Donat said she didn't want to come.) We thought of casting George Brent in the role, but he didn't have the dash and color we needed.

Minna asked me to consider Errol. He wasn't an admirable character, but he was a magnificent male animal, and his sex appeal was obvious. Jack and I took a gamble, and gave him a test. It seemed not to matter whether he could act. He leapt from the screen into the projection room with the impact of a bullet.

His first day at work was astonishing. He arrived late, in a bad temper, with no idea of the lines he was to speak, and no idea of how to act them. He was to give a long speech in the hall of the Lord High Justice of England. But the results were better than we dared hope. Errol's delivery was extraordinary in its intensity and conviction. He was one of those rare personalities with whom the camera fell in love. He couldn't move or make a gesture that wasn't instantly photogenic.

About halfway through the picture, Minna came in with a demand from Flynn that we rewrite his contract. He knew the excitement his performance was creating and wanted to take advantage of it. We were so impressed by what we had seen of him on the screen that we rewrote his contract mid-picture and raised his salary to $750 per week.

This was to become a pattern. Every time we got ready to start a picture with Errol, he demanded an increase in salary. We had the choice of renegotiating the contract, or not having him in the film.

Matters came to a head on *The Charge of the Light Brigade*. Flynn was called in for wardrobe, but was nowhere to be found, having taken off for parts unknown. His yacht was at sea, headed for the West Indies and Cat Cay, a privately owned island belonging to Erwin Wasey, an advertising man in New York. It boasted a captain's house with accommodations for guests, several cottages along the beach, tennis courts, a small golf course, as well as a harbor for sport fishing boats. Cat Cay could only be reached by yacht or by charter seaplane. We sent William Guthrie of the Warners staff to Miami. He chartered a seaplane from Chalk's, and wangled permission to land. After several hours of negotiating with Errol, during which his salary was again doubled, Flynn returned for the picture.

The Charge of the Light Brigade was shot in stinging cold winds in the Sierras. Errol was undisciplined and restless and hated Mike Curtiz, who directed the picture. The hotel where the cast and crew were housed caught fire and burst into flames the first night they were there. Errol ran out of his room with a blonde. His wife, Lili Damita, raised hell when she saw the photograph in the paper.

He and Lili fought as violently as Bogey and Mayo Methot. Their fights were always in the headlines, and the Legion of Decency complained, but Errol didn't care. He laughed at moralists and flaunted convention.

We had absolutely no idea of the extraordinary facts about him that have recently come to light. Had we known, we would never have kept him on the payroll. I'm sure Jack Warner never believed J. Edgar Hoover's charges against Errol.

Our biggest picture with him was *The Adventures of Robin Hood*. Errol was Robin to the life: good-humored, uninhibited, athletic. We began shooting in a marvelous forest in northern California. Unfortunately, the action scenes were not effective, and I had to replace the director in mid-production, an unheard-of event at that time. I felt that only Mike Curtiz could give the picture the color and scope it needed. The reason we hadn't used him in the first place was because Errol had begged us not to. He preferred the elegant and civilized William Keighley.

From the moment Mike took over, the picture raced along and the rushes were wonderful. His only fault was extravagance. He hired hundreds of background extras for scenes played entirely in close-up. I asked him to cut down on expenditures, and he reluctantly agreed.

Jack and I wanted a strong storybook feeling in *Robin Hood*. We even issued a Sherwood Forest gazette to people in the lobby as they arrived to see the picture.

Both Errol and Mike were at their best on this production. It is one of my favorite pictures.

No matter what else he may have been, during Errol's nine years at Warners he was the golden cavalier of our studio. But his type of picture went out of fashion early on. The genre is dead; and there was only one Errol Flynn.

CHAPTER 6

Great Lives

During the Depression, biographies of important historical figures were very popular with the reading public and the film-going public, as well. Warner Bros. made a modest beginning in the biographical film field with *Disraeli,* starring that grand old actor, George Arliss. The picture did good business, and it was felt that an expensive biographical production might be even more successful. In the early thirties we decided to make a film based on the life of Louis Pasteur, the genius who revolutionized immunology.

At first Jack Warner was opposed to the idea. "Who would want to see a picture about a chemist?" he asked. And someone in the New York office said, "Who'd want to see a picture about pasteurized milk?" But they gradually came around.

The late Pierre Collings began writing the script from a synopsis of the scientist's career. Collings, a drug addict, collapsed after a few weeks' work, and New York playwright, Sheridan Gibney, replaced him. He was very enthusiastic, and researched the subject at the Los Angeles County Hospital by studying slides of anthrax cultures and methods developed by Pasteur.

I asked Paul Muni to play Pasteur. He was a great actor, a private, withdrawn man who became considerably larger than life on the screen. His wife, Bella, strongly influenced him. When he worked, she stood behind the camera where Muni could see her. If she thought some element in his performance was wrong, she shook her head, Muni froze, and the whole scene would have to be redone. When Mrs. Muni nodded her head yes, we could all relax. Only because he was such a fine actor did we tolerate this very eccentric behavior.

William Dieterle was the perfect choice to direct *Pasteur*. He was a German, he understood the European background, and he got along well with Muni. Dieterle was a perfectionist. He had a great sense of lighting, composition, and mood, but he also had idiosyncrasies. He and his wife were deeply into astrology, and everything they did was dictated by the stars. One day Dieterle came to me and asked if he could shoot an insert of a poster on a brick wall four days before the scheduled start of the picture. I knew immediately what prompted this. Dieterle had received word from his wife that the picture should start shooting on the eighth, when the stars were right, instead of the twelfth, so we made a shot on that date to make it official. When I came on the set about 9:00 that first day of shooting and looked around for Dieterle, he was nowhere to be seen. I asked the assistant director where he was, and the assistant said, "He'll be here at ten minutes after nine." Sure enough, at ten minutes after nine, the stage door opened, Dieterle came in, took his position back of the camera, and yelled, "Roll 'em." His wife had warned him not to start shooting until ten minutes after nine.

He had another quirk. When an actor or actress was being tested for a role in his pictures, he examined their horoscopes. Those born on the wrong day of the wrong month were frowned upon, and sometimes failed to get the part.

The studio did a major job of research on *Pasteur*. Herman Lissauer of the research department went east to study the files of the Mayo Clinic trophy room in Rochester, and those of the Bausch-Lomb Corporation Library of germ life in New York. Censor Joe Breen passed our script with flying colors, insisting only that we change "God forbid" to "Heaven forbid," and that we must only *suggest* the sight of sheep being inoculated. Dead or dying sheep must not be shown.

Perc Westmore and I had a difference of opinion over Muni's makeup. Westmore was a great artist, but he tended to draw attention to his art by overdoing the faces. He had Muni sit for hours, aging him from thirty to thirty-eight. I pointed out there would be little difference in that period of time in a man's life, that he would acquire just a few more lines and perhaps a gray hair or two. The beard Westmore gave him, with a white streak through black, looked like a dead skunk. I had the whole makeup changed.

The success of *The Story of Louis Pasteur* convinced me that we should proceed with another biographical film. Medicine was the theme of our first picture, and I felt it should also be the theme of our second.

Robert Lord, one of our best producers, wanted to make the life story of Florence Nightingale, the heroine of the Crimea. I liked his concept. Originally, he was going to base it on Lytton Strachey's study of Miss Nightingale, with Josephine Hutchinson in the starring role, but we decided to cast Kay Francis instead. Walter McEwen, our very able story editor, suggested we hire Pierre Collings to write the picture, but he was very ill by now. Sheridan Gibney came back from New York again to do the script.

As in making *Pasteur,* we began extensive research of the period. We cabled London, seeking information on characters and atmosphere of the era 1850–1860. We wanted pictures (contemporary photographs, where possible) of St. Thomas's Hospital; uniforms of the Crimean War; photographs of Queen Victoria, Dr. John Hall, Sidney Herbert, John Sutherland, Andrew Smith, and Lord Raglan. They sent back an enormous number of lithographs, drawings, and photographs, and art director Anton Grot did unusually fine sketches for us based on them. Sir Edward Cook's excellent book, *The Short Life of Florence Nightingale,* informed us that Crimean War soldiers wore unattractive uniforms of gray tweed, with ugly scarves of brown holland. They had to be modified, of course.

We were faced with problems at the outset. Told by the Lord Chamberlain that we could not portray royalty on the screen, we protested that Florence Nightingale's presentation to Queen Victoria was a high point of the production; however, we were advised that Miss Nightingale would have to curtsy to a throne, the occupant of which must not be fully identifiable. The same day, the Breen office told us we could not have any brutality on the screen. And this was the story of one of the most horrifying wars in history, in which disease and death were rampant.

I had our London representative talk with the Lord Chamberlain, and it was arranged that long shots would be permitted of the Queen; we would simply make cuts for England, and show her in full in America. And we watched the script carefully for shots of excessive violence.

We tested a number of actresses for Queen Victoria, but none satisfactorily. Finally we found an actress who looked exactly like her, but spoke with a Brooklyn accent, so we did something most unusual for the time. We hired the actress and dubbed a perfect English voice (that of the British actress Doris Lloyd) to her lip movements. The result was harmonious, and pleased everyone, particularly our British audiences.

Not all of Dieterle's casting was as effective. There was one soldier who cropped up in every scene (in the hospital in the Crimea, in England, and on the battlefield) simply because the actor was a friend of Dieterle's and he seemed to like the look of his very ugly beard. I lost count of the memoranda I sent insisting the man be used in backgrounds only.

I also objected to Dieterle's old trick of cutting in the camera, giving us nothing to cut later. And I felt that he should have gotten more emotion from Kay Francis. In scene after scene, reacting to the sight of the injured, or clashing with an official who refused to see things her way, she looked completely blank. At one stage Dieterle took a day scene and changed it into a night scene without telling me. It all had to be redone.

We weren't too happy with the picture. *The White Angel* was well directed, but miscast, and Kay Francis had lost the box office appeal she once had. It was one of our box office failures, but there seemed no point in crying over spilled milk. We were already committed to another biographical vehicle: *The Life of Emile Zola* starring Paul Muni.

Jack Warner was very much against our making it. He had predicted that *Pasteur* would never make money, as it was "the story of a milkman." Now he told me that nobody would see this picture because it was the life of a scribbler. Later, he received the Legion d'Honneur for having "made" both pictures.

Zola's life was a wonderful theme for a film. In the Depression, millions of people could identify with a story of injustice and oppression. We decided to focus on the story of Zola's passionate defense of captain Alfred Dreyfus, who had been falsely accused of treason in 1894, stripped of his rank, and sent to Devil's Island. Zola's conviction that Dreyfus had been wrongfully accused led him to write his famous "J'Accuse" letter to the president of the republic, denouncing the general staff associated with his condemnation. The Dreyfus case divided the country. Zola went to prison for his letter, and Dreyfus was court-martialed and again found guilty. In another hearing, on July 13, 1899, Dreyfus was exonerated, decorated, and raised to the rank of major.

The story was brought to us in late 1935 by a German writer,

Heinz Herald. He produced a first draft with another European, Geza Herczeg, which I had rewritten by the very skillful Norman Reilly Raine.

Then we received disturbing word that Pierre Dreyfus, wealthy son of Alfred Dreyfus, was very concerned about the script's portrayal of his father. Our representatives in Paris assured him that the portrait would be a flattering one. He accepted this assurance, but wrote that his chief worry was that the military command that had condemned his father might be portrayed in an unflattering light! He spoke, he said, not as a loving and loyal son, but as a Frenchman: "I do not want to see emphasized the brutality of the military command before a foreign public . . . because that public might deduce regrettable generalizations." He added: "I desire that the artists portraying my father and my mother remember that my parents were quite simple people, good middle-class French people. . . . It was only a tragic destiny that made them celebrated and their only grandeur was that of an heroic courage as profound as a family sentiment of honor." We were fascinated to learn that Mme. Dreyfus, who had stood beside her husband in his severe need, was still alive. I reassured our Paris representatives that neither Pierre Dreyfus nor his mother would have cause for worry.

I handed over the Dreyfus letter to the writers so that they could better understand Dreyfus the father. His son's letter reflected clearly his own strong sense of honor, patriotism, and duty. I wrote to Pierre Dreyfus on December 18, 1936, and told him he need have no fear: both his parents, as well as Emile Zola, would be portrayed in a most sympathetic light, and the general staff would not be condemned. We would introduce only one imaginary scene: Mme. Dreyfus coming to see Zola at his house to plead her husband's case.

We invited Pierre Dreyfus to come to Hollywood to see the picture in production, but he declined. However, he did agree to read the script, and, with minor suggestions which we adopted, he approved it wholeheartedly. (Later, when he saw the film itself, he wrote me he was greatly touched by Joseph Schildkraut's accomplished portrayal of his father.) He signed a waiver of all privacy rights for himself, his mother, and his sister—and we were free to proceed.

The script, originally entitled *The Truth Is on the March,* was completed at the beginning of 1937. But Matthew Josephson, author of a biography of Zola, obtained a copy of our script and charged us with plagiarism. Finlay MacDermid, of the research department, went back to all of the sources given him by the cowriters and came up with an impressive list of actual court hearings, French documents, and out-of-print books. The case took a serious turn after the picture was released. We even reshot several scenes because our lawyers felt they were too close to the book. To settle the matter once and for all, we paid for the rights to the book, and added a mention of it in the credits. Despite this fact, Josephson and his agent insisted on more. We finally paid $10,000 to obtain the necessary clearances.

Then a well-known but impoverished German playwright named Hans Rehfisch claimed his play, *The Dreyfus Affair*, had been stolen by Heinz Herald. Herald, he maintained, was the play's agent in the United States. Herald admitted he had known the playwright in Berlin, and had even seen the play. It turned out that Gilbert Miller had produced the play in New York, and Paramount had an option on it. Herald protested that his script with Herczeg had nothing in common with the play, that Dreyfus did not appear in the stage play, and that Zola was a minor character in it. Rehfisch was adamant. He pursued the matter in the London courts, and the case dragged on for years. He was interned as an alien in 1939, imprisoned for four years, but continued to fight the case. Rehfisch finally accepted a settlement of $5,000 in 1944, long after the picture had outlived its commercial success.

Joseph Schildkraut was superb as Dreyfus, and Paul Muni gave a great performance in the title role. His speech of accusation in court was one of the finest scenes played in my career at the studio. I still have the memorandum I wrote to Dieterle to that effect.

When *The Life of Emile Zola* was completed, we began to prepare *Juárez*, the story of the Mexican patriot, and the ill-fated Maximilian and Carlotta. Besieged from the outset by offers of published and unpublished books on the subject, we received letters and diaries, and scores of people wanted to act as technical directors. We also received threats from the family of a Maréchal Bazanine in Paris, who warned that on no account must we portray him in our picture. We had no intention of doing so.

We based our script on Bertita Harding's best-selling book, *The Phantom Crown*. But we soon saw that the character of Juárez, the stubborn, authoritative Mexican hero, was even more interesting and exciting than Maximilian or Carlotta, and would be perfect for Paul

Muni. I asked Aeneas MacKenzie to develop the first-draft screenplay accordingly.

We bought Franz Werfel's play, *Maximilian and Carlotta,* because it contained many powerful situations we wanted to use. Unfortunately, because of that decision, we were placed in the unpleasant situation of having to pay a Nazi publisher for the rights.

For a time we called the picture *The Phantom Crown,* but changed it as the character of Juárez predominated. Muni, who was very powerful at the time, worked with MacKenzie on the script, along with John Huston. John supplied many exciting ideas, as did Wolfgang Reinhardt, Max's son. It was Reinhardt's suggestion that *La Paloma* be a plaintive theme of the picture.

We received word from Mexico that there would be trouble there if the picture was in any way inaccurate or cast a bad light on the country's patriots. We reassured our Mexican office, but nevertheless received a visit from politician Carlos Baz, who warned us that MGM's *The Girl of the Golden West* had infuriated the Mexicans.

Henry Blanke, William Dieterle, Paul Muni, and I went to Mexico City to familiarize ourselves with the backgrounds. Dieterle's Chinese houseboy accompanied him to take care of his meals and make sure that his clothes were in order. We enjoyed the visit and learned a great deal.

Muni, who was shy and withdrawn, even a little humorless, rarely showed his feelings in public. But he relaxed and grew warmer in Mexico City. One night, after a few tequilas in a fashionable nightclub, he rose tipsily from his seat, made his way to the stage, borrowed a violin, and began playing along with the orchestra. Another amusing incident took place on the return trip. We came in through El Paso, Texas, and as we got off the train at the border, the head of immigration said to Dieterle's Chinese houseboy, "Mr. Muni, I'm very glad to meet you. I enjoyed you so much in *The Good Earth.*"

Once the script was completed, it was essential that the Mexicans approved it. We mailed it off to Pedro Hurtado in December 1938. He returned it with the comment that one element must be changed. We must not make it seem that the execution of Maximilian was a result of the hatred and lack of forgiveness of the Mexican people. It must seem the result of fate—of an impersonal destiny.

He also told us that the Empress Eugénie must not be portrayed as a blonde; that the Emperor Napoleon III was almost sixty, not forty, and was ravaged and dissipated by drink; and that Porfirio Díaz was not in any of the places we showed him. These seemed modest changes, and they were made.

Brian Aherne was the perfect choice for the unfortunate Emperor Maximilian—he looked exactly like the contemporary photographs. Bette Davis agreed to play the comparatively minor part of the Empress Carlotta, and Paul Muni was brilliant as Juárez.

Perc Westmore's makeup contributed a great deal to the picture's success. After trying various masks, modeled on sculptures of Juárez, he finally achieved the dark, brooding, Indian look through the use of makeup alone. Muni had to check in at six o'clock every morning to have it applied, a process that took three hours.

As I have said, Wolfgang Reinhardt wanted *La Paloma* to run as a refrain throughout the picture. At the end, when Maximilian was shot, he felt the horror of the scene would be softened by the haunting melody. It was a traditional piece of music, in public domain, but an arranger who had redone it for a current sheet-music publisher, sued us for plagiarism. This was quickly disposed of, but it was a nuisance for several weeks.

The preview, held at the Egyptian Theatre in Hollywood, was a disaster. There were laughs in all the wrong places, and many people left before the ending. The comment cards were very bad. I held an emergency conference with Blanke and Dieterle, and decided to cut two thousand feet to give the picture momentum and vitality. We trimmed all sixteen reels, and gradually the picture looked better.

But we postponed the New York opening by several weeks. I wrote to Jack Warner on April 11: "Because of the juggling of sequences and because the picture is so important and we have so much money in it, we should definitely have another sneak preview to see what we have done in terms of audience reaction before opening. The preview the other night proves that you cannot sit in a projection room and look at pictures and think you have it right on the nose. In a picture as complex as this, and as long as this, an audience will have to tell us if we are right. . . ."

In its new form, the picture was successful. But, inevitably, we were faced with another plagiarism suit. A man named Miguel Contreras Torres, a well-known Mexican director, claimed that we had stolen the Juárez picture he had scripted in 1931–1932 and produced in 1934. In 1935 an English version had been dubbed, and Torres claimed we were responsible for the fact that it still had not found a distributor in this country. He asked $1 million in damages for unfair competition, as well as theft of his concept and approach.

Nobody connected with our picture had ever seen or heard of the Mexican production. No sooner had we received notice of this suit than we had threats of further suits from descendents of families who claimed they were sure to be misrepresented in our picture. Then a writer named Jean Bart claimed she had written the original script of Torres's movie in the English version, and threatened us with action.

The case continued after *Juárez* was released. In May 1939, Miguel Contreras Torres went to New York and had his friend, the Mexican consul, run the film in the presence of a notary public and stenographer. Then they ran a print of ours. With a complete list of the excellences of their own production and the historical "faults" they claimed to find in ours, Torres went to Washington and told the Mexican ambassador to put all possible pressure on the Mexican population of the United States to boycott and even picket the showings of our picture.

The situation was becoming ugly, and Jack Warner decided to seek a compromise. Although we knew Torres had no case, we felt that in the interests of the picture's successful release, we must appease him. We knew that he had powerful friends in Mexico and could have *Juárez* banned there.

Jack invited Torres to the studio. Using his considerable charm to relax the man, Jack told him over coffee that he would buy his picture and release it worldwide. Torres beamed. He cabled President Cardenas of Mexico that all was well, and an agreement was reached. I sent a cable to our man in Mexico City, Pedro Hurtado: PROCEED WITH OPENING AS PLANNED. As a result, *Juárez* did open in Mexico, and became a great success there.

We parted company with Paul Muni after 1939. We had him under contract for a limited number of pictures, but he was extremely critical of the roles offered him, and turned down part after part.

One he did like was *I Was a Fugitive from a Chain Gang*. It was the true story of one man's experiences on a Georgia chain gang. We never met Robert Burns, the author. The authorities were still looking for him. We corresponded through a third party, and were able to supplement his original material with other factual incidents that helped make our picture the success that it was.

Finally, it became too difficult to find material for Muni because he would only play very important historical characters or roles with social significance. After he left us, his career was never the same, and sadly, he was reduced to playing in very inferior pictures later in his life.

In 1938 we decided to take a chance and make Dr. Ehrlich's life story. It was a forbidden subject: the story of the scientist who found the cure for syphilis. Only Edward G. Robinson could play the part. He had Ehrlich's rugged honesty, compassion, and strength.

Dealing with the official bodies began. The surgeon general and Will Hays were jointly approached before I went to the Breen office.

The surgeon general wrote to me on August 12, 1938:

My dear Mr. Wallis,

It will be a great pleasure to give you any possible help in connection with your proposed film on syphilis. Early in July, in company with Dr. Paul de Kruif and Dr. O. C. Wenger, I had a conference with Mr. Will Hays to ascertain his attitude toward such a film. Naturally, he did not wish to commit himself on the abstract questions involved except to emphasize that the motion picture industry was primarily for the purpose of entertainment and not for educational propaganda, however meritorious such propaganda might be.

As it turned out, this reply meant that Hays was not taking any stand, and the surgeon general referred me to Breen.

On October 28, 1938, Breen read about our plans in a Louella Parsons column and wrote me a stern note, warning me that the code was very restrictive vis-à-vis the discussion or portrayal of sex hygiene or venereal diseases, and that, though pictures had progressed considerably, the fact of that progress did not affect the rules of the code that prohibited such subject matter. He concluded: "If asked to render an opinion on a motion picture dealing with the subject of sex hygiene or venereal disease, we would have to withdraw any such approval in advance."

I decided to proceed anyway.

Norman Burnside worked on the first draft of the script, later assisted by Heinz Herald, whose German background made him an ideal choice. Wolfgang Reinhardt was the associate producer. However, we had difficulty in obtaining research material for these writers. No biography of Ehrlich could be found, and the papers and references we needed were to be found only in libraries on the East Coast.

Gradually, we discovered more and more interesting information about the man. Ehrlich infected himself while experimenting with tubercular bacilli, thus permanently affecting his health. Unwittingly, he caused the death of a patient through the use of Salvarsan, a derivative of arsenic, and his struggle to escape charges of destroying a human life made for major drama. He was defiant, remorseless, a man against death.

There was a double motive in making the picture. I see from my memoranda at the time that we were angered by Hitler's widely quoted statement in 1938 that "a scientific discovery by a Jew is worthless." When Jewish organizations had asked us to prove that statement wrong with another picture, we were very happy to do so.

It seemed that no film on a public figure could be started without problems. There was no plagiarism suit on this occasion because there was no published material. But in November 1938 an announcement appeared in the *Hollywood Reporter* that a company called Collective Film Producers was going to make *606: The Life of Paul Ehrlich* from a play by Dr. Maurice R. Rosen. We decided to ignore Collective Film Producers, and indeed their picture was never made.

It became necessary to contact members of the Ehrlich family. By coincidence, Ehrlich's daughter, Mrs. Schwerin, was in town that Christmas, so I took her to lunch, and she talked charmingly of her father. She was wealthy and told me she had no interest in receiving money for the picture, but she mentioned that her mother was in Germany and it was impossible to get funds to her. I promised to help. George Schwerin, Ehrlich's grandson, proved to be extremely difficult. He called from New York, complaining that our European representative, Herbert Erlanger, had been harassing his mother in Switzerland, telling her that if she failed to send photographs and documents by the eighteenth of March, we would abandon the picture. I replied that this seemed untypical of Erlanger's behavior. Schwerin proceeded to insist that a very large sum of money be paid to the family for the right to use Mrs. Ehrlich's name. I pointed out that we had never paid Zola's daughter or Dreyfus's son. Jack Warner said he was disinclined to pay the Ehrlich/Schwerins anything, but our legal adviser, Roy Obringer, felt we should reach a settlement to avoid a suit.

There were also script problems that spring of 1939. Heinz Herald had done a well-written first draft, but it was cluttered with clinical detail, too literary, and the characters all talked in the same stiff manner. I asked John Huston to come in and do a new draft. With his gift for writing fluid, idiomatic dialogue, he did a fine job of making the story smooth and believable and all the characters very much alive.

There were still problems with the Ehrlich estate. Even though we brought Ehrlich's secretary's memoirs, we needed more information from the family, and George Schwerin was proving impossible. Countless letters and memoranda went to and fro. Jack Warner insisted we drop Mrs. Ehrlich from the script, but that would have left us with no feminine interest—something unheard of in those days. We contributed to a fund to help Mrs. Ehrlich in Europe. Soon after, we found out that she was a very rich lady. By June, Schwerin was still refusing to cooperate, and we still did not have a finished script.

One bright note in this period of struggle was Edward G. Robinson's approval of the screenplay. He cabled from the Hampshire House in New York on July 23:

> TREMENDOUSLY MOVED BY THE EHRLICH SCRIPT. IT IS MAGNIF-
> ICENT. A MASTERLY BIOGRAPHY OF A GREAT SCIENTIST AND A
> SIMPLE SOUL. IN THE FACE OF SO MANY DESTRUCTIVE FORCES
> THREATENING THE WORLD TODAY IT WOULD BE PARTICULARLY IM-
> PRESSIVE TO GENERAL AUDIENCES TO TELL THE STORY OF A HUMAN
> BENEFACTOR. I HOPE I MAY MEASURE UP TO ITS STATURE. LOVE
> FROM GLADYS. EDDIE.

I sent the screenplay to the surgeon general, who forwarded it to his aide, R. A. Vondarlehr. Vondarlehr approved it with two tiny cuts. This was wonderfully flattering to our writers, and John Huston was overjoyed, as was our research department.

Only the Schwerins were unhappy with the script. Jack Warner sent me a telegram from New York after a particularly difficult meeting with them:

> I WISH WE COULD CUT THE MOTHER OUT OF THE SCRIPT AND TELL
> THEM TO GO TO HELL.

And we were still up against the Breen office. The surgeon general had talked with Will Hays and everything seemed clear, but both Hays and Breen expressed their conviction that syphilis must not be the overpowering theme of the picture. I tried to argue that syphilis was an important social theme that was a fact of life. The matter remained unresolved for weeks.

In September, with no approval from the Breen office or the Schwerins, war broke out in Europe and communication with Mrs. Ehrlich became impossible. We ended up paying the Schwerins over $50,000, with an additional sum in lawyer's fees. In return, we received little more than permission to proceed with the picture, along with some scrapbooks, diaries, notes, fragments of an unpublished autobiography, and a very long and complicated letter from George Schwerin demanding changes in the script. Fortunately, because of the terms of our final contract, we could ignore them.

We went ahead and made the picture.

Jack wanted Gale Page to play Mrs. Ehrlich, but I felt Ruth Gordon was far more suitable. Dieterle directed, and the box office was good.

We had made pictures about scientists, writers, and patriots, and now it seemed time to make a biography of a sporting hero. Robert Buckner suggested we do the life of Knute Rockne, and I wrote to Notre Dame seeking their cooperation. When Buckner went to South Bend to contact Father Cavanaugh and Rockne's charming widow, Bonnie, they were very cooperative, but insisted on script approval and the right to select the cast.

We wanted James Cagney to play Knute Rockne, but Mrs. Rockne and everyone associated with Notre Dame flatly refused to have him because he was associated with gangster pictures, and thus was quite unacceptable. In vain, we pointed out that he was a fine actor who could play any part, and had even been in musicals. They were adamant: Cagney must not play Rockne. They wanted Spencer Tracy, but MGM refused to make him available, so we settled on Pat O'Brien. Notre Dame wasn't aware of him, so we sent them a print of Pat in *The Fighting 69th*. They liked the picture, accepted Pat, and indeed he was ideally cast.

MGM suddenly announced a short on the same subject, but, with great difficulty, we made them withdraw it.

Buckner wrote a good script, but Mrs. Rockne had a number of objections to it. She said that her husband did not chew cigars down to a frayed stub; he was not sloppy in dress but always elegantly turned out; he was a scholar and a teacher, as well as an athlete, and this should be emphasized; the fact that he gave guidance and help to young boys should be illustrated in several scenes; and, most important, there was too much football in the story. Buckner's rewrite took care of most of these problems, but we didn't cut down on the football. That was what most moviegoers would be coming to see.

There was the usual lawsuit, this time from the author of a radio script on the "Cavalcade of America" program who said we had used some of his ideas. To save trouble, we settled out of court once more.

The late director, William K. Howard, began the picture, but he drank heavily and had to be replaced. Lloyd Bacon took over and did a fine job.

Ronald Reagan gave a marvelous performance as the great George Gipp. We dealt very carefully with the Gipp's rise to fame under Rockne's coaching and his tragic death before the end of his senior year. Whenever Rockne wanted extra effort from his teams, he urged them to "win this one for the Gipper," or asked "And what will you give for the Gipper?"

I had a very pleasant visit to the campus during the shooting. Faculty and students at Notre Dame expressed unanimous pleasure in the picture, and it was a great success.

The last of the cycle was *Sergeant York*. This great American hero was a simple Tennessee hill-country man who, for more than twenty years, had resisted all efforts to tell his life story on the screen. Jesse L. Lasky, who joined us in 1940, had dreamed of producing this story. I liked the idea, Jesse sold us his option, and, with a writer named Harry Chandlee, he traveled to see Sergeant York and visited his birthplace, Pall Mall. Gracie York gave us copies of Alvin's love letters from the front, his scrapbooks, and diaries of his lecture tours. Lasky and Chandlee did a fine job of researching the story. In addition, each member of York's squad was contacted and paid clearance money so we could depict them by name in the picture.

We were preparing the film in Hollywood when we received an ugly letter from a man claiming to be a squad member. He wrote that York had been a coward, masquerading as a hero, and had gone mad with fear when confronted with the challenge of going "over the top" in the trenches. Fortunately, the letter turned out to be a fake. We were also harassed by a man who said he had written the only authorized life story of York. This, too, proved to be untrue.

Jack Warner and I agreed that only Gary Cooper should play Sergeant York, but for some strange reason Cooper did not want to do it. After several unsuccessful attempts to get him to come in and talk about it, we learned he had gone to New York, and Jesse Lasky followed to conveniently bump into him at restaurants, theaters, and dinner parties. After much persuasion, we came to an agreement, and Cooper did the picture. It resulted in his getting an Oscar for best performance of the year.

Borrowing Cooper from Sam Goldwyn was a major problem, because Goldwyn refused to release him unless we lent Bette Davis for *The Little Foxes.* We finally agreed to this: $150,000 for Cooper in return for $150,000 for Davis, but neither Goldwyn nor Gary's manager, Jack Moss, would let us know when Cooper would be available. We waited for months until at last Goldwyn said we could have him—six months after we had contracted for his immediate services, and long after Bette Davis had been supplied.

It proved equally difficult to find a director whom Gary Cooper approved. He would not accept Curtiz, Paramount refused to loan us Henry Hathaway, Universal declined to provide Henry Koster, and MGM would not release Norman Taurog or Victor Fleming. I decided to hire Howard Hawks, whom Gary liked, and whom Goldwyn lent us for an exorbitant price. Hawks was a fine director, particularly of action pictures, but he wanted to play Mrs. York as a sexy Jane Russell type, and even suggested that Jane play the part. I wanted a simple, country girl, and chose Joan Leslie.

Cordell Hull and General Pershing wrote me, saying they were overjoyed that we were making the picture. A pleasure to work with, Cooper portrayed Sergeant York just as good-natured, honest, and slow-speaking as I had imagined.

There was a huge reception for Sergeant York at the premiere in New York: Broadway blacked out its lights for half a minute in his honor, Mayor LaGuardia greeted him at a reception after the ticker-tape parade, and a special train from Washington brought senators to the screening. Al Jolson took a special ad in *Variety,* congratulating us on making the picture.

I was very proud.

CHAPTER 7

The War Effort

Because Jack Warner and I were deeply concerned over the crisis in Europe in the late 1930s, we decided to undertake a policy of opposition to Nazism in our pictures, despite the very strong possibility that isolationist elements in America would severely criticize us.

In 1938, Leon Turrou of the Federal Bureau of Investigation was working for J. Edgar Hoover, exposing espionage in our cities. Hoover contacted me, suggesting that we do a picture illustrating the operative's undercover work. In June of that year, Turrou had completed sample chapters for an unpublished book of reminiscences, and we decided to buy the work, hire Turrou as technical adviser, use his name and likeness on the screen, and put him in our trailer.

I talked with Robert Lord about the project at some length, while Jack Warner conferred with Roosevelt. The president was extremely enthusiastic about the project, and he and Hoover promised extraordinary cooperation in the venture.

Milton Krims, a writer I liked and trusted, had been working on a script for Edward G. Robinson (the life of Beethoven, I believe), but it wasn't working out, and I decided to hire him for the Turrou project. Krims was intensely anti-Nazi. He had covered the Munich crisis for *Collier's* with great skill, and came close to winning a Pulitzer Prize.

In August of 1938 I instructed Krims to go to New York, disguise himself as a Nazi, and attend meetings of the notorious German-American Bund, the organization devoted to subversion in our country. At great risk to himself, he made notes at night about the Bund meetings, and sent them back to us by a staff member who made laborious journeys by train to and from New York over a period of several weeks. Krims also attended the trial in which the leaders of the Nazi spies were investigated and condemned, took detailed notes, and even managed to obtain actual Nazi files and records.

With Krims assisting him, Turrou prepared a series of articles that ran in the *New York Post,* infuriating J. Edgar Hoover. He had forbidden Turrou to use classified information, but Turrou felt privileged to do so because of his position. When Hoover dismissed him, Turrou proceeded to write a best-selling book about his experiences.

The articles and a treatment for the picture were sent to the White House from Jack Warner's office. They came back severely cut: certain highly placed figures had been filtering material to the Nazis, and all references to these people were deleted.

We were now faced with a major problem. Could we legally use the names of those who stood trial as spies? I sent a twenty-eight-page memorandum to Maurice Ebenstein, our legal representative in New York, along with some sample pages of the script. After investigating the matter, and despite the fact that most of these people were in jail, it turned out that we could not depict them on the screen without clearances. To our considerable disappointment, we had to fictionalize the characters and give them pseudonyms.

Under the working title of *Storm Over America,* later changed to *Confessions of a Nazi Spy,* we began work in earnest in December 1938.

Anatole Litvak would direct; Edward G. Robinson was obviously the best man to play Turrou; and Francis Lederer, a Czech, passionately anti-German, was cast as the informer who turns against the other Nazis, played by Paul Lukas and George Sanders. I was worried that Sanders might not hold his own with the foreign players, but his German accent was so perfect that he was even more convincing than the Hungarian Lukas or the Czech Lederer.

We were faced with several problems before shooting began. Hedwiga Reicher, cast as the wife of Paul Lukas, begged me to remove her name from the credits because she had relatives in Nazi Germany, and was terrified there would be reprisals against them if her name appeared on the screen. We changed it to Mildred Embs, for the purpose of the production.

Bizarre letters came in from people offering to play actual historical figures. One N. Polisson of 430 West Fourth Street, New York, sent me a telegram reading: YOUR DIFFICULTY IS SOLVED. I WILL PORTRAY HITLER.

I cast Martin Kosleck, a New York actor little known in Hollywood, in the important role of Dr. Goebbels. As soon as this was announced, Goebbels responded angrily by having a secretary telephone our Berlin office that the German film industry would soon prepare propaganda films focusing on corruption in the American government.

Threatening letters poured in. Robert Lord, Edward G. Robinson, and I all received letters from unknown people saying that if we proceeded, we risked death. We ignored them. More serious, the Nazi government lodged complaints with the State Department in Washington, and high-ranking Nazi George Gyssling, consul general in Los Angeles, came to see me and asked me to call off the picture. On Hitler's express instructions, Fritz Wiedemann, the Führer's commanding officer in World War II, his closest personal friend, and now consul general in San Francisco, tried to stop our film. We stood firm. Our art director began to build eighty-three sets. In January 1939 we went into production.

But the difficulties continued. Paul Lukas was shooting a picture for Hal Roach, and, because of the timing, we had to share his services, which delayed our picture considerably. Anatole Litvak made a habit of shooting many takes and printing all of them. Needless to say, we broke him of that habit.

Because of legal problems, we were not allowed to have a preliminary statement saying that all Nazis in the picture were living and in jail. But in other respects, we were able to get away with a great deal.

Even after the picture was finished, Jack and Ann Warner had their lives threatened by anonymous notes, and the German-American Bund sued us for $500,000. But the case had to be dropped because Fritz Kuhn, head of the Bund, was jailed for stealing Bund funds.

Confessions of a Nazi Spy was banned in many European countries, including Sweden, Yugoslavia, and Germany itself. The German ambassador, Hans Thomsen, delivered a message to Secretary of State Cordell Hull denouncing the picture as an example of "pernicious propaganda poisoning German-American relations." Fortunately, the critics took no notice of such attacks.

But I had cause to remember them. In 1939 I set off on a motor tour of Europe with Henry Blanke and another associate, Jack Saper. We were crossing from Austria into France when we suddenly realized we had to make our way through a tiny area that was German. When Nazi soldiers stopped and questioned us, we were very nervous. Knowing of Goebbels's hatred of what we had done in the field of movie propaganda, we were afraid we might be held and even imprisoned. The Nazis went into a small office at the frontier post, spent considerable time going through a large card index of names, but finally emerged, stamped our passports, and allowed us to proceed to our destination.

Our next propaganda picture was *Underground*, a story by Oliver H. P. Garrett and Edwin Justis Mayer which later became a book, published by Simon & Schuster. It has been submitted to several studios, including Columbia and Selznick, but was considered too controversial for a film. The story of treachery and conflict within the Nazi ranks, it showed illegal radio stations, torture and murder of Jews, and betrayal by servants of their masters. Charles Grayson wrote the script, and I asked John Huston to polish it. Eric Sevareid came from New York for a mere five hundred dollars to do our prologue. But we had casting problems from the beginning, and the picture was not a major success.

Soon after, we made a companion piece, directed by newcomer Vincent Sherman, entitled *All Through the Night*. This was the story of Nazism in New York: a gangster besting German subversives on the principle of "it takes one to catch one." It was played largely for comedy.

We offered the female lead to Luise Rainer, who, after winning two Academy Awards at MGM, mysteriously left the studio. She turned down the role. We wanted Walter Winchell to play the gangster who uncovers the Nazis, and felt that the publicity attached to the casting would more than make up for any defects in Winchell's acting. Walter was very excited about doing it, but the pressure of his work made it impossible for him to take eight weeks off to make the picture. After we had cast George Raft, he backed out and Humphrey Bogart took over. Judith Anderson, who scored a great success in *Rebecca* as the menacing housekeeper, Mrs. Danvers, agreed to play a major role, despite the fact that she was already appearing in *King's Row* for us. She had to go from one sound stage to another, changing from modern costume to period clothes, and from one character to the other, without a break. She carried it off like the supreme professional she is.

Vincent Sherman fell ill during production, and another new director, Curtis Bernhardt, took over for a time. When Sherman returned, his slowness infuriated Jack Warner. He sent me a memorandum reading: "Friday's dailies were over before I could get my cigar lighted. That great, no director can be."

The picture's timing was more perfect than we could possibly have predicted: it was finished exactly one month and one day before Pearl Harbor.

We were equally fortunate with our production of *Dive Bomber*. The navy encouraged the project and gave us an extraordinary amount of cooperation, including the use of the San Diego Naval Base, PBY5 Consolidated bombers, interceptors, torpedo bombers, aircraft carriers (including the U.S.S. *Enterprise*), as well as several technical advisers.

The purpose of the picture was to illustrate techniques of training navy pilots, copilots, and navigators, particularly in hazardous night-flying by instruments. We dealt with the danger of high-altitude flying; blacking out when pulling out of dives; nervous problems that developed in intensive combat; and the strain of separation from loved ones at home. In addition, we wanted to show the considerble might of the San Diego Naval Base and its surrounding installations. With no thought of any warlike attitude on the part of the Japanese, our chief concern was to make the public aware that our country was fully prepared in the event of an attack by Nazi Germany.

We decided to cast Errol Flynn in the role of the naval air force corps surgeon who survives the problems of dive-bombing to become a full-fledged hero. We did not suspect Flynn's unusual enthusiasm and unheard-of interest in shooting on the *Enterprise* and in the restricted areas of San Diego. Ralph Bellamy and Fred MacMurray were added to the cast, with Robert Lord associate producer and Mike Curtiz directing.

Everything went well at the beginning. I often drove down to San Diego and stayed at the famous old Coronado Hotel where Errol, Ralph, Fred, Bob, and Mike were billeted. It was a happy company, and Mike was in good form.

Trouble began in the hotel itself. Errol had a dog with a tendency to misbehave, like its owner. It would jump up without warning on girls' laps and prove unduly affectionate. When dislodged, it brought the tablecloth to the ground, shattering glassware and dishes. On one occasion it took a bite out of a waiter's leg and he fell to the ground, carrying a heavy tray with him. On another occasion, when Adolph Spreckels, the San Francisco sugar tycoon, picked on Errol, calling him "a fairy," the two got into a fistfight that ended up with Errol decking his opponent.

Worse trouble came on the U.S.S. *Enterprise,* that very famous aircraft carrier from which we catapulted planes in some of our more spectacular sequences. Mike Curtiz, who seemed to think he was secretary of the navy, screamed at the admiral (in front of his men lined up on deck in white uniforms), "The ship's smoke is going in the wrong direction!"

The admiral became very red in the face. He said icily, "And what, Mr. Curtiz, do you suggest I do about it?"

"Turn the ship around in the opposite direction!" Curtiz replied.

The admiral's answer I have fortunately forgotten.

Curtiz ordered the crew up and down the deck until they were ready to kill him. In revenge, the chief gunnery officer ordered a violent fusillade to be fired from the decks throughout the night as a form of gunnery practice. We got no sleep at all.

Despite Mike's behavior and constant problems with the weather, we made a good picture. But there was a strange aftermath. The picture was sent to Japan as a normal film export, since there was no thought of a possible attack from that quarter. The detailed shots of the *Enterprise,* the shots of the naval installations at San Diego, and the techniques of catapulting planes used by our navy unhappily proved of great interest to the Japanese.

In the spring of 1941 we began work on an even more ambitious project, *Captain of the Clouds,* suggested to us by two people: Joseph W. Clark, of the Canadian Department of National Defense Air Service, and John Grierson of the Canadian Film Board. They outlined plans for a picture to illustrate the gallant work of the Canadian air force in the war against Germany. The film would show bush pilots at work, turning their skills to military uses in wartime. To this end, we bought a property entitled *Bush Pilots,* a magazine story by Arthur Horman that had been brought to my attention by the Canadian actor, Raymond Massey.

Although James Cagney was perfect casting for the hero, he

didn't like it, and felt the material was too familiar. Jack Warner was determined to have him, and persuaded him that he would be combating Nazism by undertaking the role. Jimmy agreed on condition that his brother, Bill, be the "line" producer.

Making *Captains of the Clouds* proved to be by far the most extensive and difficult venture in location work undertaken by Warners since the silent period. We had to shift an entire unit—cast, crew, and colored film stock—to Canada. All had to be triple-checked for security purposes before crossing the border. (Italian cameraman, Sol Polito, almost didn't make it, as Canada was at war with Italy.)

The story called for the first part of the action to be set in a trading post on a lake, complete with pier, hangar, stores, sheds, and surrounding trees. Writer Norman Reilly Raine flew up ahead of us to collect military information and seek out a location similar to the one he had described, but it proved impossible to find, and we finally built a complete trading post on North Bay in Ontario. It later was augmented and actually used.

We decided to center our action in and around Ottawa: film our street parades and a Wings ceremony there. Unfortunately, with every hotel in Ottawa jammed because of wartime conditions, we had to house the crew in an army camp and feed them army food. They grumbled loud and long, and twice we came close to a strike on the picture. We had to rent trucks from private contractors to haul our heavy gear from one location to another. Twice, trucks crashed, causing equipment to be damaged. Inexperienced local laborers were injured in loading and unloading, and we had to meet heavy bills for hospitalization.

We hired a Canadian Royal Air Force officer named Owen Cathcart-Jones to act as technical adviser. I flew to Ottawa with Bill Guthrie, our liaison for military affairs, at the beginning of July, and checked into the Hotel Château Laurier, which we used as our headquarters.

Mike Curtiz was our director, and his assistant directors were Byron Haskin and Eric Stacey. We had late-night conferences at the Château Laurier, working out the incredibly complex task of coordinating our movements with those of the Royal Canadian Air Force. I also had many enjoyable lunches and dinners with Air Marshal William Bishop, who was totally cooperative at every possible level. Without his help, we could not have completed the picture.

One of the most difficult sequences to shoot was the Wings ceremony, a high point of the picture. We began on a windy morning in late July at Uplands Airport, with hundreds of RCAF officers and enlisted men lined up on the parade ground. Our script called for a plane flown by Cagney to perform stunts over the ceremony, showing the character's contempt for officialdom which later changed to patriotism. Timing the famous stunt pilot, Paul Mantz, as he flew over Air Marshal Bishop giving a speech to the ranks was extremely difficult.

On our first day of work, the plane flew in on schedule, but the air marshal was late. We sent a radio message for the Mantz plane to come in again, but a sudden rainstorm ruined the effect, and we had to call off shooting. Next day, the weather was good, but Mantz developed engine trouble and had to abandon the flight. The following afternoon, the ceremony was held up for hours because there was not enough light in the sky for the color cameras. No sooner had the scene begun than one of the cameras malfunctioned, and by the time it could be fixed, the sun had gone for the rest of the day and we had to quit work.

A week dragged by. Every morning, hundreds of badly needed airmen had to be pulled from active duty to form their lineup for the picture. The air marshal, who was very busy, had to reemerge and give his speech while Paul Mantz looped-the-loop and performed other stunts. But rain, technical mishaps, and problems of every kind continued to dog us. We finally had to piece together fragments of film footage from the many days of shooting in order to achieve a finished result. In the picture, however, it looks as if the whole sequence was shot at high noon in optimum sunny conditions.

With Curtiz, Cathcart-Jones, and Sol Polito (miraculously recovered from a heart attack), I flew to North Bay by amphibian to begin work on the next phase of the picture. The problems there were major. Cagney, Dennis Morgan, and Brenda Marshall were housed in a second-rate hotel, along with Bill Guthrie and me. Tourists and local citizens swarmed through the lobby to see the movie stars, and made it impossible for our cast to come and go freely. After an emergency meeting, Bill Guthrie and I secured private accommodations for them.

One morning, a bus driven by an inexperienced driver plunged off a steep road down an incline, and three of our crew were hurt. Two of them had to be flown home to Hollywood.

All of the scenes in North Bay called for ideal weather conditions, but every morning, after an hour or two of fairly good light, it rained. Some of our cars got stuck in flood water caused by beavers damming up the storm drains during the night, and one of the grips stumbled into the lake and almost drowned.

Jimmy Cagney insisted on being his own double in a scene in which he was knocked into the water by a seaplane propeller. The scene was so realistic that he suffered a slight concussion. After it was all over, our technical adviser informed us that the propeller would normally be turned off long before the plane drew up alongside the pier, and that we had gone through this experience for nothing.

Then a local pilot insisted on making a landing, and bounced the plane so badly that he broke a strut in a pontoon. Instead of grounding the plane for repairs, he defied Paul Mantz and went back for a second fly-in. The plane went into the water on its side, and was out of action for days. Another plane had to be flown in from Toronto at great expense. Still another seaplane cracked up in Trout Lake, and that also had to be replaced.

The weather worsened. By mid-afternoon each day, our sets were flooded. Lightning struck our reloading shed and burned it to the ground.

At last, we struggled to finish. It was exhausting, and the location was a headache for all concerned.

We returned to Hollywood with great relief and pieced the film together. Mike Curtiz did a great job, and the picture was excellent.

Because of Jack Warner's special relationship with Hap Arnold, chief of the army air force, the government encouraged Warners to promote the cause of the air force. We decided to make a series of patriotic shorts. The most outstanding of these, in my opinion, was *Beyond the Line of Duty*, made under the direction of Gordon Hollingshead. It showed Captain Hewitt T. Wheless downing eighteen Japanese Zeros.

My friend, Ronnie Reagan, and Burgess Meredith, both lieutenants, starred in a short named *Rear Gunner*. We made *Wings of Steel, Commandos of the Skies, Safety in Aviation, I'll Tell You What the Army Air Force Is, Takeoffs and Landings,* and *Thirteen Aces.* We also made one of the longest films in history: the twenty-four-reel *105 HM Howitzer.* We put all of our technical resources into these pictures, and handed over the old Vitagraph Studios in New York to the army air force's motion picture unit.

In other war efforts, 95 percent of our employees subscribed to war bonds—$20,000 worth of bonds and stamps were sold each week —and Bette Davis and John Garfield ran the Hollywood Canteen.

The Office of War Information sent Jack Warner and me a memorandum asking us to concentrate our efforts on six main categories: the enemy, our allies, the armed forces, the production front, the home front, and the issues.

Errol Flynn had been turned down for service in the army and navy because of tuberculosis, so he fought for the Allies on the screen. He made *Desperate Journey* for us, about an RAF bomber shot down in Europe. His health was poor during the shooting, and he collapsed twice. As a result, the picture, directed by Raoul Walsh, was over budget and over schedule. I was called down to the set one day to arbitrate a confrontation between Flynn and Ronald Reagan in which Flynn demanded that a scene of Ronnie's be given to him. I ruled the scene remain Ronnie's. Flynn also made *Northern Pursuit* and *Edge of Darkness.*

We made *Wings for the Eagle,* about the Lockheed plant, and *Across the Pacific.* The latter, starring Humphrey Bogart and Mary Astor, and directed by John Huston, proved prophetic. We made it before the war, but our last scene showed the bombing of Pearl Harbor. When history caught up with us, we had to change to the bombing of the Panama Canal.

One of our biggest pictures was *Air Force,* based on the famous flight of a group of B-17's to Clark Field, Manila, (via Honolulu) at the outbreak of the war. The action culminated in the Battle of the Coral Sea. Captain Hewett T. Wheless and Captain Sam Triffy helped me prepare this complicated production.

One of our problems was that we could not use a California airfield to stand in for Clark, as many in the military were convinced a Japanese submarine invasion of the West Coast was imminent. So we moved the entire location to Florida, where we matched up the layout of Clark Field at Hickham Field and Drew Field.

Shooting the Battle of the Coral Sea in that spring of 1942 was a major undertaking. We decided to match documentary footage with new material to be shot in the Pacific at Santa Barbara. We issued a warning through the coast guard that a full-scale naval battle would take place about three miles off the pier, and asked that people be evacuated from that part of the coast for several weeks. We made arrangements to turn the Santa Barbara pier into a combined studio and workshop, and fixed places where we could tie boats and other water equipment to the dock and set up derricks. We rented a barge in San Pedro, and tugged it down to Santa Barbara so we could ship our cameras out to sea. We borrowed the mock-up of a B-17 from Paramount, which included fuselage, instrument panels, pilot controls, bomb doors that opened at the press of a button, and propellers that turned at a director's instructions.

Dudley Nichols wrote a fine script involving characters that were a cross section of the Allies: an Irishman, a Pole, a Swede, a Jew, a Welshman, and an Englishman. We asked Dudley to present the Japanese as well-trained, highly intelligent men, neither pushovers nor invincible. There was a problem with length, however. In order to show the details of the heroic flight to Manila, Dudley had to pack in a tremendous amount of action and character, and the screenplay ballooned to 207 pages. I felt we needed a leaner, tighter draft and Howard Hawks, our director, agreed.

Dudley and Howard condensed the script to about 160 pages, and Joe Breen made more cuts on censorship grounds. His changes were amusing and maddening. He wanted army air force men to talk like choirboys, but my objections were in vain. Typical cuts were "You S.O.B."; "Let's go after those sons of heaven"; "This place is a hell hole"; "He's a pain in the pants"; "My mother was scared by the Empire State Building"; "This is a lousy war"; "You're a louse"; or "Go thumb your nose at him." Corrections like these were a constant annoyance. Any reference to hell, heaven, God, or even the Empire State Building was forbidden. I never understood the one about the Empire State Building, and Howard Hawks blew up about it to Joe Breen, but wasn't able to get an explanation. Hawks told me in a memorandum that he assumed Breen considered the building as sacred as a church.

In August 1942, Hawks and a very large cast, headed by John Garfield, John Ridgely, and Arthur Kennedy left for Tampa, Florida. Unfortunately, our schedule demanded we work in that hot month and humidity was high and tempers short. There was no air conditioning in those days, and no relief from the heat at night.

There was trouble as usual on location. Hawks had a tendency to rewrite dialogue. On *Sergeant York* I was able to control this in the studio, but when he went to Tennessee on location, he tried to rewrite the screenplay in its entirety. He misbehaved equally when separated from me on *Air Force,* and Tenny Wright, my production manager, reported constant changes and rearrangement of scenes. I wired Howard to stop meddling with the script. Under great pressure at the studio and unable to go to Florida, I became more and more furious at the rapidly escalating budget caused by added sequences and Hawks's slowness.

In late August, the rains came, making it impossible to shoot. One actor suffered from heat prostration and was confined to bed for several days. The crew complained about living in air force quarters, and eating air force rations. Sometimes, the sky cleared and shooting began; a few minutes later, it rained.

Since a real war was going on, the planes were frequently needed for training purposes, and we could only use them on certain days. One B-17 used in long shots hit a coconut palm on landing and tore off a wing tip. One of our men was flying it, so we were responsible for repairs.

On August 19, I lost patience, and demanded that Hawks wind up production and return home immediately. He flatly refused to do so, insisting he had three more days' work—shooting a flight of B-17's coming back to the airfield at dusk. As they shot the scene, the generators failed and the cameraman, James Wong Howe, asked Hawks, "What shall I do? We can't light the airstrip!" Hawks told him to solve the problem as best he could, and Jimmy came up with flares lining the tarmac. It made a great shot. Then we received word that all the B-17's were being withdrawn from shooting and dispatched to Clark Field, Manila. Fortunately, we had enough long-shot footage to complete the picture.

As in *Captains of the Clouds,* I wanted what we call sketchy lighting in the plane, rather than hard lighting which illuminated completely and wouldn't be found in a B-17. I disliked shots in which you couldn't see the cabin roof. I felt, and Hawks agreed with me, that we needed a sense of claustrophobia and that a muslin roof wouldn't do. The problem was how to light this tiny, cramped set.

I had a consultation with Jimmy Howe, a wizard, and one of my favorite cameramen. He took a globe from his pocket and put it on my desk. No larger than an acorn, it was controlled by a rheostat, which he could press with his thumb. This little bulb was called a peanut globe, and could be hidden in the actual machinery of the plane, creating tiny areas of light on the instrument paneling which would cast a faint glow on the faces. It was marvelous, and just what we wanted.

In 1941, Irving Berlin's career was at its peak. His hit show, *This Is the Army,* was exciting audiences with its wonderful songs and strong patriotic feeling. I traveled to Chicago to see the production, and Jack Warner and I decided to film it.

I asked Casey Robinson to write the script. Irving came west for preliminary work with Casey, Mike Curtiz (who was to direct), and me, and then we accompanied him back to New York by train, the Santa Fe Chief. We worked on the script from the time we left Union Station. Somewhere in the Middle West, we got stuck in a snowdrift overnight, and had to be dug out with snowplows. We were hardly aware of it. As the snow piled up around the train, we outlined the whole production. Irving disappeared from time to time into the adjoining bedroom to compose new songs, which later became classics. He sang lustily as he worked, quite oblivious to the fact that we were snowbound.

We continued working in my suite at the Waldorf Towers in New York, and at Irving Berlin's house on Seventh Street in Greenwich Village. Fanatically Irving went over every page of the script, constantly making corrections. He was never satisfied, and Casey, who had taken on the job as a commitment to the war effort, was miserable. Finally, Irving took over entirely, and Casey went on to another project.

Back in Hollywood, there was a great excitement when Kate Smith, the queen of radio, agreed to come to Hollywood and sing "God Bless America" in our film, *This Is the Army.* I met her personally at the train, something I hadn't done since the silent days when I was in charge of publicity.

I found Kate charming, and my wife and I entertained her at our home. Irving Berlin doted on her. She is a jolly, outgoing lady with a superb voice, and her rendition of "God Bless America" was one of the two highlights of our picture. The other was Irving's own wonderful performance of "Oh, How I Hate to Get Up in the Morning," sung in an army barracks. Both these numbers brought down the house at the previews, and the picture was a roaring success.

The profits from the film were given to the Air Force Benevolent Fund, and all of us involved in the making of the picture worked without salary as a contribution to the war effort.

My first photograph.

Uncle Maurice introduced
me to baseball.

Mother and my sisters
Minna and (*standing*) Juel.

With Al Jolson, discussing the publicity campaign for *The Jazz Singer.*

As publicity head of Warner Bros., I am at the railroad station in Pasadena to welcome Lenore Ulrich to California. To my left is Harry Warner, his daughter Doris, Mrs. Warner, Lenore, and director Millard Webb.

Greeting Rin Tin Tin and
his owner Lee Duncan
on their return from a
publicity tour.

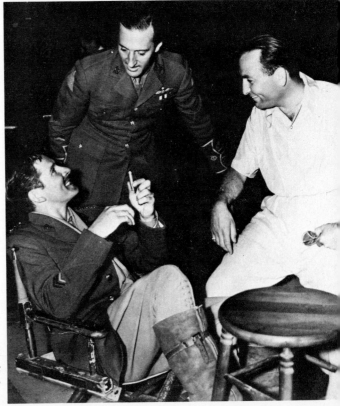

Visiting with Errol Flynn
(seated) and Basil Rathbone
on the set of *The
Dawn Patrol*.

With my bride Louise Fazenda on our wedding day.

Paul Muni entertains our group at a post-premiere party. *Standing, left to right*: Jack Warner, Paul, director William Dieterle, and me; *seated, left to right*: Cecil B. De Mille, Charlie Chaplin, and author H. G. Wells.

Showing off my first Irving Thalberg Award for "general excellence of production" in 1938.

A happy evening with my mother and Louise.

Gathered together to help dedicate Marion Davies's
new bungalow at Warner Bros. Studio. *Standing,
left to right*: me, Louis B. Mayer, Joan Blondell,
Mary Astor between two unidentified gentlemen,
Marion, and Frank McHugh; *seated*: William
Randolph Hearst and Lyle Talbot.

With my son Brent.

With Louise at the premiere of *Little Caesar*.

At a banquet with Bette Davis following the premiere of one of
her pictures.

My sister Minna with her favorite client—Clark Gable.

A scene from *Now, Voyager*, starring Bette Davis and Paul
Henreid. The year was 1942; the director, Irving Rapper.

Brent and I visit Pat O'Brien on the set of *The Fighting 69th*.

Louise and I visiting our Malibu Beach home while it is still under construction.

Receiving congratulations from Jack Warner on the success of my program of pictures.

A scene from *Yankee Doodle Dandy*, starring James Cagney. That's Walter Huston as "Uncle Sam," with Joan Leslie on his left.

One of Busby Berkeley's fantastic camera setups for *Footlight Parade*.

CHAPTER 8

Casablanca

Five days after Pearl Harbor, I found a script on my desk that was destined to become my toughest assignment, the most famous picture I ever made, and a legend that has lasted until this day.

It was an obscure play entitled *Everybody Comes to Rick's,* and it had been turned down by every studio in town. It was written by two unknowns: Murray Burnett and Joan Alison. Just before war broke out in Europe, they had visited a nightclub in the south of France, called La Belle Aurore, a gathering place for raffish expatriates, where a black pianist played the blues. Burnett and Alison had turned the experience into a romantic melodrama involving characters: Rick Blaine, a tough American running a nightclub in Casablanca; Sam, his black piano player; Captain Louis Renault, the French Prefect of Police; and Ilse Lund, Rick's former girlfriend, involved with a Czech underground leader named Victor Laszlo. Through the play, the song "As Time Goes By" was played by Sam as a refrain.

The script needed a great deal of work, but I liked it. The story of a laconic American solving the problems of Europeans would have definite appeal in those troubled times. I decided to seek the opinions of people at the studio whose judgment I valued. I was particularly anxious to have the comments of producer Robert Lord, who wrote: "I suspect that with enough time and effort a picture could be got from this very obvious imitation of *Grand Hotel.*" He went on to suggest that since it was written as a play, we might finance its production on the stage in exchange for the motion picture rights. If the play were successful, it might also be successful as a picture, but he added a warning: "Somehow most of these characters and situations seem conventional and stereotyped. If we buy this thing, I would not pay much money for it."

David Lewis, another producer, said the story had possibilities: "The background is colorful and modern and the characters romantic. I think the story needs work but it is an attractive setup." Jerry Wald, an up-and-coming writer-producer, thought it might make a good vehicle for either George Raft or Humphrey Bogart, adding that it could be tailored along the lines of *Algiers,* which costarred Charles Boyer and Hedy Lamarr.

Jerry had gotten to the heart of the matter. This could indeed be another *Algiers*—a romantic story in an exotic setting. Two days after I received the play, I bought the rights to it for $20,000.

I wanted Aeneas MacKenzie to write the script. He was a gifted man with a flair for writing believable dialogue for European characters. I called him in for a discussion, but his reaction to the material was lukewarm. He felt there was a censorship problem involved— that the suggested relationship between hero and heroine was overtly adulterous and that the Breen office, guardian of industry morals at the time, would complain. He was right. They did.

But Aeneas contributed some excellent ideas. He sent me a memorandum, dated December 17, 1941: "Behind the action and its background is the possibility of an excellent theme. The idea that when people lose faith in their ideals, they are beaten before they begin to fight. That was what happened to France and Rick Blaine. The chances for action are limited. But possibilities present themselves for several very emotional scenes and the construction of the play can be materially strengthened by having the dialogue of the characters reveal their varying national attitudes in the present chaos of viciousness, despair, decadence and courage. . . ." I asked him to read the play again and give me a further memorandum. In his second memo, he said: "I feel the material presents very serious problems indeed. . . . in my opinion this material will require drastic revision, because the situation out of which the action arises (between Rick and the girl) is a highly censorable one. . . . This is a tough job for anyone to whom it may be assigned."

As a result of this note, I decided Aeneas would not be the ideal adaptor, and offered the picture instead to the very gifted Julius and Philip Epstein. They were enthusiastic, tremendously excited by the idea. And I liked everything they suggested, particularly their ideas for opening up the story and making the American girl a foreigner. I gave them the assignment.

Then, to my dismay, they announced they were leaving Hollywood to work with director Frank Capra in Washington on a series of government propaganda pictures entitled *Why We Fight*. They assured me they intended to keep working on our story, but to be on the safe side, I hired Howard Koch (who had worked well with me on *The Letter*) to write an alternate screenplay.

Now I needed a title. Since *Algiers* had been such a hit, I decided on *Casablanca*, and on December 31, 1941, sent a memorandum to all departments: "The story that we recently purchased entitled *Everybody Comes to Rick's* will hereafter be known as *Casablanca*."

William Wyler was my first choice for director. I rushed the play and a short outline to him at Sun Valley Lodge in Idaho, where he was enjoying a winter vacation, but I never heard from him. When I called writer Norman Krasna, who was also staying at the lodge, to find out why Wyler had failed to respond, he reported that Willie was playing gin rummy with Darryl Zanuck until two-thirty every morning and couldn't be bothered. I then approached Vincent Sherman, an able studio director, and William Keighley, who had made some very good pictures for me. Neither seemed excited about the project, so I ruled them out.

Michael Curtiz told me he disliked doing this type of story, but I talked him into reading it, because I knew he would be good for the picture. He was masterful at keeping scenes moving, crowding them with atmosphere and suspense. Of all the people I sent notes to, Mike was the only one who didn't respond in kind. While we were skeet shooting at his farm in the San Fernando Valley, he told me with great enthusiasm that he wanted to do the picture.

I had casting problems right away. When George Raft turned down the part of Rick Blaine, I was not entirely surprised. He often turned down parts, preferring to go on suspension without salary rather than play them. His reasons were varied—and very strange. For example, he wouldn't act in *High Sierra* because the character died in the last reel. He was very superstitious.

My next choice was Humphrey Bogart. I felt Bogey would be great as the cynical, world-weary, essentially kind-hearted Rick Blaine, but he was irritable about playing another part George Raft had rejected. And there was an even more serious problem. Warners badly needed Cary Grant, who was under contract to Columbia, to star in *Arsenic and Old Lace*. Columbia's boss, Harry Cohn, would only lend us Cary Grant if we would lend him Bogart for a picture named *Sahara*. We had been forced to agree, and weren't sure when we could have Bogey's services. Columbia kept switching dates on *Sahara,* and we had to cast Bogey without even being certain we would have him.

I wanted Ingrid Bergman for the part of Ilsa. She had just made a tremendous success in *Intermezzo,* and I felt that she was the only actress with the luminous quality, the warmth and tenderness necessary for the role. But getting her, too, was a major problem. She was under contract to David O. Selznick, who was notoriously difficult when it came to lending his stars. His brother, Myron, was a powerful agent whose demands for his clients were so excessive we often had to bar him from the studio. And David was an agent at heart, endlessly putting people he seldom used under long-term contracts, and then farming them out at inflated prices.

Knowing I wanted and needed Bergman, Selznick avoided me, and failed to return my phone calls. When I learned he was in New York at the Hotel Carlyle, I flew back, checked in there, and called him on the house telephone. It paid off. He agreed to see me, and I managed to persuade him to lend us Ingrid Bergman for *Casablanca*.

I had two aces in the hole. Ingrid wanted very badly to do *Saratoga Trunk* (a novel by Edna Ferber we had just bought) and Selznick wanted Olivia DeHavilland for a picture. So I made the deal based on our supplying Olivia, and promising Ingrid the Ferber project. I got Ingrid for the very reasonable sum of $60,000 for the picture. This was a modest star salary for those days, and Ingrid was still not in the front rank.

The Epsteins returned from Washington and went back to work on the script. Using Ingrid was presenting more problems. We could only have her for a limited time, and every single decision on her presentation—hair, makeup, and wardrobe—could only be reached after consultation with Selznick. Though it was an irritating situation, there was nothing whatsoever I could do about it. Selznick kept an iron grip on his stable of stars.

Neither Bogey nor Ingrid was happy with the script. Bogey was wondering if he would be doing our picture first, or *Sahara*. Bergman was afraid she had lost a part she coveted, Maria in *For Whom the Bell Tolls,* because Selznick had lent her to us. In addition, they couldn't make sense of the characters they were to play.

We began casting. At first I thought of using a woman in the role of the black entertainer who plays and sings "As Time Goes By." At first I recommended to Warner that we seriously consider the brilliant singer Lena Horne, who was then appearing at The Little Troc in Los Angeles: "She is a stylist, singing soft, throaty rhythm and torch numbers in a very intimate manner." I also recommended Ella Fitzgerald, "a more exuberant colored stylist. Of course, neither of these girls are pianists . . . strictly singers. I will therefore check on Hazel Scott's possible availability."

Finally, I decided to use a male pianist, so we went back to the character of Sam in the play. Clarence Muse was considered, but he seemed too much of a caricature of a black type in the test, and we didn't want broad comedy in the romantic scenes played around the piano. I had seen *Cabin in the Sky,* MGM's all-black musical, liked Dooley Wilson's performance as Little Joe, and decided to test him. He couldn't sing or play the piano, but his personality was just right. Once again, however, we were faced with a problem. Dooley Wilson had been signed to a long-term contract by Paramount, and he was on loan-out to MGM for the picture *Cairo* until June 1. Even though we were supposed to start our film in early May, I decided to take a chance and sign him to begin *Casablanca* the day after *Cairo* finished.

Dooley managed to get over to see us on a day off so that we could dub in somebody else's voice to his lip movements. We also taught him to finger the piano, and then laid in the music played by a professional pianist. However, the voice substitution didn't work. Finally, it was determined Sam shouldn't be too professional, and we went with Dooley's own voice. It was a lucky decision. His throaty, half-speaking, half-singing proved to be a great success with audiences, and he was well worth the $3,500 a week Paramount forced us to pay for his services. That was $375 a week more than we were paying for Ingrid Bergman!

More cast difficulties loomed. The whole town knew we had a May start date and had to cast many important parts in a hurry. The agents had us over a barrel.

One important role was that of the villainous Nazi commandant, Major Strasser. I wanted Otto Preminger, who was directing and acting for Zanuck at Twentieth Century-Fox. His bald head and evil looks made him perfect casting for this menacing character, but unfortunately, Zanuck proved to be the greater menace, demanding $7,000 a week for Preminger. I declined. The only other possible choice, Conrad Veidt, was under contract to Louis B. Mayer at MGM. Mayer, knowing how desperately we needed him, asked $5,000 a week for his services for the length of shooting! This was almost $2,000 more than our female star was getting, but we had to pay it.

Claude Rains was a perfect choice for Captain Louis Renault, the Vichy police chief. He was a free-lance actor whose salary soared to $4,000 a week on our picture.

Peter Lorre, ideal for the sniveling Ugarte, was on loan-out from Universal. We paid $2,750 a week to get him back.

There was an important part of a waiter threading through the story, leading the audience from one group to another in Rick's Café. Curtiz and I both knew only one person could play it: S. Z. ("Cuddles") Sakall, whose habit of grimacing, shrugging, and pinching his chubby cheeks delighted audiences. Sakall refused the part, saying that he would go on suspension (he was under contract to us) rather than play it. As a result, we had to increase his salary to $1,750 a week.

We wanted Sydney Greenstreet for Señor Ferrari, the black marketeer and owner of the Blue Parrot Café. He also was under contract, and he also refused the part, compelling us finally to pay him the extraordinary sum of $3,750 a week for what was virtually a bit part. We agreed to pay it for two weeks, but eventually paid for twelve because of the many delays in shooting.

Another serious casting headache was Paul Henreid, whom we wanted for the part of the underground leader, Victor Laszlo. A Czech, he had the dignity and integrity the role demanded, but was tied up in my current production of *Now, Voyager* with Bette Davis. The picture was behind schedule, and it would be several weeks before we could get Paul. Claude Rains was also working in *Now, Voyager*.

By March 20, 1942, I had only sixty satisfactory pages of script. On Sundays, Mike Curtiz and the writers came out to my farm in the San Fernando Valley, and we spread the pages out and tried to combine them into a satisfactory draft.

Selznick was giving me so many headaches on Bergman's contract I even considered dropping her and replacing her with actress

Edwige Feuillere, whom I saw in a film called *Sarajevo*. But Feuillere was in Occupied Europe, and the next day I succeeded in straightening out the problems with Bergman.

I had two songs written for the story by March 31.

By April 2 our problem with Bogey was acute. Jack Warner sent me an inexplicable memorandum which read, "What do you think of our using George Raft in *Casablanca*?" I discreetly ignored it.

Worried that Henreid would not be free in time, I tested Jean-Pierre Aumont for the role of Victor Laszlo on the recommendation of a friend, Buster Collier. But Aumont was much too young, and I decided to wait for Henreid.

Even getting a cameraman was a problem. I wanted James Wong Howe, probably the best man we had, but he was working on *The Hard Way* with Ida Lupino. So Arthur Edeson, who had done a very good job on *The Maltese Falcon*, got the job.

Max Steiner was assigned to write the score, Owen Marks hired as editor.

With an incomplete cast—and about half a script—it was advisable to postpone production two weeks, until May 25.

I had intended to begin shooting in Rick's Café, but because Dooley Wilson was still working in *Cairo* and Henreid was still tied up in *Now, Voyager,* I had to rearrange the schedule and begin with the Paris scenes. Bogart was available because his Columbia picture was postponed until August.

There was trouble immediately.

First of all, the Paris sets done for us by the usually reliable art director, Carl Jules Weyl, were unconvincing and had to be redesigned and rebuilt. Then the whole first day's work was ruined by a technical mistake. Bogey and Bergman were fretful. I came down on the set to calm them—though I was anything but calm myself.

Three days into the shooting, I had another shock. There was an important scene in which Bogey and Bergman drive from Paris into the countryside. Their dialogue was vital to an understanding of their love affair. Without warning, Curtiz simply dropped all the dialogue. When I demanded to know why, he had no explanation. At great expense, the entire sequence had to be reshot with the dialogue in it.

On June 4, *Now, Voyager* was completed and Paul Henreid was free at last. We needed him immediately for the first scene in Rick's Café, but he became ill, and his doctors ordered him to bed.

Conrad Veidt and Peter Lorre were finally sprung loose from their respective studios after an uphill battle and the ridiculous payments I have mentioned. So, about two weeks into production, we more or less had a cast, but we still did not have a script.

As soon as Paul Henreid was well enough, he told me he did not want to play Victor Laszlo. He felt the role of an underground leader who appeared in a white tropical suit and hat in a famous nightclub and talked openly with Nazis was ridiculous and redolent of musical comedy. I promised to build up his part, and Casey Robinson handled this. Henreid joined the cast.

Work went on. Nobody was very happy. Bogey complained constantly about the dialogue and the fact that new pages came in every day.

The cast kept saying they had no idea what they were doing. We still had no ending. We didn't know if Rick or Victor Laszlo would get the girl, and both actors were insisting they had better be the one. Ingrid kept saying, plaintively, "Does Bogey get me in the last scene—or is it Paul?" I had to referee all these differences. Bergman became fretful when she heard there was a chance for her to do *For Whom the Bell Tolls,* and she was not free.

I felt Rick's Café was much too brightly lit. I wanted a dark, moody atmosphere, and insisted on the use of sketchy lighting: a great deal of contrast, with shadows and highlights to give visual excitement to the scenes.

There was one scene in the script in which Ilsa comes into the café and asks Rick if he has taken care of everything in covering up for Victor Laszlo. To my amazement, Curtiz failed to shoot the scene. I asked him about it, and he told me he had simply forgotten it. Unheard of!

By July 10 we were still dealing with a recalcitrant director, a cast who hated most of their lines, actors being overpaid to sit around for weeks doing nothing because we weren't sure we would need them again, and a female star who was desperate to be free to start in *For Whom the Bell Tolls.* Mike and Bogey argued so frequently I had to come on the set to control the quarrels. I also had problems with the composer of the score, Max Steiner. Even before he started work, he told me he hated the song, "As Time Goes By," obviously upset because he had to use somebody else's theme. I insisted he accept it, and also that he use a favorite of mine, "Perfidia," in the picture. We argued about a scene in which the German forces in the club and the supporters of Free France clash. He wanted the Germans to sing the "Horst Wessel" while the French sing "La Marseillaise." I pointed out that the "Horst Wessel" was not normally sung by high-ranking officers, who probably despised Hitler, and we chose a more appropriate song. Steiner grumblingly began his work.

As if we didn't have enough problems, the Breen office complained about some of the dialogue, which had to be changed. Rick was not allowed to shoot Major Strasser in cold blood, but had to be provoked. We had taken the risk of shooting the scene without an official approval from Breen, and had to reshoot it in its entirety.

By August 7 we were still in production, nine days behind schedule.

We needed a good punch line for the ending at the airport as Bogart and Rains walk off into the fog. We were so uncertain that we shot two. One line was: "Louis, I might have known you'd mix your patriotism with a little larceny." The other, which I confess I thought of and which became world famous was: "Louis, I think this is the beginning of a beautiful friendship."

We had an ending, but we did not have a good beginning. To start the film importantly, I ordered a spinning globe of the world, with voice-over narration like that used in the *March of Time* series. The globe would come to a halt on North Africa, and we would be plunged into the intrigue and drama of this crossroads of the world.

At last we finished—eleven days over schedule.

Now we put the jigsaw puzzle together. Editor Owen Marks and I ran and reran the picture until we finally succeeded in getting a fast-moving, forceful film. Under great pressure, and with countless arguments, Max Steiner produced a rich, romantic score, weaving together "As Time Goes By" and "Perfidia."

We took the picture to Huntington Park for a sneak preview. The audience seemed to like it, though they didn't rave, and indeed several cards suggested we should show Rick and Louis escaping Casablanca, as it looked as if they would be arrested when they got back to town. We wrote a new scene in which they were seen with refugees on a freighter, and even got Claude Rains back from New York to do it, but finally decided against it.

Then we had a tremendous stroke of luck. In November, the Allies landed in Casablanca. Soon after that, the summit conference of Churchill, Roosevelt, and Stalin was held there. Casablanca became a household word. One of my publicity staff had argued against using the title because it sounded like the name of a beer. And Jack Warner suggested we use the conference as a climax!

Bergman was rushed into *For Whom the Bell Tolls*. She whooped with delight when she heard the news. Bogey went off to his yacht. The other actors, who had held us over a barrel, went home with their pockets full of money. Selznick cabled me: THIS IS A SWELL MOVIE AND AN ALL ROUND FINE JOB OF PICTURE MAKING. He congratulated Curtiz and me for the "superb handling of Ingrid," adding, "the part seems much better than it actually is, and I think it will be of benefit to her and of course to me." I was delighted: I had overridden his initial doubts.

The picture opened in New York and Hollywood around Thanksgiving of 1942, and received rave reviews. There were lines around the theater for blocks even in record blizzards. By the end of 1943, the picture had become a classic by general consent. It was something I could never have foreseen that difficult summer when we made it.

Oh, yes. While I was doing the final cutting, a number of those involved in the writing and production had seen the picture in the projection room, and wrote me their opinions of what was wrong with the picture and what should be done to correct it. I kept a file of these letters in the top drawer of my desk, but did nothing about them, as I was satisfied with the reaction of the preview audience. Then *Casablanca* opened, and public acceptance was truly fantastic. In later story conferences, whenever there were violent disagreements or differences of opinion, I merely took out the file on *Casablanca* and ended all discussion.

At the Academy Awards in March 1944, we won eight Oscars, including Best Picture, Direction, and Screenplay, and I was given my second Irving Thalberg Award for consistent high quality of production.

Mike Curtiz, in accepting his Oscar, said, "So many times I have a speech ready, but no dice. Always a bridesmaid, never a mother. Now I win, I have no speech."

I started up the aisle to receive my award.

To my astonishment, Jack Warner leapt to his feet, ran to the stage, and received it ahead of me.

Almost forty years later, I still haven't recovered from the shock.

But more of that later.

CHAPTER 9

Independence

A great joy in the early 1930s was the birth of my son, Brent. Louise and I had longed for a child, but it seemed this was not to be. After years of disappointment, Louise made a pilgrimage to Lourdes and then to Sainte Anne de Beaupré, a religious shrine in Quebec. Soon after, she bore a son, a wonderful boy who brought much happiness into our lives.

As a child, Brent went to Highland Hall, a little school not far from our home. A reclusive boy, perhaps because he was an only child and didn't have the rough-and-tumble of brothers and sisters, he was extremely studious and was chiefly interested in curling up in a chair with a book. His closest friend as a boy was Ricky Arlen, son of the well-known actor Richard Arlen. But apart from visits with Ricky and with Manny Robinson, Eddie Robinson's son, Brent grew more and more introspective and withdrawn.

One day a complete stranger came to the gate of the ranch and announced that he was a physical training expert. Was there anyone in the family who needed building up? Louise welcomed him with open arms. Those were the days you could ask strangers into your home without the slightest fear. This man took Brent in hand and turned him into a fine, robust youngster, and Louise and I were delighted. Brent still works out regularly and today has a movie-star physique.

As Louise's career faded, she became more and more involved in charitable work and philanthropy. She visited invalids and shut-ins who were total strangers, and took care of their needs, paying their bills, unbeknownst to them, and bringing them books and food. Brent went with her on these visits.

One poor woman they saw often was a schoolteacher who lived alone in an isolated area. When she died, we were amazed to discover she had substantial property. She left Louise over one hundred acres of land in northern California near San Luis Obispo. She felt that if America lost the war, a special place must be reserved for Jewish people like us to escape the clutches of Adolf Hitler.

The brilliant comedienne ZaSu Pitts was perhaps Louise's closest friend. They were birds of a feather, great in silent pictures, and very much in accord temperamentally. She was also very fond of Bess Meredyth (Mrs. Mike Curtiz) and Mrs. Raymond Griffith. Another close friend of Louise's, Edith Ryan, was her press agent. There can be very few press agents who are buried in their clients' family plots, but Edith was one of them. Louise made sure that Edith had a place next to her in Inglewood Cemetery.

Brent used to enjoy visiting Edith with Louise. Her place was very colorful. She lived in a darkened room, the walls covered with anti-Roosevelt cartoons. Her fuel was a burning hatred for FDR, and it kept her going for years.

Brent's introduction to motion pictures was very strange. He says today he was traumatized at an early age by seeing movies as I cut them at home. He would walk in as the film was starting and a minute later it would be over. Or he would see the plot out of order: somebody would be shot dead and a minute later they would be introduced. For a child, this was very unsettling. After a while, I simply arranged special evenings for him to see the latest Westerns or Disney pictures. There was scarcely a night I wasn't cutting, so that seemed only fair.

Brent attended Occidental College and spent a year at Stanford University before serving two years as a first lieutenant in the air force. He took his doctorate in psychology at the University of Florida and practices today in San Francisco. He was a constant joy to Louise and me. I am very proud of him.

Shortly after Brent's birth, I stepped down from running the studio to simply being a producer at Warner Bros. It was something I had wanted for some time, as the job of supervising this vast and growing organization was becoming more and more exhausting. I had no rest, no home life, and now that I had a growing son who needed his father I was more conscious than ever of the need to reduce the pressure.

My deal with Jack Warner was that I would make no more than

four pictures a year. The studio would provide the financing, and I would have a drawing account and get a percentage of the profits. I was to have first call, first choice of everything they acquired: books, plays, and magazine stories. I made eight pictures under our agreement—among them *Casablanca, Now, Voyager, Air Force, King's Row, Saratoga Trunk,* and *Watch on the Rhine.* This rich period for me was followed by a severe rift with Jack Warner, which led to my departure from the studio for good.

First of all, Jack did not live up to the terms of our contract. He often acquired material I never saw and never had an opportunity to consider for my own productions. This was totally unacceptable to me. Then Jack began to inject himself into my company's decision making, attempting quite arbitrarily to overrule me in some cases.

After my second year I was determined to leave Warner Bros. I had to make pictures my way or not at all.

Matters came to a head that Oscar night. After it was announced that *Casablanca* had won the Academy Award for Best Picture of the Year, I stood up to accept when Jack ran to the stage ahead of me and took the award with a broad, flashing smile and a look of great self-satisfaction. I couldn't believe it was happening. *Casablanca* had been my creation; Jack had absolutely nothing to do with it. As the audience gasped, I tried to get out of the row of seats and into the aisle but the entire Warner family sat blocking me. I had no alternative but to sit down again, humiliated and furious.

The next day Edwin Schallert, dean of the motion picture writers, protested with a column in the *Times,* and the Academy apologetically sent me another Oscar, but nothing could make up for what Jack had done. I should have expected it: I remembered that he alone received the French Légion d'Honneur for *The Story of Louis Pasteur* despite the fact that he had had no interest in making the picture!

Later on, when we were friends again, Jack wrote a very lengthy anecdotal memoir without once mentioning my name. Such are the ways of our industry.

One of the problems we faced constantly at Warners, both before and during my period of independence, was casting. It is surprising that with the great pool of available talent at the time, we were often unable to find ideal players. I was always searching for new stars.

One that got away was Gregory Peck.

While working on a project in New York with Casey Robinson, I saw this fine-looking young actor in a play. Though he had not yet made his mark in the theater, his personality intrigued me and I made an appointment for him to come to the Waldorf Towers to discuss a possible contract with Warner Bros. I telephoned Jack Warner, told him my reaction to the actor, and that Peck could be signed to a contract for a period of years beginning at $1,000 per week. Warner said, "Who is this guy, I never heard of him, and we certainly aren't going to pay $1,000 per week for an unknown." Remember, at the figure quoted there was no limit to the number of pictures that Peck could have done for us. It was a weekly salary, and we could have put him in two, three, or four pictures a year, had we chosen to do so.

In any event, Warner turned him down and Casey Robinson, who planned to leave Warners and start his own independent company, asked me if I objected to his talking to Peck about a contract. I told Casey he was free to proceed. He did, and signed Peck for five pictures. Though Peck's first picture was not a great success, it did introduce him to films and gave other production companies an opportunity to see him on the screen. As a result, Robinson sold the remaining four pictures of his contract for a handsome profit.

The contract between Casey and Peck was nonexclusive, permitting Peck to make outside pictures. Jack Warner, having now seen him on the screen, made a deal with Peck's agent for a single picture at $125,000. This would have paid his salary for two years on the basis originally proposed.

We had problems casting *The Man Who Came to Dinner,* the famous comedy based on the character of the temperamental and extravagant Alexander Woollcott. Monty Woolley had played the irascible Sheridan Whiteside on the stage, but we felt that his name was not sufficiently known to justify starring him in the motion picture.

Charles Laughton was desperate to play the part, and even offered to test for it. His agent, Phil Berg, sent me an endless stream of notes urging me to consider him. Jack Warner was afraid that Laughton, a homosexual, might be effeminate in the role. Director Edmund Goulding handled his test very carefully, but Jack turned out to be right. We had to tell his agent that his client was out of the question.

Laughton, a very emotional man, broke into tears when he heard the news. Berg called and asked me to give him another chance. "He'll be able to get his teeth into the character in two days," he said. "I promise you he won't swish the next time around."

I was touched by the call and gave Laughton another test. But it was a disaster, worse than the first. When he left the studio, Laughton's face was a picture of despair.

We tested the enormously fat and very talented Laird Cregar, then making his mark at Twentieth Century-Fox in such pictures as *The Black Swan* and *Blood and Sand*. But he was overblown and extravagant, and he too had to be ruled out.

Robert Benchley was excellent in his test but too mild mannered.

Bette Davis (cast at her request as Maggie, Whiteside's secretary) urged me to use John Barrymore, but I couldn't risk it. The dialogue in *The Man Who Came to Dinner* was tremendously complicated, and Barrymore was drinking so heavily that he had to read his lines from cue cards.

Suddenly, Orson Welles turned up and announced that not only would he appear in the film, he would also direct it. He wanted $100,000 to act, and $150,000 to direct, a very hefty sum in those days. We finally agreed that he would act in the picture but *not* direct. He then specified that he would work only with directors Leo McCarey or Howard Hawks. McCarey was busy and so was Hawks. While we were sorting this out, we got a phone call from George Schaefer of RKO Radio Pictures flatly advising us that Orson was under contract to them and would not be permitted to make *The Man Who Came to Dinner*. Then Eleanor Roosevelt telephoned me that only Orson Welles could make the picture! I referred her to George Schafer. Apparently even her unique powers of persuasion could not overcome that tough man's decision.

Things looked bleak. Jack suggested Cary Grant, but I felt he was far too young and attractive.

Fredric March was tested.

Bette never stopped begging for Barrymore.

Six months after we had started planning the picture, we still had no leading man.

In desperation, we went back to Monty Woolley. Jack was afraid that Woolley's homosexuality would be obvious in the scenes. Bette Davis hated him and threatened that she wouldn't work with him, but we tested him anyway.

He was excellent. His acid, piercingly sharp delivery of the lines, spoiled-child mannerisms, and outbursts of petulant rage were perfection itself. We felt that Bette and a strong enough cast could make up for the fact that Woolley wasn't a box office name. Certainly there was no hint of effeminacy in his test, his performance powerful and entirely masculine.

We began work.

Bette grumbled about Woolley but gave her usual superb performance. Then a crazy accident took place. A dog bit her nose . . . and she the president of the Tailwagger's Society! She retreated to her home in New Hampshire and didn't come back for weeks.

She sent me the following telegram:

IF I THOUGHT IT POSSIBLE TO WORK ON MONDAY I WOULD OF MY OWN VOLITION BE THERE. SCAB NOT OFF YET AND HOPING IT WILL BE ALL RIGHT BY THURSDAY WHEN I GET IN. WISH THERE WAS SOMETHING I COULD DO TO HURRY ALL THIS.

A few days later another telegram was sent, which read:

MY NOSE IMPROVING RAPIDLY. SHOULD KNOW SOMETHING THIS WEEK MY DEFINITE DATE OF RETURN. MY BEST.

When Bette did come back, she drove straight from the station to my office. Her nose was covered by an alarmingly large bandage, but at least she was there, and I could stop sending get-well telegrams such as

HAPPY TO HEAR YOUR NOSE RAPIDLY IMPROVING or DON'T BLOW IT TOO HARD.

We shot for two days with Bette's back to the camera. This was fine, except that every time the other actors saw her, they broke into fits of giggling led by Monty Woolley. It became impossible for them to speak their lines.

Bette eventually recovered and resolved her differences with Woolley. The picture was finished on schedule and was very well received critically and commercially.

Each picture presented its own problems. *King's Row,* one of my independent pictures, was no exception.

Buying the property was difficult. After haggling for weeks with agent Anne Watkins, who represented the author, Henry Bellamann, we finally closed for $50,000, a lot of money in those days.

King's Row was a harrowing account of life in a small country town. It depicted the incestuous relationship of a pretty young girl and her father, a sadistic doctor who operated without chloroform, a handsome young man whose legs were crushed under a falling freight car, grim scenes in a lunatic asylum, and indications of syphilis and inherited madness. In spite of all this, the book was basically inspiring, its central character a young doctor who defies the forces of evil and disease to become a force for good in King's Row.

I wanted Max Reinhardt's son Wolfgang to be associate producer, but he told me flatly he didn't believe it could be made. He said the censors would never approve such a story. Fortunately, David Lewis, an associate producer working in my independent unit, liked the story and wrote me: "It has the makings of a big, fine picture. In fact, I am more enthused about this than any other project. . . ."

I felt the perfect writer for the adaptation would be Casey Robinson. With his great sensitivity and gift for authentic American dialogue, he would be ideally attuned to Dr. Bellaman's concept.

But I was in for a shock. Casey had just left for a vacation in the Orient, on one of the last cruises before Pearl Harbor. When he received the book in Hong Kong, he cabled to say he thought it was hopeless material for a picture. I cabled him to read it again. He says today that while sailing between Manila and Bali, he finally tossed the book into the sea, thinking that I was crazy to have bought so downbeat a property.

Then something very strange happened. As he saw the book floating on the waves, he suddenly realized how he could lick the subject: make it the story of an idealistic young doctor challenged by the realities of a cruel and horrifying world. He cabled me he would go ahead at once. I was delighted with his approach to the theme, and cabled him in Bali to start work immediately. Unfortunately, he couldn't, as the book had already been consigned to the waves. He spent the rest of the journey in a state of acute frustration.

Back in Hollywood, I decided to hire Sam Wood to direct *King's Row*. I liked his direction of *Kitty Foyle*, which won an Oscar for Ginger Rogers, and felt that Sam had handled Christopher Morley's story of a young girl in New York with great skill. His warm response to our project encouraged me further. Although Sam was a fine director of people, he needed to work with an art director who could visualize the scenes for him. We hired the best in the business: William Cameron Menzies.

Menzies was the genius who did such a superb job on *Gone with the Wind*. The rich look of that film owed everything to his talent. *King's Row* was set in period, in a world of white fences and clapboard houses and overstuffed rooms with potted palms.

With Casey's sensitive writing, Sam's brilliance with actors, and Menzies's visual eye, all we needed was a great cameraman. The greatest was James Wong Howe, whom I had under contract and assigned to the picture.

We began work on the script following Casey's return in the spring of 1941. Before we had submitted a single page to the censor, Joe Breen told us flatly we simply could not make *King's Row*.

He sent a memorandum which read, "Any such picture would be rejected in full. . . . We see illicit relations between Parris and Cassandra and Drake McHugh and his girlfriend Randy. . . . There is much loose sex everywhere. . . . There is a suggested affair between Drake and two local girls, the Ross sisters. . . . There is a mercy killing of Parris' grandmother. . . . There is a sadistic characterization of a doctor. . . . Any suggestion of sex, madness, syphilis, illegal operations, incest, sadism, all must go. . . . If this picture is made [Breen was warming to his theme] it is likely to bring down the industry as a whole . . . decent people everywhere will condemn you and Hollywood . . . even if you rewrite the script it will be against our policy and the policy of the whole industry to allow such a picture to be made. . . ."

Jack Warner, David Lewis, Casey, and I went to see Breen to argue our case. We pointed out that far from bringing disgrace on the industry, the picture would illustrate how a doctor could relieve the internal destruction of a stricken community. Casey carried the brunt of the argument and I could see Joe Breen was impressed. He agreed to reconsider the screenplay if we removed all reference to incest, changed Cassie's nymphomania to dementia praecox, and did not specify that Parris and Cassie actually went to bed together. We also removed the mercy-killing aspect and (to our great annoyance) the young kids skinny-dipping: a nice period touch.

We returned to Breen with a second-draft screenplay, but he again turned it down. Third and fourth drafts were submitted until he was satisfied. In the long run I felt it was all to the good: audiences had a great deal to swallow in the picture, and too much grimness might have wrecked its chances at the box office.

Once again, casting was a headache. Henry Fonda and Tyrone Power were my first choices to play idealistic young Parris Mitchell, but they were under contract to Darryl Zanuck and he would not release them. I tested Michael Ames several times. Young and handsome, he had a fresh, open quality that made up for the fact that he had no name. But he was drafted into the army and lost his chance for stardom.

Finally, I settled on Robert Cummings. He was actually too old for the part, not quite right, but was helped considerably by an extraordinary supporting cast. Ronald Reagan, who played his friend Drake McHugh, gave a very fine performance. Ann Sheridan, Charles Coburn, Judith Anderson, and Nancy Coleman were all excellent.

One of the most important roles was unhappy, mad Cassie, with whom Parris Mitchell had his first love affair. We offered it to Ida Lupino, but she turned it down because she was committed to *Ladies in Retirement* at Columbia. Bette Davis wanted to play it, but we all felt the picture would be thrown off balance because of her fame and talent.

James Stephenson, a fine British actor who worked for us in *The Letter,* was cast as the tragic Dr. Tower, who kills Cassie and himself because of his guilt over fathering the child of an insane woman. We were no sooner into his wardrobe tests than he collapsed and died of a heart attack. After a midnight emergency conference, we decided to replace him with Claude Rains, who could match Stephenson, even surpass him, in the role. We called Rains at his home in Chester County, Pennsylvania, and he declined instantly. But we tried again, rushed him the book, and he finally agreed to break off his much-needed vacation and make the long train journey west. His refusal to fly meant a considerable delay in our schedule.

Because of the postponement, Robert Cummings had to fulfill another commitment, a Deanna Durbin picture at Universal called *It Started with Eve.* Understandably, he was very nervous, making two pictures at once—one a lighthearted musical comedy and the other stark tragedy. Bob had to drive from Burbank to Universal and back again every day, changing costumes and characterizations en route. It was a major headache. Less so, but still an annoyance, was the coincidence that Judith Anderson was also making two pictures at the same time, our spy thriller *All Through the Night,* as well as *King's Row.*

We still didn't have our Cassie. Casey Robinson had written the part brilliantly, and I felt Olivia DeHavilland would be interesting as the fragile, doomed girl. She agreed to a test but backed out. After playing Melanie in *Gone With the Wind,* she felt audiences would not accept her as a sex-mad, mentally disturbed girl. I considered waiting for Ida Lupino to finish *Ladies in Retirement,* but she told me that she, too, was afraid of the part. She had played several mad-women in a row and wanted a change of pace.

Even though Breen had approved the script provisionally, he raised endless petty objections. He said we could not have a scene in which Drake McHugh said to his friend Parris, "You have to bunk with me. I hope you don't mind the change." In vain, we protested that these two men and the actors who played them, Ronnie Reagan and Cummings, were entirely masculine and the line contained no suggestion of homosexuality, but Breen was adamant. We had to change the line to, "You have to bunk with me. I hope you don't mind, Mr. Mitchell!"

Sam Wood gave us another problem. He didn't want Drake McHugh's legs amputated after the freight car accident because he was afraid the audience would assume castration and regard Drake as a freak. I pointed out that legs were normally amputated just above the knee. Drake might be affected psychologically but not sexually. Wood refused to accept this. He insisted that the surgeon who hated Drake would have wanted to take his manhood. It took a great deal of time and much additional dialogue to convince Sam.

We began shooting in late summer. We still had no Cassie, and Jack Warner made some ridiculous suggestions, among them Joan Leslie, Susan Peters, and that buxom example of normal, middle-class, healthy womanhood, Priscilla Lane. In mid-August, I was still trying to get Gene Tierney, whose unusual face and temperament made her ideal casting, but Darryl Zanuck got her first.

Marsha Hunt, Laraine Day, and Anita Louise were tested and found wanting. Marlene Dietrich's publicist announced that she had won the role, which gave us all a much-needed laugh.

When only Cassie's scenes were left to shoot, we took a chance with an actress we had tested earlier. Her name was Betty Field.

She was superb . . . astonishing. But she had a curious shortcoming: she was marvelous the first time she did any scene, but couldn't sustain the emotion, burned it up quickly, and had nothing left for later takes. She was great in the test she made with Cummings, but completely flat when she did it again in the actual film. So we used the test, and the first take of everything else. The results were just what we wanted.

Because of delays and problems, we finished up twenty-two days over schedule, but the effort was worth it. Audiences were fascinated by the picture and it became a classic. We were very proud of it.

Yankee Doodle Dandy was one of my favorite pictures as an independent producer. The life story of George M. Cohan, the composer and musical star, it presented us with remarkably few problems. One great advantage of the story was that it dealt with an extremely patriotic person. By using scenes of World War I, we could say a great deal about America as a defender of freedom in World War II.

I had seen Cohan, already an old man, in his dazzling performance on Broadway as the president of the United States, in *I'd Rather Be Right*. I knew then that James Cagney was the only actor to play him. I telephoned Cagney's brother Bill, who controlled his every move. I didn't call Jimmy because we had never gotten on well together. He referred to me not by name, but as "the front office." Bill Cagney was friendlier and knew I had Jimmy's interests at heart. He promised to get in touch with him and I confidently awaited an excited long-distance call from the East. I was sadly disappointed when Cagney refused to make the picture. He said he was going into independent production and had absolutely no interest in Cohan.

I asked Bill Cagney to put everything on hold. In record time, I had a skilled writer named Robert Buckner write a treatment and rushed it to Martha's Vineyard.

No response.

I called Bill again. He was lukewarm, but I got the impression I had made a dent in Jimmy's armor.

I had Buckner write the entire script with Jimmy in mind and enlisted Cohan's aid. He was terminally ill, and I believe his great desire to have Jimmy play the part touched that hard-bitten man. Cagney suddenly agreed to make the picture.

He worked hard on the dances. It had been many years since he had danced, and it took him quite a while to master the stiff-legged, jerky style of Cohan. But once he succeeded, despite two sprained ankles, he was a knockout.

Mike Curtiz directed the picture for me. He was as tough as Cagney, and once Cagney recognized that fact, they got along famously.

Despite the fact that Cagney gave his greatest performance in the picture and won an Academy Award for it, he was never cordial to me from the first day of shooting until the last. I was, and still am, "front office" to him.

George M. Cohan was bedridden when we ran *Yankee Doodle Dandy* for him. It was a joy for that grand old man to see Cagney impersonating him so brilliantly and it made his last days happier.

One of my favorite independent productions was *Now, Voyager*, which was also one of Bette Davis's best pictures. It was set in her native Massachusetts and certain elements of the story were similar to situations in her own life. She had been an awkward, shy girl who broke free of a dominating mother and a strait-laced background to become an attractive and appealing woman. Charlotte Vale in *Now, Voyager* was a pathetically awkward ugly duckling who discovered romance with an architect on a cruise to Rio.

Olive Higgins Prouty's novel had been a big best-seller and I was determined to buy it. We began negotiations with Mrs. Prouty's agent, Harold Ober, in October 1941, and closed with him for $35,000, quite a bargain.

I sent the novel and a synopsis to Edmund Goulding, suggesting that he write the script as well as direct the picture. No sooner had I done so than I received an immensely long memorandum from Mrs. Prouty. Beginning with glowing praise of my previous pictures, clearly a softening-up tactic for what was to come, her letter contained very definite and rather imperious ideas. She wanted to make the picture experimental in character, with the present-day sequences in sound and the flashbacks silent with subtitles. I had visions of the entire audience moving quite rapidly into the street.

She pressed on. She wanted the heroine to alternate narration with the hero and sometimes use both voices at once. She even laid down a scheme for actual sequences: "The opening sequence will show the bright, brilliant blinding Italian sunshine [the novel was set in part in Italy] and the dour, dread, dreary dark of the moon on Marlborough Street, Boston. . . . Technicolor should be most ideal, the flashbacks being shown in subdued colors as if seen through a veil." Unable to find a way to respond to this letter, I decided the best policy would be not to do so.

Eddie Goulding came up with a more rational idea. He suggested that Casey Robinson do the screenplay, and I assigned him at once. In December, just after Pearl Harbor, Robinson began work on Goulding's treatment.

I was under pressure from the studio to change the title, but I thought it ideal and retained it. I felt the story could have the same success as Charles Boyer and Irene Dunne's *Love Affair,* and I thought of them as perfect casting for the leading roles. I also offered the picture to Norma Shearer, who liked it but had already decided to retire from the screen because of eye problems. Irene Dunne heard that her agent Charles Feldman had discussed the script with Norma and, under the mistaken impression that he was playing one actress against the other, she declined.

I sent the book to Leland Hayward for Ginger Rogers, who loved it and left for her ranch on the Rogue River, promising me an early decision. Weeks passed. I wired her on February 2, 1942, but she did not respond.

Bette Davis wanted to play the part, and we finally went with her. She was last choice, and a lucky one.

We delayed production because Bette was involved in the Democratic Convention at Madison Square Garden. She had had disastrous notices in *In This Our Life* and the preview cards had criticized her makeup and costuming. *Now, Voyager* called for her to become a beauty one-third of the way through the picture. There couldn't be any mistakes.

I signed Sol Polito as cameraman because of his superb lighting of the stars. He had been assigned to a Jack Benny picture but I asked Jack Warner to transfer him and he agreed.

Eddie Goulding fell ill and I asked Mike Curtiz to take over for him as soon as he finished *Yankee Doodle Dandy.* Mike and Bette didn't get along, and he asked me to reconsider, so I decided to go with a new director named Irving Rapper, a pleasant, amusing Englishman. Rapper liked Bette and she liked him.

A very strong actor was needed for the part of Dr. Jaquith, the psychiatrist who cures Charlotte Vale in *Now, Voyager.* I felt Claude Rains would be ideal, but he turned down the part, insisting it was too sketchy. Casey Robinson built up the role, and Rains agreed to do it for the then enormous salary of $5,000 a week. I offered him $25,000 for six weeks but his agent Mike Levee was adamant and we went ahead with the required arrangement.

Another difficult part to cast was that of Charlotte's tyrannical mother, Mrs. Vale. Ethel Griffies was too much the maid, too little the matriarch of a clan. Dame May Whitty, a stalwart of the MGM stock company, was too warm and charming. Alma Kruger, who had made a great hit as a vicious old woman in *These Three,* was too obvious and melodramatic. Irving Rapper suggested the great British actress Gladys Cooper. Although her test was disappointing (she spoke much too softly), I felt that if she could be made comprehensible to American audiences and more aggressive in her playing, she would be good in the part. What I could not have predicted was that she would fully match Bette in the dramatic scenes. It was a battle of champions.

I told Orry-Kelly to design extremely simple, beautiful, timeless clothes for Bette to wear after her transformation. I did not want to overdo the ugliness of her costumes or makeup in the early scenes, and insisted that she be presented at all times in a style appropriate to her position.

Our old nemesis, the Breen office, made ridiculous demands again. On April Fool's Day, 1942, Breen sent me a lengthy memorandum. He said that when Charlotte and a ship's officer climb out of a car in which they have been kissing, Charlotte's hair must not be mussed to suggest a close embrace. Despite the fact that the entire picture centered on the affair between Charlotte and her lover, Jerry, there must be no suggestion that they go to bed together. In a scene in which they are stranded for the night in a cabin in Brazil, it must be made clear that they are under separate blankets. We protested that it was unlikely there would be a blanket in the place at all, certainly not two. Breen said that if the lovers were covered by only one blanket he would not permit the picture to be released.

The result was that a chief element in the story, Charlotte's loss of her virginity, was eliminated. This was very serious, but there was nothing we could do about it. It made nonsense of the character of Jerry, implying that he was a man who could have an attractive, loving woman in his company for an entire night and do nothing about it. Fortunately, Paul Henreid acted the part so sensitively that audiences accepted a man who was either neuter or a saint.

I asked Orry-Kelly to design a very special hat for Bette to wear in the first scene after her metamorphosis. The hat was to shade her face to indicate that she was still shy, despite her emergence as an attractive woman, and was deliberately designed for this effect. Jack Warner sent me a note after seeing the tests: "I am much afraid of Davis' hat. You will have to guess what she's thinking about. A large hat may be all right and again it may not but we must see the people's eyes when they are acting." Since this was an independent production, I consigned the note to the wastebasket, where it belonged.

The script was criticized by our Rio office, who said that Brazilians would reject the picture out of hand because it showed an inept taxicab driver driving the hero and heroine off the side of a cliff into a canyon. We were also told we should not show a bumpy, dusty road in the scene of the accident. This note found its way into the same wastebasket.

In the scene in which Charlotte Vale arrives in New York after the cruise, I wanted to show her female relatives amazed and impressed by the change in her appearance. Under Rapper's direction, they showed no surprise, and the entire scene had to be reshot, and in part rewritten, in order to strengthen it.

Gladys Cooper was excellent, but she was working all night at the USO and often came on the set exhausted and unprepared.

I had Rapper reshoot Bette's entrance at the beginning of the picture. Casey and I had worked out a shot in which we moved from her feet up her thick, shapeless legs to her fat figure and plain face. Later, we would repeat the shot to show how attractive she had become. Irving began the shot correctly, but then suddenly cut to a close-up, which ruined the effect. I asked him to do it in one continuous shot without a break.

Going over my memoranda today, I find countless notes reading, "Please step on it, Irving . . . we are far behind . . . enormously over budget and schedule." Irving Rapper blamed Gladys Cooper's poor memory and Bette's constant demands for dialogue changes as reasons for the delays. But the picture turned out very well and Rapper's direction was skillful.

The preview at Huntington Park had a mixed response, however, and we made some cuts. Harry Warner wrote Jack that he hated the scenes of Bette and her lover's daughter on a driving trip, feeling the scene slowed up the second half considerably. Fortunately, I had the final say, and no further changes were made.

Although we had completely ignored her suggestions, Olive Higgins Prouty wrote me a letter of glowing praise. She saw the picture at her home in New England with twenty-five friends, all of whom applauded at the end. She wrote, "The plot follows very closely that of my book and the personalities of the various characters have been carefully observed and preserved."

Despite mixed reviews, the commercial results were excellent.

Another Bette Davis picture that worked well was *Watch on the Rhine,* which had been a great stage success starring Hungarian actor Paul Lukas. Lillian Hellman had written it with great passion, inspired by her political beliefs. It was the story of the daughter of a Virginia family who returns home after marrying a Jewish underground fighter to find her right-wing clan completely opposed to her commitment to anti-Nazism.

The play opened just before Pearl Harbor. The Roosevelts attended it and gave a great party at the White House with Lillian Hellman as guest of honor.

We were happy and proud to acquire the rights. War had broken out, and although the theme of isolationism no longer applied, we felt there were sufficient elements of appeasement in the community to justify our proceeding.

Miss Hellman was busy and suggested that her intimate friend Dashiell Hammett write the script. He had injured his back and was laid up at his farm in Pleasantville, but I corresponded with him and he agreed to do it. Though he was extremely slow, and communication at that distance was difficult, nevertheless, he did very fine work.

Once again, Irene Dunne was considered for the part of the wife and once again we finally settled on Bette Davis. Miss Hellman very much admired her, which made our choice easier.

Bette, with her usual sense of fairness, insisted that Paul Lukas have first billing, and we reluctantly agreed. Her name on the top of the marquee would have aided the picture commercially, but she would not change her mind and we very much wanted to please her.

Herman Shumlin, who directed *Watch on the Rhine* on the stage, directed the film as well. He was a great friend of Hellman and Hammett.

The picture worked without problems, although Shumlin's lack of experience with the camera often resulted in clotted compositions (too many characters crowded together in the frame) and too many lines coming on top of one another. We corrected this quickly.

Miss Hellman is good enough to say today that the picture was everything she wanted it to be.*

Saratoga Trunk, from the novel by Edna Ferber, was much more difficult. First of all, the heroine was partly black, and Joe Breen was shocked by the idea of her having an affair with a white man. She also had a black servant whose role was so large and important that it was beyond the range of many actresses of that time. We cast Flora Robson in the part. A further problem was that the story fell awkwardly into two halves. The first half was a story of revenge in which the heroine seeks to humiliate the aristocracy of New Orleans for scorning her. The second half deals largely with the story of the Saratoga Railroad.

Casey Robinson found a way to combine the two stories, and we cast Ingrid Bergman against type and coloring as the quadroon. With a black wig and dark makeup, she looked stunning. We costarred her with Gary Cooper, repeating the electric casting of *For Whom the Bell Tolls.*

The Maltese Falcon, like *Casablanca,* was another picture that far surpassed our original expectations. None of us could have foreseen that what appeared to be a run-of-the-mill melodrama would become a classic.

We made the picture at the suggestion of John Huston, the lanky son of Walter Huston, who worked as a writer on our biographical pictures. He asked if he could direct as well as write the script and I decided to gamble with him.

Once again, we ran into casting problems. George Raft foolishly turned down the leading role. His loss was Humphrey Bogart's gain: Bogey *was* Sam Spade, the tough San Francisco detective.

Geraldine Fitzgerald was to play Brigid O'Shaughnessy, the seductress with whom Spade reluctantly falls in love, but Gerry wanted to go back to New York and gave up what could have been the biggest opportunity of her career. We cast Mary Astor instead, and she was brilliant in the part.

I had seen an actor named Sydney Greenstreet in the play *There Shall Be No Night* by Robert Sherwood. Enormously fat, almost 350 pounds, he seemed to rejoice in his size. He had a deep chuckling laugh, a fruity voice, and a manner that was alternatively genial and

* Higham's Note: Miss Hellman told me if she ever did another picture, she would want Wallis to produce it.

menacing. I felt he would be perfect for the part of the fat man (appropriately named Gutman), who was the villain of the piece. His test was marvelous. We only had to tone down a slight effeminacy in the playing to make it perfect.

Peter Lorre, the sly, witty star of the Berlin stage, made a perfect homosexual crook: Joel Cairo.

John asked me if he could use his father Walter in the wordless part of a man who staggers into Spade's office carrying the falcon wrapped in rags. I agreed and the scene worked well.

Huston also hit on an unusual idea that I don't think has been repeated since. He took the entire cast to lunch every day at a country club near Toluca Lake, resulting in an extraordinary intimacy in the group playing.

It would not have seemed normal if Joe Breen had not complained about our script. The picture dealt with a tough guy up against a gang of villains, and Breen refused to allow the sight of anyone drinking in the picture! We pointed out that a man like Spade would get through a large amount of liquor in a day and that if he turned into a teetotaler the audience would consider him very strange. Breen responded: "Some drinking may be permitted. But please keep it to an absolute minimum."

We were not allowed to have the line, spoken by Sam to his secretary, "You'll come tonight?" We could not show Joel Cairo as a homosexual. When he leaves the office, Sam couldn't say, "Just smell those gardenias." Instead, Sam had to sniff the air and remark, "Hmm! Gardenias!" Sam couldn't slap Brigid or indicate that he had slept with her. The Fat Man had to say, "By gad, sir!" not, "By God, sir!"

John Huston had never directed, but after the first day's rushes I knew I had made the right decision. His only problem was tempo. Bogey drawled his lines instead of snapping them out, and the action was too slow, deliberate, careful.

Huston responded to my memo on June 13, 1941: "I am shrinking all the pauses and speeding up all the action. You understand so far I have done all the slow scenes of the picture. After Brigid's apartment scene, the story really begins to move. By the time we reach the Cairo–Brigid–Fat Man scene, it will be turning like a pinwheel . . . this picture should gather momentum as it goes along . . . otherwise the very speed with which I would be playing the opening sequences

110

would become very monotonous . . . nevertheless I am doing as you say . . . making Bogart quick and staccato and taking the deliberateness out of the action . . ." John was right. By shooting the picture in sequence, gradually increasing the speed until the gripping confrontation at the end, the excitement was intensified. Audiences were spellbound.

CHAPTER 10

At Paramount

During the late 1940s, Louise and I were dealt a severe blow. At breakfast one morning we received a letter from the board of education stating that they were requisitioning twenty-two acres of our land in the San Fernando Valley for the building of a junior high school. We were to deliver the land to them free and clear of any building, which meant tearing down the house we had lived in happily for almost twenty years.

Neither of us believed a home could be ordered demolished by an official body, but we were wrong. Anybody's home in California can be pulled to the ground if the land is required for government use.

The shock of losing our beloved ranch almost destroyed Louise. Her health deteriorated rapidly. Our lawyers fought the order and the studio pulled every string possible to change it, but it was useless. Though the courts wrangled for months over the amount due us, it was nominal compared with the true value of the property. And no amount of money could compensate for our emotional investment in it.

Louise began house-hunting. She heard that the Walter Wanger–Joan Bennett home was on the market and called me in New York to tell me about it. On South Mapleton Drive in Holmby Hills, it was a lovely French provincial dwelling built for the Wangers by architect Wallace Neff. Louise liked it very much, and I told her to go ahead and buy it even though I hadn't seen it. We remodeled it completely and South Mapleton has been my home ever since.

Another upheaval in my life in the forties was my departure

from Warner Bros. I was miserable for reasons I have pointed out, and felt I could no longer work under the conditions imposed upon me by Jack Warner. I broke clean, left for New York without any plans, and holed up at the Waldorf Towers for eight weeks. Much as I loved Louise, I had a profound need to be by myself, to get away and think things out alone.

One day I got a call from close friend Joseph Hazen, a brilliant lawyer who for many years had been Harry Warner's right-hand man. Hazen had represented the entire film industry in negotiations with the attorney general concerning a decree that sought to separate studios from their theater chains. His situation with Harry Warner was similar to mine with Jack. Harry made promises Harry failed to keep, and Hazen wanted out.

I was delighted by his call. We made a date for lunch, met happily, and plunged headlong into plans to form the first independent motion picture company in Hollywood since Chaplin, Pickford, and Fairbanks founded United Artists. We wanted complete autonomy. But times had changed and we knew our company would have to link up with one of the major studios. Without knowing it, we were looking into the future of the entire industry, which eventually restructured itself along the same lines.

Word of our plans got around and several companies approached us. The most important and intriguing of these was the J. Arthur Rank Organization in Britain.

Rank was a dynamo, a self-made man whose distinctive presence was as famous in the film industry as de Gaulle's not dissimilar appearance was in politics. Rank knew what he wanted, and he wanted us. He called constantly at enormous expense, backed up his points with cablegrams running to many, many pages. He wanted us to come into his organization, and for me to take charge of production immediately. He had launched a campaign to conquer the international market with British productions of fine quality catering to American tastes.

I was flattered by the offer, but reluctant to accept. I didn't want to live in England. My son was in school in California and I wanted him to grow up with American children. Louise wasn't well and I didn't want to move her. My roots were in America, and I didn't want to disturb them.

Rank wasn't easily deterred. He suggested I divide my time

between the two countries: spend six months of every year making pictures in Britain and six months in Hollywood. The sum of money he offered was enormous. Even more appealing was the fact that Rank was prepared to give me absolute freedom, from story selection to the very last cut of every picture we made. But I declined the offer.

United Artists approached us, too.

Another attractive bid came from Nick Schenk of Metro-Goldwyn-Mayer. He proposed that I become production head of MGM with Joe Hazen as president of the company, headquartered in New York. As an inducement, he offered to buy our first two completed pictures for a great deal of money on a capital-gains basis. It would be a five-year contract with very special fringe benefits. We met with Schenk at his home in Miami but decided the situation at MGM would be too much like the one we wanted out of at Warners. We would not be truly independent.

Joe and I weighed every offer but were still undecided when Barney Balaban of Paramount Pictures called. We had several meetings with him, all extremely cordial, and finally decided to sign the superlatively good contract he offered. After we accepted the Paramount offer, Hazen and I went to see Serge Semenenko, senior vice-president of First National Bank in Boston. He agreed to set up a revolving fund of $2.5 million to finance our company, the first time this bank had capitalized an independent film organization.

With these funds in reserve, Paramount agreed to subsidize our productions in a transaction that gave us profit participation, a producer's fee, and complete autonomy in making our films. It was a splendid deal, the first truly independent setup in the business, setting a pattern for all future independent production.

Y. Frank Freeman was the genial head of Paramount in those days. When Joe and I returned to Hollywood, we found him friendly and openhanded. It was an ideal situation. All we had to do was deliver the finished negative: no interference, no nonsense. Unlike Jack Warner, Balaban and Freeman stuck to the letter of our agreement from the day it was signed until the day it was terminated.

Joe Hazen and I worked comfortably together for the entire twenty-five years of our Paramount contract, an unusual relationship in the motion picture business. Joe lived in New York and was our liaison with the Paramount executives there. We conferred on the telephone daily and he negotiated for personalities and properties I wanted for our company, and took care of all legal matters.

Paul Nathan, my former secretary at Warner Bros., became my very able assistant.

Irene Lee worked as story editor for me, first in California and then in New York. She was dedicated in her search for film material for the organization and added considerably to its success.

Jack Saper, an old friend with whom I had grown up in Chicago, worked as production assistant for Hal Wallis Productions and later became an associate producer.

Our production manager was Bill Gray, a brilliantly efficient friend who is an executive at Universal Studios today.

Ours was a lean, tight organization: people of similar taste and background working in harmony. There were no serious problems in those productive and peaceful Paramount years. They were among the happiest of my life.

Joe and I realized that in order to make good pictures we had to have stars. Because it was difficult to lure established players away from major studios, we decided to develop our own stars. We formed a stock company, put our players under long-term contract, and moved them from picture to picture until they became well known.

New performers in whom I had faith were Charlton Heston, Kirk Douglas, Burt Lancaster, Wendell Corey, Martin and Lewis, Lizabeth Scott, Shirley MacLaine, Elvis Presley, Dolores Hart, and many others. I had all of these people under contract for years. If I had no picture ready for them, I lent them to other studios, taking a page from David Selznick's book.

I met Lizabeth Scott through Irving Hoffman, a public relations man in New York. Miss Scott was a well-established model who had done a small part in *Skin of Our Teeth* on Broadway. Irving wrote items about her for Winchell's column and suggested I sign her for our growing stock company.

He arranged an interview. I found her unusual and intriguing. Different. Her photogenic face and husky voice promised an interesting screen personality. A New York photographer made a striking series of still pictures of Liz, which prompted us to send her to California for a screen test. As a result of the test, I signed her to a contract.

Lizabeth Scott appeared in a number of my pictures and on loan from our company to Columbia and RKO, costarring with Humphrey Bogart, Charlton Heston, and Dick Powell. She enjoyed a long and successful career.

At the time, there was a shortage of rugged leading men. I went east in 1945 determined to find actors of this type for our company. In the club car of the "Super Chief" en route to New York, I had drinks with the Bogarts, and Betty urged me to consider a friend of hers appearing in an obscure play called *The Wind Is Ninety*. I went to see it on a night of record-breaking June heat. Playing the part of the unknown soldier was a lithe, barrel-chested, six-footer with a mop of wavy blond hair who impressed me tremendously. He had a jauntiness, a self-confident grace that commanded attention. He was everything Bacall said he was. His name was Kirk Douglas.

I went backstage to talk with him. I found him quiet, soft-spoken, but bursting with energy and animal magnetism. At subsequent meetings he told me of his background. His parents were poverty-stricken Russian immigrants like my own, and he was the only son of seven children. He had worked in carpet factories to help his family and to pay for gymnasium classes where he developed his legendary physique. He had worked for Western Union, eked out a living as a waiter at Schrafft's, and had just come out of the hospital when I met him. Kirk had been a midshipman in an antisubmarine unit in the navy and had been injured.

Warm and grateful for his chance in Hollywood, he never gave me any trouble, nor was there a hint in his personal life of the savage quality that gave such color to his performances on film.

I costarred Kirk with Barbara Stanwyck in *The Strange Love of Martha Ivers*. I knew I was taking a risk pitting a newcomer against that powerhouse, Stanwyck, but she was extraordinarily considerate and played unselfishly with him in every scene. The biggest stars appreciate the fact that they shine brightest with a strong supporting cast.

The reviews for Kirk's performance were as good as he deserved. Critics and public alike recognized his very special star quality.

Later, I cast him as a bootlegger, a shameless double-crosser in *I Walk Alone*. He was as powerfully convincing as a gangster as he was in the part of the drink-sodden husband of Martha Ivers.

Kirk's only problem was that he occasionally went overboard in dramatic scenes. Once it was explained to him that his power was

116

greater if contained, he listened carefully, absorbed thoroughly, and learned.

There came a time when I had no suitable picture in sight for Kirk and offered my commitment to Paramount for $35,000. Paramount wasn't interested: they didn't like the dimple in his chin. I thought this gave character to his face, made him striking and individual, and said so, but they wouldn't listen. A short time later Billy Wilder wanted him for *Ace in the Hole* at the same studio, and Kirk asked and got $125,000 for the picture.

Kirk showed his great versatility in *A Letter to Three Wives,* brilliantly written and directed by Joe Mankiewicz, and hit the big time in *Champion,* playing a high-powered boxer. We drifted apart professionally, but we remain great friends to this day.

Burt Lancaster also came from a background of poverty. For years, he and his friend Nick Cravat performed a horizontal-bar act in a circus for a salary of three dollars a week and a free lunch. When an infected finger made it impossible for Lancaster to perform, he took a job as floorwalker in the lingerie department of Marshall Field in Chicago.

Like Kirk, Burt had just left the service and gone into the theater when I first saw him in New York that summer of 1945. He was in a play called *A Sound of Hunting,* a bad play, but he was excellent as the drill sergeant, a martinet with striking command and attack. Looking at Burt's huge shoulders and big, capable hands, I knew women would be delighted with him.

I went backstage, introduced myself, complimented him on his performance, and offered him a job in our stock company. Burt was cool and quite unimpressed, suggested that I see his agent to discuss terms, and closed his dressing-room door. I saw his agent, Harold Hecht, and proposed what I thought was a very generous deal: a two-picture-a-year contract with the right to make other pictures on the side. Burt accepted it as his due.

On the set of *Desert Fury,* his first picture for me, I asked him how he was getting along. He shrugged coldly. "Okay, I guess," he replied. "But I won't be doing this much longer. I'll soon be directing."

Four years later, I still had two pictures remaining on Burt's contract. I offered him the role of Wyatt Earp in *Gunfight at O.K. Corral,* but he turned it down. It was an excellent screenplay done by

Leon Uris from a factual story in *Holiday* magazine. When I was in New York several weeks later, I acquired the motion picture rights to the successful Broadway play *The Rainmaker,* in which I planned to star Katharine Hepburn. Burt telephoned me in the middle of the night to say that if I would let him play Starbuck, the lead in *The Rainmaker,* he would do *Gunfight at O.K. Corral,* and that would take care of our two remaining commitments. I agreed and they were two of Burt's best pictures.

Another discovery I made at that time was a pleasant, giving human being named Charlton Heston. Like Kirk and Burt, Chuck was exactly the type of he-man I was looking for. He was tall, rangy, bony; described by Bosley Crowther of *The New York Times* as "a rough-hewn sort of chap who looks like a triple threat halfback on a Midwestern college football team. . . ."

Unlike the others, Chuck emerged from the world of television. He had attended speech school at Northwestern University in Illinois, been in stock companies and Broadway flops (as well as playing in *Antony and Cleopatra* in the Katharine Cornell production), but really made his mark in "Studio One" at CBS. He was outstanding in *The Taming of the Shrew, Of Human Bondage, Julius Caesar,* and *Macbeth.*

I saw him in all of these and called him in for an interview. When he walked into my office, I hired him on the spot. (It will give some indication of how impressed I was that I tested both Kirk and Burt, but felt no impulse to do the same with Chuck.) Chuck arrived wearing a zoot suit—he literally had no other clothes. We took him out and bought him a wardrobe for his first picture, *Dark City.*

Heston remains a close friend to this day. He was, and always will be, a true professional.

Very consciously, I made a series of melodramatic films with strong characters and situations, films that proved to be extremely popular. Movie-going audiences had matured during the war and no longer required false and sentimental portraits of human nature. I dealt again and again with the psychology of murderers. I showed, and encouraged my writers to show, how frustration, poverty, and a desperate need for money could drive people to psychotic extremes, the theme of *So Evil My Love, The Strange Love of Martha Ivers, The File on Thelma Jordan,* and *Sorry, Wrong Number.* In every case, the motive for destruction was greed, a theme with which millions could identify. We made no attempt to glamorize, excuse, or deify villains. We explained them, that was all. The dark side of life was portrayed frankly and without compromise.

As at Warners, I regarded the writer as king. Scripts as excellent as Lucille Fletcher's *Sorry, Wrong Number,* based on her own play, or Leonard Spigelgass's *So Evil My Love* made this producer's work a pleasure.

Sorry, Wrong Number had been a one-woman radio drama, so Lucille had to flesh out several new characters for the film. The rich woman's husband who plans her killing is seen as physically strong and handsome but morally and spiritually a weakling. We made no attempt to disguise the fact that the spoiled woman who married him had bought him. He wants to kill her because she refuses to pay off his gambling debts.

The only sympathetic character in the picture was played by the Australian actress Ann Richards, a friend whom the endangered Leona calls in the middle of the night, seeking help. This ordinary woman, living with her baby in a cramped apartment, was necessary as a counterpoint to the wealthy Leona in her mansion on Sutton Place.

The whole picture was made in the studio with the aid of a very skilled art department. It was well received and successful.

So Evil My Love, from a book by Joseph Shearing, was an equally "dark" story. Joseph Shearing was, in fact, a woman: the pen name for the well-known English novelist Marjorie Bowen. Under her Shearing pseudonym, Miss Bowen specialized in stories based on actual Victorian crimes, and *So Evil My Love* had echoes of two or three cases. It was the story of an impoverished woman who becomes a companion to the sick wife of a cold and unscrupulous man. The companion becomes involved with a worthless painter and plots a murder in which the invalid wife is falsely accused.

I decided at the outset that only an English director and cast could handle this very British story. I had admired British director Lewis Allen's work on two films: *The Uninvited,* from a ghost story by Dorothy McCardle, set in Cornwall, and *The Unseen,* a thriller by Raymond Chandler. I talked with Allen and hired him.

Casting began. Allen and I agreed that Welshman Ray Milland would be perfect for the role of the wastrel painter. He had recently made a big hit in *The Lost Weekend* as Charles Jackson's pathetic drunk, and audiences would easily accept him as a beaten human being. Ann Todd was a British actress who had just made a great success in *The Seventh Veil*. I saw in her face a quality of toughness, of resolution, that suggested she would be perfect in the part of the murderess. Geraldine Fitzgerald was often cast as a murderess, but I felt it would be interesting to have her play a victimized woman for a change. She proved to be perfect in the part of the invalid wife, especially good in the powerful scene in which she is visited in a hospital by the woman who has brought about her destruction. Here both actresses were at their best.

The picture presented a problem insofar as I wanted to shoot on location as much as possible. London had changed enormously since the Victorian era, and we had to very carefully select areas that still looked of that period, arranging our shots so that electric lights, store windows, and even the pavements were not clear. We were one of the first American companies to shoot in London after the war, and crowds gathered to watch our actors stepping into carriages or hurrying in period costume through dimly lit streets.

Rationing was still in effect. Our company stayed at the Dorchester Hotel and even there the meals seemed tiny and uninviting to spoiled American eyes.

One night, Louise and I decided to take a break. We went to see Margaret Sullavan in *Voice of the Turtle,* a comedy that had been causing a sensation in London. As we left Miss Sullavan's dressing room, a crowd of fans rushed toward her. She turned, pen poised for autographs, but the crowd rushed past her and swooped down on Louise, who was as embarrassed as she was delighted. She had no idea she was still a favorite in England, and that her comedies had been enormous hits there.

We made *September Affair* in Italy. This was perhaps the first time that a major Hollywood production with an entire crew had been shipped to Europe. We worked in Rome, Venice, Florence, and Capri. *September Affair* was the story of a married man who meets an attractive woman in Italy. The plane on which both are scheduled to fly crashes, and they are presumed dead. They decide to enjoy a brief furlough from life, a romance they know will be doomed once the truth is discovered.

Joan Fontaine played the leading role opposite Joseph Cotten, whom I borrowed from Selznick. Our arrangement with her was that she could have two first-class air tickets to the Italian location and bring whomever she liked with her. She chose Hedda Hopper, one of the most powerful columnists in Hollywood. Hedda and Joan were very good friends until the time of their arrival in Naples.

Hedda expected to be treated like a queen, and we had the red carpet ready for her at the airport. We had borrowed Slim Aarons from *Life* magazine to do the stills for our picture, and he met the plane with us to photograph Joan's arrival. Joan took one look at the handsome young photographer—sparks flew—and they drove away in Slim's car, leaving Hedda to us.

Hedda was furious. I've never seen such rage. I did everything in my power to appease her, giving her a larger suite at the hotel, besieging her with champagne and flowers, but she refused to melt until Joan apologized.

Joan was occupied elsewhere. She and her good-looking discovery were nowhere to be found for two days. When at last they turned up, looking like cats that ate the cream, Joan's excuse was that she had been told she wouldn't be needed for a few days, so they took a side trip. I put enormous pressure on Joan to speak to Hedda, who threatened to fly back to Hollywood and destroy our picture in print. Joan finally did so, and a truce was called.

Things went fine on locations in Capri and Naples for about three weeks. We had ideal weather and the Italian crews worked well.

Then it happened. One morning we had a call from the production manager saying that Miss Fontaine was not at her hotel. We called everywhere. Not a sign. I was compelled to call off shooting for the rest of the day. This was in essence a two-character picture and there was no way we could shoot around Joan. Joe Cotten was furious; Hedda shrugged and started making notes; my heart sank.

The next day Joan sailed cheerfully onto the set as if nothing had happened. With someone as cool and superficial as that, I knew anger would be futile, though I was, nevertheless, angry. Without a serious apology or a tremor, she went straight into a love scene with Joe Cotten, who played the scene with anger in his heart and seraphic smile on his face, the face of a man in love. I never admired him more.

I did a Hitchcock in *September Affair*. In a scene on a narrow street in Capri, I played a tourist who stopped and looked in a window as the principals passed by. I received fan mail from all of my relatives.

In another scene an Italian fisherman walking along the beach finds the clothes belonging to Joan Fontaine, who is swimming. Unfortunately, the light went bad and we couldn't complete the sequence. We wrapped the company and gave the players a call for the next day. In the morning William Dieterle, the director, sensed something was wrong and asked the bit man if he had worked yesterday. The man said, "No. That was my brother. He couldn't come today so he sent me." This meant that we had to reshoot the entire previous day's work with the new man.

When we finished *September Affair*, I decided to return to America by ship. Joan called me frantically in Paris and said she must get on the same vessel. The French Line told her there wasn't a cabin available, but she refused to take no for an answer. Fortunately, I had some influence with the line and they managed to squeeze her into a stateroom. I went on board firmly expecting to find a bottle of champagne in my suite with a thank-you note. Nothing. I didn't see her in the dining salon that night and wondered if after all her desperate efforts she'd missed the boat. Then I ran into her playing backgammon with a group of friends. Instead of embracing me and thanking me for my efforts on her behalf, she nodded coolly and went on with the game, not even bothering to introduce me to her friends.

Not all stars are selfish and inconsiderate. Walter Huston was just the opposite.

Shortly after the completion of *September Affair*, I did a picture with him called *The Furies*, starring Barbara Stanwyck. I told him that in a scene Fontaine and Cotten play in a little inn in Naples, they put on a record of "September Song" as he had recorded it from the play, *Knickerbocker Holiday*, and that we were trying to get the right to use it. "Why not do an original track?" Walter said, "I'll be glad to do it for you." I told him that I didn't think we could afford him and he told me that he wanted to do it and would work for scale. So for about two hundred dollars, Walter Huston came into the dubbing room and sang "September Song" as it was heard in the film.

Shirley Booth was another exception. I saw her first in *Come Back, Little Sheba* by William Inge, a heart-breaking play about a sleazy, middle-aged woman living in a run-down house with a beaten husband. All she had left in life were memories of their early romance and of an adored little dog that ran away. She was a great actress. Few others would have dared look so unattractive, and they would have compromised. Shirley never did.

I decided to bring this hugely successful play to the screen. Up to now, Paramount executives had agreed with everything I wanted to do, but they were appalled by the idea of filming *Come Back, Little Sheba*. Prepared to accept glamorous men and women in melodramas of the seamy side of life, they were shocked at the thought of making a picture with beaten, unkempt, depressing people. Even the young people in the story were unattractive, morally if not physically: the tough girl who taunts the old woman, the muscular young stud who provides an unhappy sexual contrast with the defeated washout of a husband.

But the decision was mine. And I hedged only one bet, casting Burt Lancaster as the husband because of his great box office appeal.

It was difficult for this huge, virile man to look like a weakling. We dressed Burt in a sloppy, shapeless button-up sweater, padded his figure to flab out his trim waistline, and gave him baggy trousers that made him look hip-heavy. He wore pale makeup over a stubble of beard, but we still had a problem hiding his magnificent physique. We made him stoop a little, hollow his chest, and walk with a slow scuffle in bedroom slippers.

Burt went along with everything. Many male stars would have resisted, fearing that so unattractive an appearance might damage them in the eyes of their fans. But the good side of his cool confidence made any such loss of popularity unthinkable.

Come Back, Little Sheba proved to be more successful than any of us dared hope, the audience responding to the painful honesty of William Inge's writing and Daniel Mann's direction. When Shirley won an Oscar for her moving performance, she thanked me profusely in her acceptance speech.

About Mrs. Leslie starred Shirley and that very fine actor Robert Ryan. It was the story of a middle-aged woman who gives up on life until she meets and falls in love with the right middle-aged man. Bob and Shirley played their roles very sensitively under Daniel Mann's direction, but for some reason the public didn't buy it. I don't know why. It failed at the box office and Shirley did little film work after that, but enjoyed great success in television.

On *Hot Spell*, directed by Daniel Mann, Mann himself was the problem. We had worked well together on our first two pictures, but suddenly he became temperamental, ordering people off the set and becoming generally abusive. We parted company and never worked together again.

One of my earliest pictures at Paramount was *Love Letters,* a romantic mystery about an English girl haunted by a long forgotten murder. I picked up the obscure novel by a writer named Chris Massie in paperback at an airport. It was a strange poetic work and I felt it would make an interesting picture.

I wanted Jennifer Jones to play the girl. She had the nervousness, the fey quality, the sense of abstraction the role demanded. At the time, Jennifer was under contract to David Selznick, who was in love with her and dedicated to making her a major star. One didn't communicate with Miss Jones directly, only through Selznick. She was shy and withdrawn and wouldn't make a decision without him, and he was extremely protective of her. I sent him the treatment of *Love Letters* with some trepidation, but I felt certain the part was right for her.

He called me two weeks later and said he liked the material, but I remembered what I had gone through with him when I had borrowed Ingrid Bergman for *Casablanca,* and I knew it wouldn't be that easy. It was very much a case of history repeating itself, and I had to go through exactly the same procedure.

I went to New York and finally talked Selznick into releasing Miss Jones. As preproduction work began, I think that he sometimes forgot that I was producing the picture. He wanted to see and approve all of Jennifer's costume sketches and called in photographer Lee Garmes, whom he had personally asked me to use, to discuss the lighting of her face. Selznick called up daily to see how things were going. It was with great difficulty that I dissuaded him from coming onto the set and interfering with William Dieterle's direction.

At the preview in Pasadena, David bought up the entire popcorn concession so that people wouldn't make noise or be distracted while gazing at his adored Jennifer. He, however, sat with a small flashlight, dictating notes to his secretary, to the total distraction of those seated in front of and behind him. He then went home and dictated an eight-page memorandum to me with suggestions for changes, as if I were one of his own employees. I read it with interest and I believe I even adopted one or two of his ideas. But I suspect I was more influenced by the reaction of the public than by the husband of the star of my picture.

CHAPTER 11

Howard Hughes

When Howard Hughes bought RKO he wanted me to leave Paramount and head up production at his studio. I had not been in touch with him since 1930, when he tried to stop *Dawn Patrol* from being made.

An aide called to make an appointment. The appointment must not be at Hughes's office or mine, or even at our homes. His need for privacy was so compulsive that I was asked to select a place that would be absolutely private, without the remotest chance of intrusion. I selected Minna's house. Very few people knew where it was, outside of her charmed circle of friends. The press would certainly never find us there.

At the appointed time Minna and I sat and waited for the great man to arrive. We waited well over an hour. I had things to do and was becoming increasingly irritated. We wondered if we should call his office to see if something had happened to him.

At last an engine sputtered to a halt outside, and a shabby, badly dressed figure in a turned-down fedora hat got out of a dirty Chevrolet, took off his coat, and hung it over one arm. He was extremely thin, with small bones and hairy arms. His long-sleeved shirt was now short-sleeved. Quite obviously he had cut off the sleeves above the elbows with a pair of nail scissors. He knocked timidly, avoiding the doorbell, looked furtively right and left, then went back and wound up the windows of his car and locked the doors.

Looking like a bum instead of a man worth $100 million, Howard entered Minna's living room. He wouldn't shake hands. He was terrified of germs and wore gloves. In view of his fear of germs, it is astonishing that he was so lacking in personal cleanliness.

He sat down and immediately got to business. Praising me lavishly and extravagantly far beyond my worth, he offered me total freedom if I would join him, and seemed surprised when I didn't jump at the opportunity. I was well aware of his reputation for interference and knew that if I went to work for this eccentric man, it would be without the independence and latitude I enjoyed at Paramount. I honestly believe he had a contract in his pocket and if I had said yes to his proposal, would have signed me then and there without an agent or manager present. He left empty-handed but called constantly, begging me to change my mind.

I finally arranged a second meeting to be held at the Flamingo Hotel in Las Vegas in the company of my associate, Joseph Hazen. We flew to Las Vegas and were met in the lobby of the hotel by one of Hughes's men, who told us that Hughes would see us at 11:00 P.M. Meanwhile he had arranged for us to have dinner and see one of the Las Vegas shows.

At eleven o'clock we appeared at the designated suite and were received by Hughes's representatives. Hughes had not yet arrived. In about fifteen minutes there was a knock on the door, and he entered. Without a word, he searched the suite—bedrooms, sitting room, bathrooms, even the clothes closets. Satisfied that no one was eavesdropping, he returned to greet us, making certain not to shake our hands.

The results of the meeting are best summed up in a memo that can be found at the end of the book and that was written by Mr. Hazen as a record of what had transpired.

We re-signed with Paramount and made pictures there until 1970. I never saw Howard again and was never sorry I had not accepted his offer.

CHAPTER 12

Magnani

I first saw Tennessee Williams's powerful play *The Rose Tattoo* on its opening night in Chicago and knew at once that I had to buy it. It was sure to be a great success. Audiences would identify with its earthiness, its sexuality, its deeply felt emotions and naturalistic dialogue.

I went backstage after the show, knowing Tennessee would be there. He liked to attend his own first nights, fascinated by the idea of seeing his work performed. I found him quite different from the flamboyant personality I had read about. Quiet, sober, professional, and very personable, he was familiar with my work and liked it, so that when I offered to buy the rights, he agreed on a handshake. In no time at all my agent had spoken to his agent and we were in business.

I was delighted. Now I had to cast the picture.

As far as I was concerned, there was only one actress on earth who could play his tempestuous Italian heroine, the warm, passionate, angry and exciting, utterly feminine Serafina. That woman was Anna Magnani. She was famous in Italy but not yet well known in America. Tennessee had written the play with her in mind. He had hoped he could get her to do it on the stage, but she was terrified and backed out at the last minute after months of negotiation. Tennessee had been bitterly disappointed. Brilliant though she was in the part of Serafina, Maureen Stapleton was too young and too American for the role. Only Magnani would do.

That night in Chicago, out of earshot of the estimable Maureen, I told Tennessee it would have to be Magnani. He became very excited, shyness and reserve dissolving into a broad smile. When I told him I was on my way to Europe and that the Paramount company head in Rome, Pilade Levi, was a close friend of Magnani's, Tennessee gave me his blessing, and I flew to Italy with Louise.

Pilade Levi, a charming man, assured me that Magnani was interested but still afraid. He wouldn't say why. We went to her apartment one afternoon for cocktails. She lived atop the Plaza Altieri, not far from the Pantheon, a crowded, noisy neighborhood. She had a full view of St. Peter's from her balcony, but no air conditioning and the windows were opened wide to admit the bedlam that was Rome: honking cars, shouting drivers, whistles, every kind of street noise. The maid, a nervous-looking woman with unkempt hair, fairly trembled as she ushered us into La Divina's lair.

We waited for her for a very long time. Tennessee told me that in Italy the longer a star keeps someone waiting, the bigger they are. We realized how important she was as each hour went by.

I looked around the apartment. Everything was heavy, ornate: dark velvet curtains, thick carpeting, somber paintings, Italian antiques almost threatening in size. A handsome young man wandered in and out: one of her stable of lovers, Pilade explained. At last she exploded through the door, and she was quite something to see. Like a prizefighter maneuvering for position, she strode in, planted her heroic legs wide, placed her hands on her hips, and glared straight into my eye, getting the measure of me. She was wearing a tight black satin dress cut low to expose her breasts.

She was magnificent and very conscious of it. She snarled at me in Italian, smiled, frowned, seemed on the verge of tears, then broke into peals of laughter and scowled again. I understood at once her lusty, bawdy attraction and why she had charmed many men half her age. I also understood why she was afraid to work in America: she didn't speak a word of English. Pilade had to fight to keep up with his translation of her volcanic flow of words.

Meanwhile, she plied us with large quantities of Johnnie Walker Red Label, the only thing she liked to drink, apart from wine. The sum total of her outburst was that the play was "beautiful" and "wonderful," she would die to play Serafina, and she would master the English language in one night if necessary. She was prone to monumental exaggerations.

She insisted on driving us back to the hotel in her own car. Given the amount of liquor she had consumed, I was nervous as we descended into the courtyard in a private elevator to select one of her several automobiles. But she was a fine, if daring, driver, talking incessantly, weaving around cars, zipping through traffic lights. I was in a cold sweat—not because of her driving but because I knew we faced a terrible language problem. We were scheduled to start in a few months and *Rose Tattoo* was full of long, dramatic speeches. But Anna *was* Serafina. She must play the role.

I got to know Magnani better. We met her son, a frail cripple walking on crutches, whose condition was the agony of her life.

She had a beach house not far from Rome. It was a rambling structure built on a rocky promontory overlooking a small private beach on a beautiful little bay. I drove down one golden Italian afternoon and found the house full of people, who told me that Magnani was waiting to see me, and a servant led me down the path to a sight I shall never forget.

Magnani rose out of the water like a galleon in full sail. She was wearing the briefest of bikinis, her entire body displayed in Rubens-like glory. She was happy with her heaviness, proud of it, in fact. Her black hair was damp and she tossed it about her face as she embraced me. I got wet too and she laughed and put her arm around my waist and walked me up the steep steps to lunch.

It was a sumptuous meal, served with great flair. Magnani presided over it like an empress. We could scarcely get up from the table after pasta, veal, heavy sauces, and vintage wines. Most of the guests flopped onto their beds or onto the beach to sleep. Magnani and her agent joined Pilade and me for negotiations with a half-asleep interpreter.

We closed our deal, and I returned to New York and had meetings with Tennessee on the script. He worked hard and well and only had one quirk: he carried a raincoat over his arm even when it was sunny. On close inspection, a pocket was seen to contain a whiskey bottle. Like so many other writers, he needed a snort to get him going. Months later, when *Rose Tattoo* was finished, and Tennessee saw it for the first time, his secretary kept coming into the screening room with cups of "water." He enjoyed the picture even more after a couple of cups.

In his screenplay, Tennessee described Serafina's home as a corner house made of wood on a plain dirt street with a small boat in the front yard. The art department did a fine job with the sets but I hated studio "exteriors" and wanted to shoot them on actual locations in Key West.

With my production manager and art director, I flew there and began scouting. A man from the local chamber of commerce drove us around, but nothing appealed to us. At the end of a long day of driving, we had given up hope when our guide remembered a place off the beaten track, a last resort. When we got there, I felt a sudden stab of excitement. I was looking at the house Tennessee had described. It was old, run-down, a typically Floridian frame dwelling with a proper porch. The only problem was that it had a tiny yard. Tennessee had big scenes involving the principals in a spacious yard.

I was delighted. I said to the chamber of commerce man, "This is ideal. But do you think we could get the owner to take the fence down between this and the adjoining house?"

He smiled. "No problem," he replied. "The adjoining house belongs to Tennessee Williams!"

I was flabbergasted. Privately I wondered why Tennessee hadn't recommended it and why the man hadn't shown it to us in the first place, but I was too happy to be annoyed. The house was perfect, and I made an immediate deal with the owners.

Magnani came to Hollywood to start work, but she absolutely refused to fly and no power on earth could get her on an airplane. Tennessee made the trip with her from Naples to New York, a voyage that took about two weeks. When she reached New York, I begged her to fly to the Coast. She still refused, and perhaps it was all for the best. During the two-week boat trip and the three days on the *Super Chief,* Tennessee worked with her on the script. By the time she arrived in Hollywood, she had made remarkable progress in English. We prepared a script for her with the scenes written in Italian on one page, translated into English on the facing page.

I still had doubts about her being able to carry off this difficult part, but I needn't have worried. When the cameras started to roll, she was letter-perfect.

After a period of shooting in Hollywood, we packed up to travel to our locations in Key West. Magnani still refused to fly, so we concentrated on shooting scenes in the studio in which she did not appear. During this time, she was on her way to Florida by train.

We began shooting the exterior of the old frame house, and frequently we could see Tennessee peeking out through the curtains, watching us. He was working on another play at the time, but usually joined us for lunch set up on picnic tables in the yard between the houses.

Magnani fell head over heels for her costar, Burt Lancaster. He was just her type of big, broad-shouldered he-man. But he wasn't attracted to her and she got nowhere and gallantly settled for friendship. Though they both had enormous egos, they were unselfish in their playing and respected each other's talent.

Soon after we started shooting in Key West, we experienced a torrential tropical rainstorm. The noise of the rain on the roof of the church in which Magnani played a very important scene was like machine-gun bullets. It was impossible to hear a word she said. Later she replayed the scene in the cold atmosphere of a recording studio, matching her own lips perfectly, not losing a thread of the emotion.

Eventually, we finished our filming in Key West and made preparations to fly back to the studio for the final scenes. There was the usual confrontation with Magnani about flying, but this time she yielded, possibly because she was deeply involved in the picture and enthusiastic about getting on with it. She agreed to fly only if I sat next to her to give her courage.

We took off in good weather but near Chicago we flew into a blinding snowstorm. For more than an hour we circled, with a great deal of turbulence. Magnani was as white as a sheet. Again and again, she asked me what was going on and why we weren't landing. I questioned the stewardess and her reply scared Anna even more. She said that a small plane had taken off in the storm, couldn't be located, and was flying at random through the stacked-up aircraft. Magnani turned green. We bumped through blinding snow until the announcement came that the plane had been located and we could land. Needless to say, we made the rest of the journey by Santa Fe *Super Chief* and finished the picture in Hollywood without further problems.

The Rose Tattoo was a great success. Anna won an Academy Award for Best Performance by an Actress that year, and our cameraman, James Wong Howe, was honored with an Oscar for his cinematography.

Later, I decided to star Magnani in a picture called *Wild Is the Wind,* a different sort of Western with a sheepherding background. It was the tormented love story of two men involved with a lusty mountain woman. George Cukor agreed to direct. But it was not the happy experience that making *The Rose Tattoo* had been. First of all, Magnani found fault with the script. She argued about it constantly, and on one occasion was seen driving down the freeway, yelling and railing at the script propped up against the windshield. She wanted to postpone the starting date until she was completely satisfied. We were supposed to start on May 1, but she wouldn't agree. I said to her, "Anna, we can't delay. It just isn't possible."

She looked at me with those great burning eyes and said plaintively, "Why?"

I gave it to her straight: "Because we can't reschedule nature, even for you!"

"What do you mean?" she asked.

"I said, "You know the script. We have our big scene when the lambs are born."

"So?"

"You have to understand the lambs are dropped only on a certain date. The sheep aren't going to change their habits just because you aren't satisfied with the script!"

She shrugged impatiently. I honestly think she felt nature *could* wait for Anna Magnani. She was grudging and ill-tempered and began to be very difficult.

The journey up to the Nevada location with Magnani, Tony Franciosa, Tony Quinn, George Cukor, and the unit was an ordeal. It was intensely cold and there were snow flurries. Often, we had to wait for the road to be cleared by snowplow, and trekked like pioneers. Magnani didn't like it at all, screaming Italian invectives at her unfortunate driver every inch of the way.

The weather shifted from day to day and we had to match the shots. We drove up from plateau to valley and back again when scenes called for no snow and snow fell.

Magnani was in a perpetual state of fury. One day, a high wind blew over a metal reflector, missing her by inches. She took it personally and exploded. She was livid because there were no telephones available during the day for her to call out and complain about her plight.

We stayed in a motel and drove up to the hills every morning as dawn broke. The air was exhilarating and the locations magnificent. But it was bitter cold, snow and wind every day.

Magnani sulked like a spoiled child. From time to time Cukor asked me to discipline her, and I did, in a few choice words. She would brood, look me in the eye, then suddenly chuckle and go back to work. Finally, she became impossible so I stopped talking to her, paid no attention to the great Magnani at all. She began staring at me, casting smoldering, suspicious looks from under those hooded lids, but I continued to ignore her. After three days of this silent treatment, George came to me and said, "Hal, for God's sake, talk to her. She's going mad." I said I'd drop in and talk to her after shooting. I went over to her trailer as promised and found her having a drink with Franciosa and Cukor, legs spread wide as a lumberjack's. When I walked in, she gave a great cry. "You son of a beetch!" she shouted, flinging her arms around me. We were friends again.

My production manager, Bill Gray, spent many hours with Anna, trying to placate her. One night, she developed an unexpected swelling in her knee. She had hit herself with a buckle while lashing out with the belt in a scene. At 1:00 A.M., Bill drove very fast to a tiny hospital in the area to obtain medication to ease her pain. It was oil of wormwood, used since the beginning of time for rheumatic problems. When Magnani saw "oil of wormwood" on the label, she became hysterical. Based on a rather sketchy knowledge of Shakespeare and the Bible, she thought it was some kind of poison. Bill told her he had suffered from arthritis all his life and knew what oil of wormwood was and that it was the best possible thing for pain. She screamed and wailed but finally slapped on the oil. In minutes, she was relieved and grinning.

Her motel room in the mountains was like a battlefield, and the one hard-pressed maid who was forced to clean up after her was in despair. Magnani had Italian food brought in by plane from her favorite restaurant in Los Angeles and sent the bill to us. She threw the food about in fits of rage and the walls were streaked with spaghetti sauce and pasta. We had to repaint the entire room after she checked out.

Her two leading men, Tony Quinn and Tony Franciosa, were young, good-looking, and virile. The first day of shooting Magnani looked them up and down with all the expertise of an Italian woman of the world. Tony Quinn was not interested, but Franciosa was instantly attracted to her and the result was predictably dynamic. Both Franciosa and Magnani were powerful personalities and struck sparks off each other. Their quarrels and makings-up filled the night air and were the talk of the entire unit. Preoccupied with problems of production, I was only marginally aware of what was going on. But the affair created endless headaches for us all.

Franciosa had been having a fling with Shelley Winters, and indeed, at the time he met Magnani, had promised to marry her. She heard rumors of his infidelity and called him at the motel each night for reassurance. Magnani exploded at the mention of Shelley's name and violent quarrels ensued.

Shelley, who was every bit as strong as her fiancé and his Italian mistress, knew just what to do. She made a hazardous drive up the narrow mountain path to the location. Our parked trucks filled most of the road, so she was cliff-hanging all the way, but nothing stopped her. She literally dragged Franciosa from Magnani's arms.

Shelley got what she came for: she married Franciosa on location in Carson City, spent her wedding night with him there, then flew back to Hollywood. He returned to Magnani.

Meanwhile, all of us had fallen in love with Dolores Hart, a lovely girl who costarred in the picture. I'll never forget the surprise I felt when she asked me to release her from her contract to allow her to become a nun. She is now Mother Dolores, of Regina Laudis Convent, Bethlehem, Connecticut. We still correspond.

The dust, the wind, the altitude, the cold, the restless sheep and their strange habits, all made the location a major endurance test. Worst of all, it was shearing season and we had to pull the sheep out and bring the shearers back later, which cost a great deal in payments to the farmers and postponed the wool crop by several weeks that year.

We had one very bad episode. We had built a bridge across a mountain stream for the sheep to cross in a particular scene. The crew built it out of telephone poles which Bill Gray somehow got permission to chop down. (Phones in the area were cut off that week and it was quite some time before they were back in service.)

It was extremely cold the day the sheep made the crossing. As the wranglers walked them out onto the bridge, they followed each other with their usual blindness, their herd sense. But before we could stop them, they were all on the bridge at the same time and tumbled by the dozen into the stream. At least a hundred fell. The water was moving very fast and was full of chunks of ice. Sheep can't swim in fast water and they were drifting away and drowning. The crew and the wranglers jumped into the stream after them. There is nothing heavier than wet sheep, and they were bleating with terror as they struggled, threatening to carry our men down with them. Amazingly, all were saved.

As if this were not enough, we endured a series of landslides that buried cameras in rocks, so that more cameras had to be flown in.

Lights were smashed. Road crews had to blast us out. In one place called Ebbett's Pass, we were stuck for two days without provisions.

We finally dragged our weary selves back to Carson City and then to Los Angeles for the editing. It was a difficult job shaping our straggling footage into a coherent whole. And then, after all our struggle to complete this most difficult of motion pictures, it failed to meet our expectations at the box office. There was nothing to do but shrug and go on to the next one.

I never worked with Magnani again, though not from choice. It was just that I was unable to find a vehicle suitable for her unique talents. But she forgave me and I forgave her and I shall never forget her.

CHAPTER 13

New Stars Are Born

The most difficult and unpleasant star I have ever worked with is Shirley MacLaine. Extremely talented, she was excellent in my pictures *All in a Night's Work* and *Hot Spell,* but she hasn't a grain of gratitude in her. I started her career in films and she refuses to acknowledge that fact.

One night I was in New York and went to see the musical *The Pajama Game.* I felt a twinge of disappointment when it was announced that Carol Haney, whom I had come to see, had twisted her ankle and was out of the show. She would be replaced by her understudy, Miss MacLaine. I rose to leave the theater, but changed my mind and sat down again. I'm very glad I did, because Shirley was extraordinary. Electrifying, an instant star, she took the audience by storm.

After the show I went backstage to see if I could find her. I saw her walking up a flight of stairs to the bit players' dressing rooms. I called out, "Miss MacLaine?"

She looked down, eyes wide, pointed to herself, and asked, "Who? Me?"

I said, "Yes," and quickly explained who I was. She got very excited, but was shrewd enough to arrange for me to meet her later with her manager, Steve Parker, whom she subsequently married.

We met at the Oak Room in the Plaza just after midnight. She had no money, and, up to that moment, had been a chorus girl living in a cold-water flat. But I knew at once she would be trouble. After a few days of listening to her demands, I predicted that she would give me more trouble than anyone I had ever placed under contract. I was right.

In her memoirs Shirley wrote that I chased her around a desk. I was younger then, and certainly could have caught her if I'd wanted to. The scene she painted was totally fictitious. She also said that when we met that first night at the Oak Room I didn't eat anything because I was mean with money and worried about the size of the check. The truth was that I had dined earlier. She and Parker ordered the most expensive items on the menu and ate everything in sight. I encouraged them to do so, as I was sure they had never been in anything better than a cheap chain restaurant in their lives. I enjoyed their obvious pleasure in a gourmet meal.

She complained that I made money lending her out to other producers, but neglected to note that I paid her a bonus for this in the form of a mink coat and a sports car. Obviously, gratitude is a word not included in her vocabulary.

I see Shirley occasionally on TV. She usually has a large dose of the cutes, and also fancies herself as some kind of political leader. Just recently, I saw her on the "Merv Griffin Show." She referred to working with me as "her slave days," and said she got "six dollars a picture." She has quickly forgotten that I discovered her as a chorus girl, brought her to Hollywood, and gave her the opportunity to become a star. I paid her thousands of dollars a picture, just what she was worth at the time.

Audrey Hepburn was an utterly different human being. I got to know her when I was preparing the film version of Tennessee Williams's *Summer and Smoke* and was convinced Audrey would be perfect as the spinster schoolteacher in this fragile, poetic work. She would give the character just the right touch of delicacy and purity.

She was interested, so Tennessee, I, and my late associate Paul Nathan flew to Rome to see her. We were invited to dinner and drove out to the farmhouse where Audrey was living at the time. Her husband, Mel Ferrer, was shooting *War and Peace* and working late, so we sat and talked until he arrived. Audrey was a witty and charming hostess.

At ten o'clock the servants presented an enormous platter containing one huge fish. The head was still attached and the eyes glared in our direction accusingly. Our host and hostess greeted it with great enthusiasm. Paul Nathan looked ill and declined a portion as politely as he could. I whispered to him, "I have a feeling if you don't eat that, there won't be anything else. It's obviously the entire dinner." I was right. There was neither soup, dessert, nor coffee, not even garnishings. Nathan went hungry. Audrey, dainty as a Dresden figure in her Givenchy gown, consumed a large portion of the sea beast with great relish.

We thanked our host and hostess and left at a convenient moment after "dinner." We were in a convertible and as we drove away, we looked back at the Ferrers framed in their doorway. As if in a film scene, Ferrer picked up Audrey in his arms and she waved good-bye to us. Tennessee grunted, "Lunt and Fontanne did it better."

It was a tremendous act. But despite the fish dinner and the romantic movie fade-out farewell, the episode was essentially a waste of time because we couldn't get Audrey to agree to our terms. Though she liked the play, she didn't want to portray a spinster, didn't want to look dowdy. When she suggested that Givenchy design her clothes (as a small-town schoolteacher in America), I'm afraid I got tough.

Instead, we made *Summer and Smoke* with Geraldine Page and Laurence Harvey. Gerry was a dream. She had just the detached, virginal quality the part called for. And Larry played well with her.

He was a charming, easygoing young man. Although he lacked the power and virility of Gerry's husband, Rip Torn, who probably would have been better in the role, he was a bigger name at the time and had scored a huge hit in *Room at the Top*. We felt he was better insurance at the box office. A raconteur with a great fund of risqué stories, he was also an antiques dealer. He had phones in his dressing room and on the set and constantly disappeared to make business calls. In the middle of a highly dramatic scene, Larry would leave the set, answer a phone call, then come back to embrace Gerry Page and carry on acting. Some critics said he seemed distracted during the picture. Hardly surprising.

Larry's great weakness was Pouilly-Fuissé. He drank enormous quantities of this wine. When we were in Japan preparing *A Girl Named Tamiko,* he held us up at restaurants all over the country, ordering and consuming wine without ordering food. Appropriately, he owned a vineyard in France which supplied him with Pouilly-Fuissé year round. He even had his name on the labels with vintages such as Laurence Harvey, 1950.

He smoked very heavily, was stricken with cancer, and died at forty-three. I remember he had to fly from Hollywood to London for treatments and was in such pain that he always bought two seats next to each other so that he could lie down during the journey.

Dean Martin and Jerry Lewis: what memories these two names evoke. When I discovered them, they were playing in a nightclub and had never made a picture. Louis B. Mayer saw their act and considered them for a contract at MGM but finally thought better of the idea. "The guinea's not bad, but what would I do with the monkey?" he asked.

Dino started as a crooner, a single; Jerry as a stand-up comic on the Borscht Belt. Together, they were dynamite. Nobody seeing them separately could possibly imagine how brilliantly funny they were as a team in those days.

I heard about them from several people, and when I was in New York, I dropped by the Copacabana to see what the shouting was all about. Nightclub comedy is not my favorite form of entertainment, and I expected very little as they came out onto the stage. They were strangely ill-matched. Dean, tall and very handsome, didn't look like a comedian and Jerry, equipped with a mouthful of oversized false teeth and a chimpanzee-like hairpiece, seemed grotesque.

But even before they began their act, the audience was screaming with laughter. Never before or since have I seen an audience react as this one did. The team (I am not given to superlatives) was an outright sensation. I knew at once that I had to sign them for pictures while there was still time. Within weeks, every studio in Hollywood would be after them.

I went backstage and congratulated them on their performance. I spoke to their agent, the very shrewd Abbey Greshler. I told him I thought they would be great in pictures and that I was interested in signing them to a contract. He said they had an engagement in Hollywood the following week at Slapsie Maxie Rosenbloom's, and we could continue our discussion then. The ex-boxer's nightery was very popular at the time.

I went to their opening at Slapsie Maxie's without actually having signed them. Greshler was stalling, hoping to generate interest elsewhere, giving him a better bargaining position. Several studio heads were there, but none made offers. I talked to Greshler again and arranged for the boys to do a screen test for me at Paramount.

I put my best test director on the job, but when I ran the finished test I felt a shock wave of disappointment. Great on stage, the two comics were awful on screen: their timing was off; they were self-conscious and stiff. The charisma that live audiences responded to so enthusiastically disappeared in the transition to film. On the screen, nothing happened. Without saying anything to Dean and Jerry, I prepared another test. It was even worse than the first. They had lost the magic of their nightclub performances.

Should I let them go? Suddenly it came to me. The reason they were terrible was that they were doing scenes written for them, playing characters. The material was excellent but it wasn't "them." I decided to make a third test in which I would just let them do routines from their stage act.

I had wanted to play down Jerry's slapstick humor with the wigs, masks, claw hands, and false teeth. I thought these burlesque routines would be too extreme for movie audiences. but I was wrong. The moment Dean and Jerry did their act exactly as they had done it on stage, they were fantastic. They burned up the screen. Everybody in the projection room was in stitches.

The question was how to use them. I couldn't risk putting them into a big-budgeted picture—it was too big a gamble. They were so special that there was no middle ground: they would either be overnight stars or flops. So I budgeted their first picture at $500,000. They themselves would be paid $50,000.

Writer Cy Howard suggested we base the film on *My Friend Irma,* the famous CBS radio series. Martin and Lewis would be teamed with Marie Wilson, the dizzy blond comedienne who had made such a big hit playing Irma. Jean, Irma's roommate, would be played by talented Diana Lynn and there would be two leading men's roles: Al, a smooth, good-looking con man, and Steve, an orange-juice-stand proprietor.

Desperate to play Al, Jerry fancied himself a handsome leading man. Since he didn't seem right for either part, we created a special role for him: Seymour, a nut who assists Steve at the orange-juice stand and who spills the juice and does everything wrong. Jerry took one look at the script, stormed into my office, and had a screaming match with Cy Howard. Cy pointed out that he hadn't a hope in hell of having audiences accept him as Al. Jerry said it was Al or nothing, and that he would never play Seymour.

We argued until well after midnight. I was so exhausted that I finally told Jerry I would have to drop him and the part of Seymour from the script entirely. He exploded again. I quietly pointed out that Dean would probably become a very big star in *Irma* even without him, looking him straight in the eye as I told him. Fond as he was of Dean, I knew he was jealous of his handsome face and figure. Jerry was very angry but he accepted the part of Seymour, sulking like a twenty-three-year-old spoiled child in his dressing room throughout the shooting. One day when I came to see him, I found a large metal plaque on the door reading MONSTER'S LAIR.

From the beginning, Jerry was as hard to handle as Dino was easy. But they had in common a mania for practical jokes. They chased each other around the set with water pistols and put boiling water in the water coolers. They set fire to reporters' notebooks or made off with their suits and ties, leaving them stranded on the set in their underwear. They smashed glasses and watches and anything else that would break, dropped water down people's backs, planted lizards or frogs in their couches, and dropped bags of rotten fruit on their heads. Sometimes they took off people's shoes and dropped them out the window or glued them to the ceiling It was dangerous to have a meal with them—it usually ended up on your head.

One day, they came into my office and asked if I would like a shoeshine. I declined but they pretended they hadn't heard and began rubbing large quantities of black shoe polish into my brown shoes. Then they flung a bed sheet around my neck and started to cut my hair—with a pair of ladies' nail scissors.

Jerry played a trick on me that Errol Flynn once played on Jack Warner. He fell into my office covered in bloody bandages, wheezing in pain. Horrified, I ran to call a doctor. When I returned, Jerry, neatly dressed in a suit and tie, was sitting in my chair smoking an outsized cigar, feet on my new blotting pad.

I put up with everything because I knew from the first day's rushes that Martin and Lewis would be superstars. My favorite scene in the picture was the one in which Jerry, as Seymour, squeezes one thousand oranges at top speed until his hand becomes a hollowed-out claw in the shape of an orange. I laughed aloud every time I watched this scene.

My Friend Irma was a smash hit, as I was sure it would be. It grossed well over $5 million: ten times its cost. Bosley Crowther wrote in his review: "The laughs were fetched by a new mad comedian, Jerry Lewis by name. This freakishly built and acting young man, who has been seen in nightclubs hereabout . . . has genuine comic quality. The swift eccentricity of his movements, the harrowing features of his face and the squeak of his vocal protestations . . . have flair. His idiocy constitutes the burlesque of an idiot which is something else again. He's the funniest thing in the picture." Even Jerry had to admit that Cy Howard and I had not been mistaken in creating the part of Seymour for him.

The public knew them as Martin and Lewis, but privately they were referred to as Jerry and Dino. They became a gold mine and I instantly set up *My Friend Irma Goes West* for them. Although this picture wasn't as good as the original, it also made a fortune.

MCA soon bought up Abbey Greshler's contract and became their agent. They continued to do radio, television, and nightclubs as well as make motion pictures.

Jerry developed an ego as tall as the Empire State Building, talking to Paramount executives as if he were running the studio, demanding more and more scenes alone, trying to push Dino into the background. He began to write his own dialogue, argued with directors, and tried to take over their work. He suggested musical themes to the composers and wanted to edit. I fought this constantly and we had many arguments. The more he screamed and threw his arms about, the quieter I got. It was all very difficult.

One of my favorite pictures with the team was *That's My Boy,* created by Cy Howard. It was the story of a former all-American football player (brilliantly played by Eddie Mayehoff) saddled with a pathetic weakling of a son. The part of this miserable bespectacled boy who fails to become the athlete his father wants, was perfect for Jerry. It was perhaps his finest screen characterization.

Cy brought the story to me when I was vacationing in Venice in 1951. We were standing out in the water on the beach at the Lido when Cy said without warning, "I've got an idea and I've got you trapped. Out here in the water, you'll have to listen." I was delighted. He said to me later, "When you ducked under the water, I knew I had you!"

We worked on the story in Venice and later on a boat on Lake Mead near Las Vegas. We sat on the back of the boat working out the story line, laughing at our own jokes until we had the picture clearly set in our minds. We felt that the earlier Martin and Lewis pictures were essentially excuses for gags, but this time we made the characters more interesting, even complex, and the two boys played them beautifully.

My troubles with Martin and Lewis really surfaced on the film

Three Ring Circus. Don McGuire wrote the picture and he delighted me from the beginning. I said to him, "Can you give me a quick premise for a Martin and Lewis picture?" He replied instantly, "Sure! GI's can study lion taming under the Bill of Rights!" I burst out laughing and hired him on the spot.

Jerry would play a GI working as a clown in a circus while studying lion taming. Dean would be a con man who was also an expert sharpshooter. I hired the entire Clyde Beatty Circus and had them move to Phoenix for our location work. They set up their tents on the fairgrounds.

At a meeting in my office with Dean, Jerry, MCA's Taft Schreiber and Lew Wasserman, and Joe Ross, their attorney, Jerry told me point-blank that he wouldn't do the picture. He had already bad-mouthed me to Don McGuire and was demanding more money. I had just increased their salaries to $75,000 a picture despite the fact that their contracts called for only $50,000.

I calmly asked Jerry, "What's the problem?"

He replied, "Dean and I should come to the circus together in the story."

I was puzzled. I said, "But you do! We early establish Dean's character as a ne'er-do-well thrown out of nightclub jobs and then you meet up with him and you go to the circus together." As I said it, I thought to myself, that's what's bugging Jerry—Dean has the first ten pages of the script alone. I said to Jerry, "If we start the opening scene with you and Dean together, is that going to satisfy you?"

"Sure," he said instantly.

One of Don's scripts was on my desk. I looked at Dean and he nodded in agreement, knowing what I was going to do. I simply tore out the first ten pages and threw them in the wastebasket. Eyeballing the group, I said, "Now, gentlemen, we can go ahead."

But that wasn't the end of it. I joined the company in Phoenix, and Dean and Jerry were to follow on an afternoon flight. When my production manager was sent to the airport to meet them, they were not on the plane. I immediately called our attorneys and they were informed by the boys' representatives that they would not do the picture. Our lawyers notified them that unless they were on the plane the next morning, we would shut down the picture and hold them responsible for all costs incurred to date, including the Clyde Beatty Circus at $30,000 a week for several weeks.

The next morning Martin and Lewis arrived and came to work. We were hardly starting the picture under ideal conditions but they left us little choice.

There were other problems. Dean and Jerry were drifting apart in their social lives. Their wives didn't get along. Each wife was protective of the relative importance of her husband in scripts, films, and publicity, and this ultimately led to the breakup of the team. Our cast stayed at the Arizona Biltmore in Phoenix. In the evenings when Dean and his wife came into the bar for a drink and Jerry and his wife were there, they ignored each other.

During the first two or three days of shooting, the boys played scenes that were supposed to be funny, and after the director yelled, "Cut!" they turned and walked off in opposite directions. They didn't speak between shots.

I had the studio send me the rushes every day. They were terrible. I called the boys in and told them so cold turkey. "These are impossible. Your work is no good. You aren't funny. And *you* are up there on the screen being judged—not the director, not me. It's going to be a lousy picture. Now if you will get down to business, forget your personal problems, and do what you are able to do so well, I will reshoot these last three days' work." Crestfallen and subdued, they agreed to retake all the early scenes.

I reshot them from start to finish. They were vastly improved and we carried on and finally completed the picture, but it wasn't easy. My emotional involvement triggered a severe gout attack centered in my elebow, and I spent the entire location with my arm in a sling.

Dino complained that his part had been cut to shreds. He told people, "All I get to do in this turkey is sing, 'It's a Big, Wide, Wonderful World,' to an elephant." He was furious when children ran up to ask him, "Hey, where's Jerry Lewis?" I realized the trouble was terminal, that the days of Dean Martin and Jerry Lewis as a team were numbered.

One amusing thing did happen on *Three Ring Circus*. Zsa Zsa Gabor, who was in the picture, stayed at a dude ranch away from the rest of the company. We soon found out why: Porfirio Rubirosa, the well-known playboy, visited her there. As he departed, piloting his own plane, reporters asked him what he was doing in Phoenix. "I was headed for Nicaragua but I was blown off course," he replied.

Shortly after completing *Three Ring Circus*, I was lunching at

Hillcrest Country Club when Jerry called and asked if he could see me. "It's a matter of life or death," he said. He came over to the club and told me, "I can't work with Dean anymore. If you force us to do a picture together it won't be any good because I can't look him in the face. Our working relationship has become intolerable. Will you give me a chance to do a picture alone? You can make pictures with us separately and you'll have twice as many commitments."

I said I'd think about it. I had a property called *The Sad Sack*, and in view of the situation I put it into work. Jerry did it on his own and was very funny in it. As a token of appreciation he sent me a gold watch inscribed, "Thanks, Mr. Hal." From that moment on, the two comedians operated separately.

Dino was excellent with the difficult Shirley MacLaine in *Career* and *All in a Night's Work* for me. He was never a problem and went on to become a superstar in his own right. We also did *Five Card Stud* and *The Sons of Katie Elder* together.

In 1964, I made *Boeing Boeing* in Paris with Jerry Lewis and Tony Curtis. From the beginning nothing went right.

Jerry arrived at the luxurious Plaza Athenee Hotel with an entourage made up of a personal publicity man, barber, wardrobe man, and stand-in/double. My production manager, Bill Gray, had booked a magnificent suite for him. He had seventy-five pieces of Hartman luggage, which filled the lobby from one end to the other, an incredible sight. Moving the luggage upstairs was a major undertaking at midnight. Two hours later, Jerry called room service to order salami and corned beef sandwiches. When this extremely elegant hotel was unable to supply anything of the kind at that time of night, Jerry flew into a temper, checked out of the hotel with his entire entourage, and swept off to the Ritz. The Ritz, also, was unable to oblige, but he decided to stay put and sent one of his people to comb Paris for the salami.

Tony Curtis was another problem. During preproduction work, he appeared to be completely rational, but when shooting began, he became a different person. After the first scene was completed, he removed his coat and held it out for a wardrobe man to take from him. The wardrobe man was not there, so he dropped the coat onto the floor and retired to his dressing room to sulk. He told me that in the future a wardrobe man must be standing next to him on the set at all times to receive his coat whenever he removed it or he would not proceed with the picture. He remained in his dressing room until I had made contact with his agents and lawyers and reminded them of the terms of his contract. We supplied the wardrobe man and he grumblingly returned to work.

When he left Los Angeles for France, we sent a car and driver to take him to the airport. He took one look at the studio's new Buick sedan and flatly refused to get into it. He said that he would only ride in a Rolls-Royce. We didn't have a Rolls handy so he traveled to the airport in his own. In Paris, he decided he would only travel in a Cadillac sedan—and it had to be black. We were unable to find a car in Paris meeting these specifications, so we sent him a Citroën sedan, a magnificent automobile. Tony refused to travel in it. Although it was identical to that used by de Gaulle, the president of France, he preferred a Cadillac and had one brought in from somewhere else.

We finished the picture in Hollywood. The last four days we were scheduled to shoot the interior of an elegant French restaurant with two hundred dress extras and Jerry Lewis, but Jerry disappeared and was not to be found in his dressing room or office. His secretary denied all knowledge of his whereabouts. Later, we learned he had left the studio and flown to San Diego to his yacht. He was having a quarrel with Paramount over billing on his pictures and he refused to return until the studio acceded to his wishes. He won. He had forced us to shut down our picture for four days at great cost, until his problems with Paramount were resolved.

Later, Jerry got the autonomy he sought from the beginning. He produced, directed, wrote, starred in, edited, and supervised the music of his pictures. There is no need to comment on their quality.

With Eddie Robinson, his son Manny, and my son Brent on the set of *The Sea Wolf*.

Mr. and Mrs. Joseph Hazen (*rear*) and Darryl Zanuck (*right*) visit Louise and me at our Malibu Beach house.

I dressed as Simon Legree for a
costume party—and was sometimes
referred to as that character by some
of my co-workers!

The beginning of the Wallis stock company
at Paramount. *Left to right*: Kirk Douglas,
Douglas Dick, Don De Fore, (unidentified), and
Lizabeth Scott.

Dean Martin and Jerry Lewis were important additions to my roster of players. Here they clown for Joe Hazen (*left*), me, and Ronald Reagan.

Signing Elvis Presley to a long-term contract was one of the high points of my independent operation.

Elvis and I had a long and friendly association.

With Elvis in Frankfurt,
Germany, making *G. I. Blues.*

With Joan Fontaine *(left)*,
the star of *September Affair*,
and Jennifer Jones, who
starred in *Love Letters.*

Left to right: Kirk Douglas, Burt Lancaster, John Hudson, and Deforest Kelley in a famous scene from *Gunfight at the O.K. Corral.*

At dinner in our home, my son and I toast Anna
Magnani for her performance in *The Rose Tattoo*.

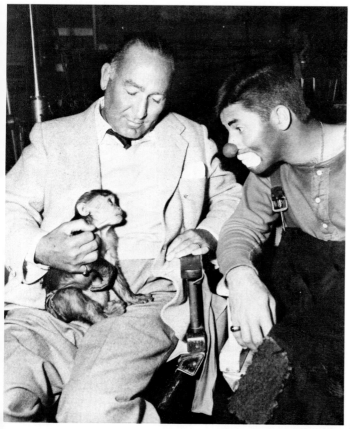

Monkey business with
Jerry Lewis.

With Robert Redford and
Jane Fonda on location in
New York for *Barefoot in
the Park*.

My prize 662-lb. catch
while on a brief vacation in
Kona, Hawaii.

John Wayne and I had a great
relationship during the making
of *True Grit*.

Here my wife Martha and I
are with Duke on location
in Colorado.

Filming *True Grit* was a happy experience.

Duke has just presented me with the Golden Globe's Cecil B. De Mille Award.

Peter O'Toole (*left*) and Richard Burton starred for me in *Becket*.

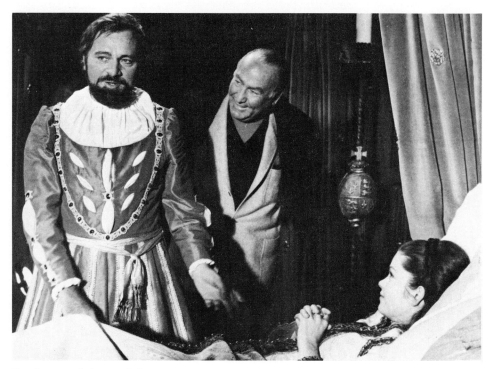

On the set of *Anne of the Thousand Days* with Richard Burton and Genevieve Bujold.

I was honored to be presented to Her Majesty Queen Elizabeth II at the Royal Command Performance of *Anne of the Thousand Days.*

The Queen Mother attended the Royal Command Performance of *Mary, Queen of Scots.*

Martha congratulates me on winning five Golden Globe awards for *Anne of the Thousand Days*.

One of the great moments of my career—being
presented with the badge of the C.B.E.
(Commander of the British Empire) in Washington,
D.C., by the British ambassador, the Earl
of Cromer, by order of Her Majesty Queen
Elizabeth II.

Discussing the films I made in
England with His Royal
Highness Prince Charles during
his recent visit to Los Angeles.

Mutual admiration society: Kate Hepburn and me on location in Oregon for *Rooster Cogburn*.

CHAPTER 14

Elvis

Elvis Presley was the complete opposite of Jerry Lewis. I made a great many of his pictures, and found him a joy to work with in every way.

The details of his early life and discovery by Colonel Tom Parker are already American legend. I found Colonel Parker as fascinating as Elvis. In his younger days, he ran a concession at a carnival, sold spun sugar, worked as a dogcatcher, and traveled around the country hawking cough medicine so successfully that he became famous in his own right. Elvis owed a large part of his success to the colonel. He is a shrewd, clever businessman and a supersalesman. I admire and respect him very much. We are good friends to this day.

In 1956 Elvis appeared on a series of CBS Saturday night television shows with Tommy and Jimmy Dorsey. Well-presented half-hours produced by Jackie Gleason, the program had been in trouble until the Dorsey brothers spotted Elvis and hired him.

I was sitting at home spinning the dial of my television set one night when I first saw this remarkable performer. Elvis was an original. He wore a sport coat that was slightly too large for him and tight black pants. At first, he looked like any other teen-aged bopper, but when he started to sing, twisting his legs, bumping and grinding, shaking his shoulders, he was electrifying. I had never seen anything like him. Those were the days of censorship, when sexuality on the screen was completely taboo. Yet here was an entertainer whose every movement excited female audiences of all ages. I turned to Louise and predicted that Elvis would soon be the most talked about newcomer in the business.

Early the next morning I telephoned Tom Parker in New York and told him I wanted to sign Elvis to a film contract. The Colonel was aware of me and my work, and listened. Clearly counting the dollars in advance, he cautiously revealed that Elvis would "probably" be out on the Coast soon and would "consider" the possibility of a meeting.

I knew instinctively that the Colonel was interested but playing it cool. He was a genius at getting every possible inch of financial mileage out of his astonishing protégé.

In March 1957 Elvis and several of his friends headed west. A snowstorm hit their plane just after takeoff from La Guardia, and the engines iced up so severely that an emergency landing was necessary. Elvis was severely shaken by the ordeal and vowed he would never fly again.

When he arrived in Los Angeles he went directly to the Coliseum to do a concert and from there to San Diego for a show with Milton Berle aboard a battleship. When he met Berle, he asked him if he knew a man named Hal Wallis and if I was "any good" as a producer. Berle assured him that I was. Elvis asked if I was "respectable" and "bona fide." Berle again reassured him. Elvis told the Colonel he would like to meet me.

Our meeting was set for the following week after he returned from a concert tour. Reluctant to fly, Elvis drove with his boys to Denver for the first concert. He was so exhausted from the trip that he collapsed in his dressing room after the performance with a fever so severe he wasn't expected to live. But he rallied unexpectedly and, having no choice, flew to Florida for another concert. His temperature was 102 degrees.

He collapsed again but forced himself to go on to New York to record his first hit album, which included "Blue Suede Shoes" and "I'm Counting on You." He wasn't well when he made the recordings but they were wonderful. I managed to get an advance copy of the album and realized I was listening to a new sound—a new style that was revolutionary. It was destined to change the world of popular music and make recording history. I vowed nothing would stop me from signing this boy for films.

I telephoned, telegraphed, and harassed Colonel Parker until he finally brought Elvis to Hollywood for a meeting and a screen test. Elvis turned up at my office in jeans and a work shirt. I expected him to be as aggressive and dynamic in person as he was on stage. But he was slender, pale, extremely reserved, and rather nervous. It was quite clear that this genius (and genius he was) very much needed the balance and strength of his practical, straight-thinking mentor. Elvis was a delicately tuned engine. Colonel Parker supplied the fuel.

A test was necessary to determine if Elvis could act. I selected a scene for him to do with that very fine actor Frank Faylen. Elvis would play a young man just starting out in life and Faylen would play his father, holding him back. It was a difficult dramatic scene for an amateur. But I had to be sure.

When I ran the test I felt the same thrill I experienced when I first saw Errol Flynn on the screen. Elvis, in a very different, modern way, had exactly the same power, virility, and sexual drive. The camera caressed him.

I met at once with Colonel Parker and arranged a three-picture deal. It was one of the toughest bargaining sessions of my career. I agreed to pay Elvis $100,000 for the first picture, $150,000 for the second, and $200,000 for the third production.

I was just in time. When "The Milton Berle Show" aired that spring, forty million people, one-quarter of the population of the country, watched Elvis Presley and fell in love with him. Every studio in Hollywood wanted to sign him. His first album went straight to the top of the charts. *Life* magazine did a cover story on him.

Elvis bought a beautiful ranch house in Memphis, but he had no privacy, no life of his own. He belonged to the public in a way even the great stars I had worked with in earlier years could not have imagined. He told me he used to rent an entire amusement park after hours because it was the only way he could entertain his friends without being mobbed by crowds.

It took a while to create the ideal vehicle for Elvis. I wanted the picture to show him off to best advantage in a plot framed around the twelve songs necessary for a simultaneous album release.

As Hal Kanter and I worked on the screenplay of *Loving You,* I was faced with the possibility of losing Elvis to the army. We were told that he would be called up in the draft, but the draft board assured us he was well down the line of 1-A's and wouldn't be called immediately.

There was no time to waste. We began shooting *Loving You* as quickly as possible. Hal Kanter's very clever script was tailor-made for Elvis. It was a simple story, but well written and perfectly suited to Elvis's talent. Because of the rush, we only had time to put together one side of an album. We didn't make that mistake again.

In the middle of the picture Elvis had his preinduction physical. Just after we finished, he was told he could expect to be drafted at any time. We were sure he'd be sent overseas and would be unavaila ble for promotion work on our picture. As it turned out, his enlist- ment was delayed indefinitely.

I then loaned him to MGM for *Jailhouse Rock*. By now, he was a very rich young man and had remodeled his Memphis estate into the famous Graceland. With five bedrooms and bathrooms and seven- teen other rooms, today it is worth millions, but Elvis paid $100,000 for it.

I decided to gamble that Elvis would not be drafted for another year and in late 1957 cast him as *King Creole*. I decided to give him the best director in the business, my dear and good friend Michael Curtiz. I warned Mike not to use his well-known shock tactics on Elvis, and on no account must he badger and bully him as he had certain stars at Warners. But Mike had mellowed. In fact, he wasn't a very well man when he did the picture.

We based the film on Harold Robbins's *A Stone for Danny Fisher,* and changed the leading character from a prizefighter to a singer. My wonderful bank robbers and hoodlums in the picture were Walter Matthau, Brian Hutton, and Vic Morrow, and Carolyn Jones gave a vivid portrayal of a prostitute with a heart of gold. Elvis was excellent in a very demanding role. In many ways, *King Creole* was his best picture.

When we shot on location in New Orleans, the crowds were so huge that we had to arrange for top security. We booked the top floor of the Roosevelt Hotel and had the elevators stop oper- ating just before reaching our level. When we shot on the streets, police and ropes were necessary to hold back the crowds. At the end of the day, it was a major ordeal for Elvis to get to his hotel room, the crowds in the lobby and in front of the hotel so tremen- dous that he avoided them by going up to a room in an adjoining building, crossing the roof, and entering his hotel by the fire escape. Pinkerton guards patrolled the elevators, the exits, every inch of the floor he was on, even his suite. One night he wanted to go to dinner at Antoine's. Colonel Parker bitterly disappointed him by telling him he couldn't. When I saw the expression on his face, I realized the price he paid for being a superstar.

I grew to be very fond of Elvis. He was utterly without guile, malice, even ego. He never addressed me as anything but "sir," spoke in a soft voice, and never lost his temper. We didn't mix socially: I was not invited to his home, nor would he come to mine. I sometimes visited him in his hotel suite. He and his boys played touch football on the carpet, listened to his favorite records, watched TV, and ate junk food. After a day's work the entire group holed up in the suite and had waiters bring in malted milks, Cokes, pizzas, hamburgers, hot dogs, and potato chips.

I was fascinated by the way Elvis recorded the songs for our pictures. He didn't feel comfortable in the recording room at Paramount; he found it too large. Because he preferred working with his own group in a more intimate area, we rented a small studio on Santa Monica Boulevard and recorded at night. Elvis hated to work in the morning or even the afternoon. Never bothering with arrangements, he and his boys noodled around, improvised, ad-libbed, and worked out numbers for hours. Finally, he would rehearse a number straight through. Night after long night I watched and listened, fascinated. Elvis was a born musician. He knew instinctively what he wanted in a song: when an instrument was wrong for a number, when a lyric wasn't right. He talked to the boys from the control room and made them repeat a number ten, fifteen, twenty times if necessary to achieve perfection. I never said a word, just observed.

Soon after we finished *King Creole,* Elvis was drafted and sent to Germany. I decided to take advantage of the situation and do a picture based on his real-life experiences in the army. Writers Edmund Beloin and Henry Garson did the screenplay. They flew with me to Frankfurt to get a feel of the background and atmosphere.

While we shot a good deal of the picture in Germany, we didn't use Elvis in any of the scenes. We knew there would be criticism of his working in a commercial picture while in the army, so we used a double for him in the long shots made there.

Elvis preferred it that way. He wanted no special treatment, even refusing invitations to attend officers' parties. We were told he was doing a fine job, was an excellent soldier, and lived just like any other recruit. He asked for no favors and overcame the mockery of his fellow GI's by keeping a low profile. Elvis Presley served his country with dignity and honor.

151

His homecoming was overwhelming. *GI Blues* was the name we gave Elvis's first postarmy film. Talented South African dancer Juliet Prowse played his girlfriend and the picture was an enormous hit.

I decided to present the new, mature Elvis in a series of pictures set in exotic locations, the first of these films being *Blue Hawaii*. In an excellent script by Hal Kanter, Elvis played a young man returning from the army to become a travel agent—once again we tried to parallel his own life with his screen personality. Angela Lansbury, one of my favorite actresses, played Elvis's mother.

I remember very clearly an incident with Colonel Parker on this picture. We had set up a complicated long shot of Elvis running out of the surf. After waiting all day for a break in the weather, the rain finally stopped and director Norman Taurog hurriedly called for action. The cameras rolled. Suddenly Colonel Parker rushed from his trailer into the shot, calling my name. The scene was ruined. I tried to keep calm. "What is it, Colonel?" I asked.

Parker replied, "Do you remember the terms of Elvis's contract?"

"Of course," I said.

"Then I don't need to remind you that *that* is out!"

I couldn't imagine what he was talking about. I followed his pointing finger to Elvis's wrist.

"That watch Elvis is wearing!" he shouted.

"Yes?"

"The contract says that Elvis doesn't provide his own clothes! If you want that watch in, you'll have to pay us another $25,000!"

Keeping a firm grip on my temper, I told Elvis, as gently as I could under the circumstances, to remove the watch and give it to the wardrobe man. He shouldn't have been wearing a watch in the surf anyway.

Such events were infrequent. The Colonel and I always got along well and still do. I visit him often at his extraordinary home in Palm Springs. It is filled with every conceivable kind of gadget. There is no recording device, record player, radio, or TV set he does not own. His Jacuzzi is a marvel in itself.

We returned to Hawaii for *Girls! Girls! Girls!* and traveled to Mexico for *Fun in Acapulco*. Those were happy days. We never had a problem with Elvis.

When his contract with me ended, Elvis and I remained very close friends. I was shocked and saddened by his death. Much that is false has beeen written about the cause of it. When I worked with Elvis, he never smoked or drank; he was on the president's committee to prevent drug abuse, and in all the years I knew him I do not believe he took anything but prescribed drugs. He died young for a variety of reasons: his weight, the pressures of his career, exhaustion —I didn't know about drugs. I knew him only as a happy, modest, clean-cut American boy. No matter what is said about him, that is what he will always be—in my memory.

CHAPTER 15

Westerns

I have always liked Western stories. At Warners, I made three popular Westerns, *Dodge City* and *Virginia City,* starring Errol Flynn; and *Oklahoma Kid,* with Cagney and Bogart. But these pictures were based on fiction, not fact. At Paramount I decided to make hard-hitting Western films debunking the myths audiences believed to be true.

The story of Wyatt Earp and Doc Holliday was, of course, a classic. There had been countless film versions of their fight with the Clanton gang, the best being John Ford's widely praised *My Darling Clementine,* with Henry Fonda and Victor Mature. Excellent though that picture was, it was still romantic fiction, fantasy.

I researched the characters and found them fascinating. Killer Doc Holliday was a charmer, but he was also a bigot who hated blacks and Indians. Earp was a cool, hard-bitten professional lawman who liked his job and did it well. Restless by nature, he moved from place to place, looking for new fields to conquer. He lived a double life after becoming marshal of Dodge City. He owned a piece of the Oriental Saloon, the brothel, and the gambling casino and accepted bribes and payoffs. But he also protected women and children and made the Maypole speech every year on May Day for all the young kids gathered round. They idolized him. They still do.

I felt a true account of the Doc Holliday–Wyatt Earp story would be dynamite movie material and it was. Leon Uris's realistic script was excellent, and I called the picture *Gunfight at the O.K. Corral.* Burt Lancaster and Kirk Douglas were cast as Earp and Holliday.

I needed a strong director to handle the action sequences so I hired John Sturges, whose *Bad Day at Black Rock* with Spencer Tracy had just the gutty quality I wanted in *Gunfight*. When John came in for discussions, I liked him at once. A tall, powerfully built man who could have been a Western hero himself, he was an expert on Western history and contributed a great deal to the success of the picture.

We shot on location near Tucson, Arizona. Our principal set was a standing replica of Tombstone surrounded by barren plains and jagged mountain ranges. We built the Clanton ranch in the hills nearby. With Charles Lang, Jr., as our cameraman, we were assured of a fine-looking production. Lang specialized in clean, sharp, hard-edged photography with extraordinary depth of focus. I wanted the picture to have the burned-out, brown look of a Remington painting, and Lang gave it to me. Remington has always been a favorite painter of mine and today several of his finest works hang on the walls of our Palm Springs home.

It was a bone-dry spring, perfect for our purposes. The look of bare, scorched earth helped establish the fact that people lived here at the mercy of the elements.

From the start, both stars asserted themselves. They reminded us constantly that they were directors as well as actors and tried to override Sturges, but John was a match for them. They rewrote their dialogue at night, but this was an exercise in futility, as I insisted that the lines be read exactly as Leon Uris had written them. Burt finally exploded, demanding that John let him play a scene his way with dialogue he had written. It was totally unrelated to the action, but John humored him. Burt played the scene to the hilt, shouting himself hoarse. The speech was out of his system. The film was also out of the camera.

The gunfight was choreographed like a ballet. John and I drew up a map plotting every move Burt and Kirk and the Clanton boys made. We asked the actors to play the scene deadpan. We assumed Western men engaged in struggles to the death didn't show emotion: they accepted the rule of the bullet and didn't question it.

I asked Burt to be especially careful about playing deadpan. In answer to his question, "What should I be thinking about when I'm in the gunfight?" John and I replied simultaneously, "Meanwhile, back at the ranch!' He listened very solemnly, and played the scene perfectly.

We wanted complete silence during the gunfight except for the stinging, cracking sound of ricocheting bullets, and some incidental sounds: a piece of tin falling off the roof, birds fluttering on a porch step, the creak of a wagon far away. We wanted the audience to clearly understand the geography of the scene, to know at any given moment exactly where Earp and Holliday and the Clanton boys were.

The original gunfight took about a minute and a half. Western men didn't fool around. That wouldn't do for us: we needed to build the sequence for maximum suspense. We stretched ours to eleven minutes and the excitement was terrific. We shot the entire sequence in three days, and each morning somehow matched the light in the sky and the exact movements of everyone involved.

Charles Lang's cinematography was exceptional. I was delighted with his work, as I was with that of Warren Low, one of my favorite editors, who cut the film expertly. When John and I ran the finished picture, we jumped up and shook hands. It was everything we had hoped for. *Gunfight at the O.K. Corral* made money and was a critical success.

Later, John and I made *Last Train from Gun Hill,* starring Tony Quinn and Kirk Douglas. This was a powerful tale of revenge, just the kind of story I like.

We went back to Arizona on location and had a great time. It was summer and the plains were green and wild-flowered. Cottonwood trees were in full bloom. We got a completely different look from what we had had in *Gunfight*.

Sequences involving a magnificent vintage steam train were shot at the studio. Unfortunately, the tracks were laid just under the office windows of Paramount boss Y. Frank Freeman and the noise drove him crazy. We had to reroute the railroad.

Tony questioned the script. In his big scene he pleads with his son to leave Kirk and return to him. After a few takes he turned to Sturges and me and said, "Goddamnit, aren't I supposed to be important in this town?"

We reassured him that he was.

Quinn added, "Then why can't I rustle up all the goddamn guys I want and go up there and shoot the ass of this character and take my boy?"

I said, "Because you're being paid not to. It's in the script. You can't do that. We're only into reel three and there are five reels to go!

If you get your boy out now, the picture will be over." Tony was sullen and sulked the rest of the day.

Another Western I enjoyed making was *The Sons of Katie Elder*. John Sturges first brought the story to Paramount's attention, but they didn't want to do it. It lay on a shelf at the author's agent's office for years until John told me about it and I asked to see it. I liked it immediately. Since John was busy elsewhere, I hired Henry Hathaway to direct it.

The story had a basic force and believability that I knew would attract audiences. Five brothers return home for their mother's funeral. One is a gunman, another a riverboat gambler, another a seed-store salesman—all very different types. They're ashamed they weren't closer to their mother and that they never communicated with her. Now that she's gone, they learn what tremendous sacrifices she made for them. She took in washing to pay for their teaching. She suffered from the town heavies—and revenge was in the air.

I wanted John Wayne to play the strongest of the brothers. No film actor had greater integrity or stature. He represented the American folk hero at his best.

I liked Duke enormously and used to enjoy visiting him at his home in Newport Beach. Big and comfortable and very masculine, it was filled with awards for a lifetime of great work and with his hunting and fishing trophies.

Wayne was exactly the same off the screen as on. He was a superb actor; there was nobody quite like him. We won't see his equal in Hollywood again.

From the beginning of our relationship, I got the measure of the man. A week before we were to leave for location work in Mexico, Duke called me in my office and invited me to his dressing room for a talk. I was greeted there by three people: Henry Hathaway; Michael Wayne, Duke's handsome son; and Duke himself. Wayne indicated that I should sit down and said, "Well, Hal, I'm going to hit you with it. I've got the big C."

I couldn't believe it. The robust, red-cheeked, two-hundred-pound man in front of me seemed the picture of health. It was incredible.

I was so shocked I couldn't speak. He told me he had gone to Scripps Clinic at La Jolla for a routine physical, which included a chest X ray. The side view disclosed cancerous lesions in one lung.

I managed a few words. It seemed futile to express sympathy, faced with so strong a character. All I could say was something practical like, "Are you going to have cobalt treatments?"

Wayne's reply was decisive. "No. None of that stuff. I'm going to have the lung removed. I'm checking in for surgery tomorrow morning." He said it matter-of-factly, much as one might say that an ingrown toenail was going to be removed.

He continued, "I'm sure you'll want to recast. It's okay with me. Fact is, I don't know how long I'll be laid up with this damn thing, and I know you're all set to start." It was typical of him to be more concerned with the schedule than with his own health. He added, "The doctors tell me it may be six weeks."

I responded at once. I told him the picture was written for him and nobody else would do. I would wait. In a daze of shock and depression, I went back to my office and postponed the picture. I would not make *The Sons of Katie Elder* without John Wayne.

I kept in constant touch with his doctors and went to see him at his home in Newport. Six weeks stretched into eight, ten, twelve, finally sixteen. But at last, Wayne was ready. He'd licked it. He grinned his famous grin, shook my hand in his giant fist, and said, "Let's go to work."

On location in Durango, Mexico, he amazed me. Even though he was functioning on one lung and had a terrible scar running down his back, he showed no signs of illness or weakness. He did his own riding, roped in steers, rounded up cattle, and handled the fight scenes without a double. Only occasionally, in high country, was he short of breath.

He gave one of his best performances in the picture. And not only on screen. Although he must have been in great pain, we never had a word of complaint from him. He won the unstinting respect and admiration of fellow players, Dean Martin, Martha Hyer, Earl Holliman, and Dennis Hopper.

I worked with Duke again on one of my favorite pictures, *True Grit*. Based on a novel by Charles Portis, it is the story of a grizzled old marshal's uneasy but ultimately affectionate friendship with a tomboy.

Portis's agents sent seven copies of the book's galleys to the major studios, and I was fortunate enough to be included on the list. I read the book overnight and told the agents I was fascinated and definitely interested. They responded by saying that the book would be auctioned. If more than one person accepted their price of $300,000, the author would have the last word on the person to whom the property would be sold.

I put in my bid for $300,000. Others did, too. Then the agents said that Portis was traveling in Central America and could not be reached. We all had to sit and wait until they found him and gave him the names of those who had bid.

He had seen and liked several of my pictures and decided I should be the one to make *True Grit*. I was overjoyed. The book was wonderful and filled with a strange, very special form of Arkansas speech that brought the characters unerringly alive. The spikey relationship between the well-worn man and the fresh-faced young girl was a delight.

Duke, interestingly enough, bid on *True Grit* himself. He was so determined to play Rooster Cogburn that he offered $100,000 over the top price to cinch it, but the agents said no. They felt accepting his bid would be unethical and unfair to the rest of us. Wayne called me and said I was damned lucky to have acquired the book and he was bitterly disappointed to have lost it. I immediately told him he could play Rooster without laying out a cent of his own money. He let out a roar of laughter and we were in business.

Now I had to find an actress to play the all-important role of Mattie Ross, the spunky young girl who stands up to Rooster. My first choice was Mia Farrow. I called her agent and she was thrilled. She drove straight to my office, plopped herself down cross-legged on my carpet, drank a bottle of wine, and accepted the part. She said she would buy a trailer and drive to Arkansas to study the manner of the people Portis had created. Her agent made the deal very difficult, but Mia overrode him and was full of enthusiasm—yet kept postponing her trip to Arkansas.

While we prepared the script, she went to England to fulfill a commitment with Joe Losey—*Secret Ceremony*, costarring Robert Mitchum. One wet afternoon in London, she told Mitchum that Henry Hathaway was going to direct *True Grit*. Mitchum advised her to avoid working with Hathaway at all costs. He predicted that sensitive Mia would hate Hathaway, who was a son of a bitch and a martinet on the set.

She was so impressed with Mitchum's remark that she urged me to replace Hathaway with Roman Polanski, who had directed her in *Rosemary's Baby*. When I refused, she cabled me that she had changed her mind and would not do the picture.

I was badly shocked. Preproduction was far advanced and I was without a leading lady. (Years later, when I was filming in England, I visited Mia and her husband Andre Previn at their beautiful home in the country. She told me over lunch that refusing to play Mattie Ross in *True Grit* was the biggest personal and professional mistake she had ever made in her life.) When I looked at the list of well-known Hollywood actresses, my heart sank. Not one of them was right for Mattie. But one night a face jumped off the television screen at me that was. Clean-scrubbed, keen-eyed, strong-boned, full of spunk and determination, this girl *was* Mattie Ross. Her name was Kim Darby.

She was completely unknown. When I contacted her agent through the Screen Actors Guild, he told me she had just had a baby and that this television job was the last acting she would ever do. She had retired.

I investigated further. She was married to a good-looking, struggling young actor named Jim Stacy. They had decided that they would concentrate on his career and she would stay home and rear the baby. They realized if they both worked, the marriage would be doomed.

I called Kim and told her I wanted to come see her. She gave no indication that she wanted to see me, but I drove up to their cottage in a canyon anyway. It was a wooden structure, casually underfurnished. Stacy and Kim were dressed in jeans.

Times had certainly changed. I found myself sitting on the floor on a large pillow, drinking wine by candlelight, begging an obscure actress to accept the leading role in a $300,000-property starring John Wayne, the world's leading box office star, to be directed by the great Henry Hathaway. It would be one of the biggest pictures of the year, and she was reluctant to do it. Certainly this was the "new Hollywood."

I used the most persuasive argument I could think of: money. They had no security. They were just two of thousands of handsome young kids who would probably never make it in Hollywood.

Stacy feigned indifference, so I focused my attention on Kim. I pointed out to her that the money she earned from the picture could provide a decent education for her child. I explained that she would not have to give up her home life. Jim would be welcome on location. We would provide a cottage for them and a nurse for the baby throughout the shooting. She would not be under exclusive long-term contract; she could make pictures for outside producers if she wished.

The conversation ended at midnight. Stacy said he would think about it and let me know. As he closed the door, he said he would want a certain amount of money if he agreed to let Kim make the picture.

A difficult two days went by. I didn't sleep as I waited for their decision. At last, the agent called and said Kim would do it. She asked for a very large sum of money, but there was no time to negotiate. I agreed at once and the deal was made.

We were fortunate in having Glen Campbell in the picture. After seeing him on television, I was impressed with his style and realized he had the talent and looks that would attract large audiences. Like Kim, he had never made a feature picture and was eager for the chance. He worked hard to make up for his lack of experience, and the chemistry was right in his scenes with Kim.

The scenery in Colorado was magnificent. Who will ever forget the golden aspen trees bordering the valley where Rooster charged Robert Duvall as Lucky Ned Pepper, yelling, "Fill your hand, you son of a bitch." Or the snow-covered graveyard where Rooster jumps the fence on his horse, asking Mattie to "Come see a fat old man sometime." We hadn't counted on snow in that scene, but when it fell we used it, working straight through until we finished the sequence.

Hathaway was Hathaway: tough, but a demon for work, and efficient. Though he was never tough with Duke, he was very hard on Kim. But she was a spunky girl, every bit as spunky as Mattie Ross, and she fought back. When Hathaway saw that she could hold her own, he respected her and we had no further problems.

As soon as I ran the rushes, I knew we had a winner. Duke was extraordinary. Kim was remarkable, too. She played Mattie Ross like a gadfly irritating Rooster's hide. Familiar as I was with the script, I often laughed out loud viewing the film Duke, like all professionals, was unselfish toward the newcomer and frequently threw scenes in her direction.

Kim was elevated to major stardom overnight, her performance loved and praised by critics and public alike. The world was at her feet, but fate was against her. First, her marriage failed, probably because she was so much more successful than her husband. Then, she made a picture called *The Grissom Gang* in which she was totally miscast as a gangster's moll. The picture flopped and her career never again reached the heights of *True Grit*.

Stacy was riding his motorcycle down Laurel Canyon very late one night when a drunken driver smashed into him and virtually cut him in half. Fellow actors and friends gave numerous benefits for him and he gradually learned to adjust to artificial limbs. Today he is well and working.

True Grit became a classic Western and a huge success at the box office. John Wayne won an Oscar for his portrayal of Rooster Cogburn. At the Academy Awards that night, Bob Hope as master of ceremonies wore a black eyepatch, Cogburn style. It was one of the most popular awards ever given and Duke received a standing ovation along with his Oscar.

CHAPTER 16

Royal Histories

I have always been deeply interested in English history. Britain, British institutions, and the pageantry of the royal court fascinates me.

One October evening, on a trip to New York, I saw Anouilh's famous play, *Becket*. It was a powerful story of crown against church; of secular against clerical; of one extraordinary man, King Henry II, against another, Thomas à Becket. I felt it could be a superb film.

Friends and associates disagreed, predicting that such a production would be static, wordy, and exorbitantly expensive. They argued that the public had lost its taste for historical pictures, but I was certain it had not. People will always enjoy the intrigue and drama of historical spectacle. I felt that audiences had become so surfeited with films of violence and explicit sex that they would welcome a story based on deep and important human feelings.

Another reason the play intrigued me was that so many exciting events happened offstage that were later described in dialogue. I realized we could dramatize these moments on screen and that a fine film could be made from the play.

Paramount told me flatly I was wrong: a picture about an archbishop and a king would have no commercial value in today's market. The company had been bought by Gulf and Western Industries with Charles Bluhdorn as president.

Bluhdorn loved movies. Even though Paramount was a comparatively minor division of the conglomerate, he regarded it as his special baby. I saw Bluhdorn in his lavish offices in New York. He was skeptical about mass-audience acceptance of *Becket* because its plot was predicated on what was essentially an intellectual argument, but he was prepared to listen.

I explained to Charles that I would flesh out the picture with action and spectacle. Audiences would be excited by the beauty of the locations, the palaces and churches, the rich period costumes. I emphasized the importance of the message of the picture. He trusted me and gave his approval.

Casting was all important. We had to hedge our bets by engaging major stars. I felt only Richard Burton could play Thomas à Becket. Others were skeptical, arguing that his reputation as a drinker and his stormy, overpublicized romance with Elizabeth Taylor would nullify his believability in the role of the archbishop. I knew he was a brilliant, sensitive, tormented man with a strong sense of moral responsibility and character.

I flew to Switzerland to see him. Throughout lunch he left the table to answer the telephone. It was quite clear Elizabeth was calling from Paris and even movie producers must wait.

To my amazement, Richard was hesitant about playing Becket. Over coffee he said, "Whom do you have in mind for Henry?"

"Peter O'Toole," I said. I was gambling. I had never met O'Toole, but through the courtesty of Sam Spiegel I had seen his work in *Lawrence of Arabia*.

The moment Richard heard Peter's name his casual indifference changed to excitement. He put his napkin down decisively and rose from the table. "O'Toole?" he said. "Marvelous. I'll do it!"

What if O'Toole turned me down? Felling very tense, I caught the next available plane to London and booked into Claridge's. By a miracle, O'Toole was in town. He was interested in playing Henry and wanted to come by the hotel to chat about it.

I had hopes and doubts. If anything went wrong . . . Peter walked into the suite and sat down with a drink. He said he wasn't sure the role was right for him. I assured him it was, but he never warmed up. The time had come to play my trump card. I waited for the all-important question and it came at last, after an hour's discussion of Henry's character. "Who will play Becket?" he asked. I took a deep breath and told him. He jumped from his chair, shook my hand, and said he would do the part.

Both Peter and Richard had commitments and *Becket* had to be fitted into a crowded schedule. I hired Edward Anhalt to adapt the play and Peter Glenville to direct. Peter did some work on the Anhalt script, but the final version was cut and pasted together on the floor of the Carlyle Hotel in New York. I spread it all out and put it back together my way, using large sections of the play exactly as Anouilh had written it.

I went to England looking for exciting and dramatic locations, the best of which was thirteenth-century Bamburgh Castle in Northumberland. Canterbury Cathedral had changed so much through the years that we couldn't use it. We built a replica of the cathedral's interior on the largest sound stage in Europe at Shepperton Studios near London.

Our set decorator, Patrick McLaughlin, was brilliant, but a stickler for period detail. He correctly hung paintings so near the top of the sets that they were never visible in the scenes. I was astonished one day to be presented with a bill for $8,000 for candles. I called Patrick and asked him to explain. He told me that in those days candles were made of beeswax, not tallow. As calmly as I could, I advised him that tallow would serve our purposes just fine.

Richard was in great form. He was in love with Elizabeth and leaving Sybil for her. Elizabeth was on the set most of the time. When Richard and Peter stopped off at local pubs after work, she telephoned repeatedly, urging Richard to come home.

Elizabeth often came out to Shepperton for long lunches. While they enjoyed their wine, the rest of us waited on the set with nothing to do. The lights were set up, very costly actors were idle, while the three stars lingered over coffee and dessert. I tried to be patient. They usually reappeared at three o'clock to have their makeup touched up and change into period costume.

Richard and Peter were pros and we had few problems with them. But because scenes shot before lunch were always better than those shot after lunch, we scheduled accordingly.

Elizabeth wasn't content with being on the sidelines. She wanted to play a small part in the picture. To humor her—and Richard—we wrote a few lines for her to speak. By the time she had been wardrobed, made up, and coiffed, it was hardly worthwhile, particularly as we did not cut the scene into the picture.

When Elizabeth read the reviews on *Cleopatra*, she had an attack of the vapors and retired to her bed at the Dorchester for an indefinite period. Her phone calls from bed to set were many, and interfered with Richard's work. He told me one morning, "If you've got a picture for Elizabeth, I think you can get her today for $25,000."

Richard and I got along famously. He told me he wanted to do another picture with me and that he liked Maxwell Anderson's play *Anne of the Thousand Days* very much. Could he please play Henry VIII? Would I buy the play for him? I had seen the play on Broadway and was struck by its powerful theme. It was the love story of Henry VIII and Anne Boleyn. Henry divorced his wife, even the Church, to marry Anne, then had her beheaded when she failed to produce a male heir to the throne. The play had great cinematic possibilities.

Becket was a huge success and I was sure Bluhdorn would want to follow it up with another historical picture starring Burton. He did not. He was violently opposed to Richard appearing in any Paramount production again. The reason was strange. Charles had asked Burton to do an introduction and voice-over on one of his pictures. Richard was so anxious to please Bluhdorn that he had agreed to do it for a modest sum, but at the last minute, he changed his mind. He called Charles and said, "I'll only do the narration if you'll buy Elizabeth a pair of diamond-and-emerald earrings she's taken a fancy to." Bluhdorn flew into a rage and told him that not only would he not buy the earrings but that Richard would never work for Paramount again.

I begged Charles to change his mind. I pointed out that my own company had bought the property specifically for Burton, but Charles was adamant. Under no circumstances would he ever speak to or employ Richard Burton.

It was a very hard thing for me to do, but I asked for a release from my long-standing arrangement with Paramount and took myself, my company, and my property to Universal, where I was welcomed with open arms.

Richard was in Rome at the time, starring with Elizabeth in Zeffirelli's *The Taming of the Shrew*. I flew there for preproduction discussions and found the Burtons ensconced in royal splendor at the Cinecitta Studios. Their dressing rooms were far more lavish than those William Randolph Hearst had provided for his beloved Marion Davies. The living room was furnished with costly antiques. There was an immense dining room, a bedroom, and a makeup room.

When I joined the Burtons for lunch, we ate off porcelain plates and drank from fine Venetian glass. The food came from the most expensive restaurant in Italy.

But lunch dragged on and on. Hundreds of extras waited on the set while the stars languished at the table in full costume. Zeffirelli fumed and paced the floor. Perspiring assistant directors appeared at fifteen-minute intervals to inform the players that they were required for the scene. The group laughed and ate and drank and paid no attention to them. I was embarrassed at the self-indulgence and lack of discipline.

Elizabeth hung on my every word. I was surprised by her attention, as there was no part in the picture for her. Over an elaborate dessert she took a deep breath and said, "Hal, I've been thinking about it for weeks. *I have to play Anne Boleyn!*"

My fork stopped halfway to my mouth. *Anne Boleyn?* Elizabeth was plump and middle-aged; Anne was a slip of a girl. The fate of the picture hung in the balance. I could scarcely bring myself to look at Richard, but he handled it beautifully. He put his hand on hers, looked her directly in the eye, and said, "Sorry, luv. You're too long in the tooth." Elizabeth took it like a trouper. I respected her for not bursting into tears or throwing a tantrum, as many actresses would have done.

Burton and I finished our meetings, and I flew to London to sign Bridget Boland to do the adaptation. Her script turned out to be far too heavy and literary and had to be completely rewritten by British playwright John Hale. There was also a problem with Maxwell Anderson's family. They had been left the rights to *Anne,* but no single heir could dispose of the property; all had to agree. A family argument ensued for months.

The script was still not perfect. I cut and transposed scenes until the Andersons finally gave in and I could firmly sign Richard Burton.

I decided to go with a new director, Charles Jarrott, whose work I had admired on television and who had received critical acclaim for his excellent handling of *The Young Elizabeth* and a very strong version of *Dr. Jekyll and Mr. Hyde.* He came to see me in London at the Dorchester and I liked him at once. His sober, measured intelligence, robust figure, and Tudor beard made him seem rather like a member of the court of Henry VIII himself.

Now I needed an actress to play Anne Boleyn, someone young enough and strong enough to play this extraordinary child-queen. No known actress would do. I began an exhaustive search for an unknown.

A miracle happened. After months of futile interviews, an agent called to tell me he had just the right girl for the part. I had heard

that many times before, but at this point I was willing to believe anything and wearily suggested he bring the footage to my screening
room.

It was three hundred feet from a Canadian film called *Isabelle,*
about the ghost of a young woman who haunts her lover. The
minute she appeared on the screen, I was riveted. I saw a tiny, seem-
ingly fragile woman made of steel—willful, passionate, intense. She
was exactly the actress I wanted to play Anne Boleyn. Even her
French accent was perfect: Anne had been educated in France. I
hired the girl without meeting her or testing her. Her name was
Genevieve Bujold.

By coincidence, she was in Hollywood, promoting her picture,
and we met and liked each other immediately. Everything about her
confirmed my prediction that she was a very special personality:
unique, perfect for *Anne.*

I signed Irene Papas to play Catherine of Aragon and top British character actors for the lesser roles. Casting in England is easy:
the country is a treasure house of fine performers.

I worked very closely with costume designer, Margaret Furse,
who duplicated exactly the garments worn by Henry and Anne in
the Holbein portraits. We wanted every piece of jewelry, every costume to look completely authentic.

I also wanted to shoot on actual locations, but Windsor was too
noisy and we could not get permission to shoot at Hampton Court.
Hever Castle in Kent was the family home of the Boleyns, and Henry
VIII first saw Anne in the window of its cobbled courtyard; we
wanted very much to shoot there. The castle today is in excellent
repair and, to my way of thinking, is quite the loveliest in the country—intimate, tastefully appointed—more a home than a castle. The
grounds surrounding it are magnificent.

Hever is now the country estate of Lord Gavin and Lady Irene
Astor and their family. We explained to them that we would like to
film some of our scenes at the castle and they enthusiastically offered
us their complete cooperation. We became warm personal friends,
and my wife and I spent several wonderful weekends with them at
Hever. On a subsequent trip to America they stayed with us at our
home in Palm Springs.

During the picture, gossip had it that Richard and Genevieve
were romantically involved. It may have been nothing more than a
lighthearted flirtation, but Elizabeth was convinced that she was

threatened. She telephoned Richard constantly, checking up on him, asking when he would be coming home.

The final scene of the picture was a very dramatic one. Henry confronts Anne in the Tower, but she refuses his royal pardon, preferring death to the disinheritance of her daughter. It was a key scene and we were nervous about it. To our dismay, the day we shot it Elizabeth decided to pay us a visit. A chair with her name on it had stood empty on the set throughout the shooting and, much as I liked her, I was glad it had. I was afraid her presence, her jealousy might affect Genevieve's performance. Now, when we needed Genevieve to be at her best, we were faced with this unwelcome visit. Elizabeth swept onto the set with her entourage and settled down into her seat.

Genevieve was fighting mad. She turned to Jarrott and me and said, "I'm going to give that bitch an acting lesson she'll never forget!" then took her position in front of the camera.

What seemed a misfortune suddenly turned into an advantage. Genevieve flung herself into the scene with a display of acting skill I have seldom seen equaled in my career. Then she stormed off the set.

Soon after filming finished, we had an end-of-the-picture party. The two actresses held court at opposite ends of the room. Richard very pointedly never left Elizabeth's side.

Anne of the Thousand Days was warmly received by the public and was nominated for ten Academy Awards: Best Picture, Best Actor, Best Actress, Best Supporting Actor, Best Art Direction, Best Cinematography, Best Original Score, Best Sound, Best Screenplay Based on Material from Another Medium, and Best Costume Design. Margaret Furse won for best costume design.

Genevieve was hailed by critics as the new Hepburn. Richard received great critical acclaim but lost the Oscar to John Wayne and *True Grit*. (I was competing against myself that year.)

Naturally, I began looking for another important historical subject with cinematic possibilities. Mary, Queen of Scots, was in the news because of Lady Antonia Fraser's big biography. I did not read it because I knew it was based on historical fact and was sure there was nothing in it we couldn't obtain from a study of history books.

The story was irresistible. Mary was a romantic figure of great mystery and appeal whose image I wanted to change from victim to active protagonist. By making her spirited and willful, with designs on uniting the thrones of Scotland and England, she would become more of an opponent, a threat to Elizabeth.

As in *Anne of the Thousand Days*, I wanted to film on the actual locations in which Mary lived out her life. I sent my production manager Bill Gray on an extensive reconnaissance throughout England and Scotland. He found that Hermitage, Bothwell's castle on the border, and Alnwick Castle were both available and he immediately made arrangements for us to use them.

Charles Jarrott directed *Mary, Queen of Scots*. We worked well together, our only disagreement coming about because he wanted to emphasize the religious aspects of the story—Mary's Catholicism in conflict with Elizabeth's Protestantism. I felt this was too heavy for general audiences, and he later agreed.

John Hale's script was excellent but complex and hard to follow. There was endless crosscutting between the lives of Mary and Elizabeth. I knew the long dissertations on Scottish law would mean little to American audiences. The problems seemed insurmountable, but Charles Jarrott was anxious to overcome them. He flew to Hollywood and we had several good sessions cutting and rearranging sequences. After two weeks we had a workable script.

We agreed from the outset that the best possible casting for Mary would be Vanessa Redgrave. Mary was known as the Long Queen: she was about six feet tall, and so is Vanessa. She fit the part physically, and we knew she could act it with great sensitivity and skill. Charles flew to London to talk with her on my behalf. They had lunch and hit it off beautifully. Fascinated by the challenge, Vanessa accepted the role at once.

I wanted Glenda Jackson for Elizabeth, but she was reluctant to play what was definitely a smaller part. For a time, the project hung in the balance.

Although without foundation historically, Schiller, in his famous play, *Maria Stuart*, took the dramatic license of having the queens actually meet. We decided to do the same thing and based the dialogue of their meeting on letters they exchanged.

Glenda still wasn't interested. She had played Elizabeth on television and was bored with the role. Universal's Edd Henry went to see her at her home in Greenwich and apparently impressed her, because she changed her mind.

But she insisted on doing all her scenes in three and a half weeks, before boredom affected her performance. All of her scenes had to be done first, which meant major reworking of the script. We wanted her, and we had to put up with it. That admirable actor,

Trevor Howard, said to Jarrott one day, "I've just spent over a year on *Ryan's Daughter*. Now I have to do this picture in three and a half weeks. Isn't there a middle way?"

Vanessa did not stop her political activities even though she was playing a queen. Weekends, she marched in the London rain for left-wing causes, and addressed the masses in Hyde Park. On location in the Loire Valley for scenes shot at Chenonceaux, she refused to eat in restaurants with the rest of us and sat out on the curb with the workingmen. I regarded her as a harmless case of English eccentricity. Her politics didn't interfere with her work, so I couldn't complain.

We shot the meeting of the queens on location in a forest near London. There was great excitement and anticipation on the set: the two actresses up for the race like thoroughbreds. As we started shooting, a plane roared overhead. Then another, and another, and another. Bill Gray frantically made calls and was informed that the airport had changed its flight pattern that morning and every plane landing at Heathrow would pass directly over us. Our sound equipment was useless for the most important scene in the picture.

Glenda and Vanessa shrugged and behaved like the troupers they are. The whole sequence had to be dubbed in the studio. The speeches were complex and charged with emotion, but both actresses played to the mechanical equipment with the same energy and style they had brought to their acting in the woods. I was dazzled by their skill.

I was proud of *Mary, Queen of Scots*. The execution scene was like a painting come to life. I was delighted with Charles Jarrott's work and was glad to see him go on to a very successful career for other producers.

Both *Anne of the Thousand Days* and *Mary, Queen of Scots* were royal command film performances. Each year one picture is chosen by the Queen's committee for a gala performance in London, with a member of the royal family in attendance. Her Majesty Queen Elizabeth II attended the premiere of *Anne*. She whispered to me as she shook my hand, "Thank you, Mr. Wallis. We're learning about English history from your films."

I made one more historical picture, *The Nelson Affair*, very different from Alexander Korda's picture of the forties starring Laurence Olivier and Vivien Leigh. In that movie, Emma Hamilton was an exquisite young beauty and Lord Nelson a handsome hero. In *A*

171

Bequest to the Nation, the play upon which I based my film, Terence Rattigan showed Emma and Nelson in tragic middle age. She had become hard and alcoholic—he was a sad, embittered man. I cast Glenda Jackson as Lady Hamilton and Peter Finch as Nelson. Margaret Leighton made a beautiful and touching Lady Nelson.

We shot in Dartmouth and several other seaside villages that still had the feel of the period. Our most beautiful scenes were shot in Bath, which still has a Georgian look. James Cellan Jones directed the picture and he did a very fine job.

CHAPTER 17

Louise and Martha

In 1962 my beloved wife Louise died of a stroke. She had been in failing health for some years but her death was a shock to us all.

I was in Hawaii filming a Presley picture when I first heard the tragic news. We were shooting at a marina. A mainland call came through for me on the dock telephone and I was told she was gone.

I couldn't believe it. Lillie, her faithful companion, found Louise's body in her bedroom. She had died during the night, her arm reaching out for the phone.

Heartsick, I flew back to California on the next plane. Services were private and she was interred at Inglewood Cemetery in a family plot alongside her mother and father.

But Louise Fazenda is not forgotten. Her gift of laughter endeared her to a generation of filmgoers. Her caring ways left a legacy of devoted friends. This warmhearted, generous woman gave so much of herself to the crippled children at UCLA hospital that a memorial fund has been set up there in her name.

Louise and I shared many wonderful years—highs, lows, happiness, heartache. No matter what happened to us personally or professionally, we admired and respected each other.

I cherish her memory.

On a spring morning fourteen years ago, I made one of the most eventful journeys of my life. It started out as a routine business trip to New York on American Airlines' Flight Two, but as I stood in line at the ticket counter, a very attractive lady caught my eye. She was blond, small-featured, dressed simply and elegantly in a Chanel-type suit, and I felt an immediate chemistry as she glanced back at me. (This eye-lock we later referred to as "the Flight Two Look.")

I recognized her. She was better looking off screen than on. Her name was Martha Hyer. Oddly enough, my sister Minna had brought her to my attention as a possibility for the feminine lead in *Gunfight at the O.K. Corral*. I turned her down for the part because she was under contract to Universal and I wanted options on the actress I signed.

I nodded. She nodded. She didn't recognize me. I could see she was trying to remember who I was.

I was seated on the plane just behind her, but the seat next to her was vacant. As soon as we were in the air, I tapped her on the shoulder and introduced myself. She had just been nominated for an Academy Award for her excellent work in *Some Came Running,* and I had read a *Life* magazine article about her headed "Nothing but the Best," referring to her good taste and business acumen in collecting French Impressionist paintings and antiques. I showed her color transparencies of paintings in my collection and felt an instant rapport. When a stewardess appeared saying that a gentleman across the aisle wished to join Martha for lunch, I was happy to hear her say she wanted to be quiet and alone.

I am a very shy man, personally. I didn't ask to join Martha nor did I feel I could ask her to join me. We talked in our separate seats, napped, played the waiting game. Just before the plane landed, I leaned forward and asked if I could give her a ride into New York. Very sweetly, she told me there was a studio limousine waiting for her. "What about tomorrow?" I asked. "Would you have dinner with me?"

"Thank you very much," she replied, "but I'm going to the country for the day."

I was disappointed but too proud to persist. I felt delicately but very definitely rejected. Resigned to not seeing her again, I leaned back and looked out the window.

After a count of about ten, Martha put her head around the seat, looked straight into my eyes, and said with a smile, "How about Monday?"

Monday night we went to Voisin for dinner, then on to a show and to Monseigneur, where we drank champagne serenaded by violins. I was smitten. I realized I had met a very remarkable human being.

Our "courtship" was a long, happy one. I traveled to see her on location in Miami, Paris, and Madrid. She worked for me in several pictures.

Martha is blessed with a good disposition and a quick, bright mind. No matter what happens, she handles it with strength and a smile. I feel relaxed with her. Always up—always happy—she sees the bright side of every situation and is a marvelous companion. She loves spectator sports as much as I do, enjoys travel, eats with gusto, and has an enthusiasm for life I find catching. Unselfish and generous in her efforts to please me, she never complains or acts possessive, never asks what I've done or where I've been. Her motto is "You hold the tightest with a loose hand."

A gregarious person, Martha mixes freely and easily with people, is kind, sensitive, affectionate. We laugh a lot—she has a great sense of humor. There are quiet moments with her but never a dull one.

Dining one evening in her beautiful hillside home, she surprised me with stone crab and key lime pie from Florida. We had spent many happy hours at Joe's Restaurant in Miami, so she telephoned and had them fly out my favorite dishes.

One birthday she called my office, asking me to cancel all appointments and spend the day with her. When I arrived at her house, a chauffeur-driven limousine was waiting. Martha's birthday gift was Disneyland—a complete set of tickets for every ride. We spent the day and evening like a couple of kids—enjoying the attractions, eating too much, just plain having fun.

We made wonderful trips to Taormina in Sicily, Bad Gastein in Austria, Capri, Venice, Mexico, Hawaii. Pre-honeymoons.

I'll never forget crossing to Naples on the Italian liner *Leonardo Da Vinci*. It was a happy cruise but we were puzzled and made uncomfortable by people's stares. I wore black sweaters and slacks almost exclusively at the time, and Martha and I seldom mixed with others on board. We are very private when we travel, enjoy our own company, and always request a table for two. Just before we disembarked, a fellow passenger and friend of mine from Hillcrest Country Club in Los Angeles came over and said, "Hal, I didn't want to bother you, but people have been speculating about you two. They finally decided that you are a Mafia don deported to Italy and Martha is your blond, young moll." We laughed about it but I stopped wearing my all-black gangster garb immediately.

I was happier with Martha than I had been for many years. We were married by a judge in Palm Springs, California, on December 31, 1966, with my son Brent and his wife Helen in attendance. A later ceremony was held at Temple Israel in Los Angeles, Rabbi Nussbaum officiating.

Martha decided to give up her career when we married and says she has never regretted it. From the beginning, our marriage has been a happy one. Martha's first husband was a very fine man named Ray Stahl, son of the famous director John M. Stahl. They lived in Japan and East Africa, where Stahl made films for television. He died of cancer far too young.

Martha moved from her lovely home into my house on Mapleton Drive. Her art collection and antique furniture blended perfectly with mine. She has a tremendous flair for decorating and I tease her that she redecorates after every film I make according to where we've been on location. After *Anne of the Thousand Days* and *Mary, Queen of Scots,* we went through our English period. After *Red Sky at Morning* and *True Grit,* we built a second home in Palm Springs to house our growing collection of Western Americana.

Actually, I had owned property on Tamarisk Country Club since the 1940s. I like to play golf and Martha and I both love that part of the country. The climate is marvelous and we have many friends living there.

Architect Harold Levitt designed an informal, Santa Fe-style ranch house for us. It is southwestern in feeling—adobe brick walls, red tile floors, beamed ceilings, and open fireplaces. Filled with Martha's Plains Indian baskets, rugs, and artifacts, it has just the informal atmosphere we wanted in our desert home.

We spend every weekend in Palm Springs and I am happiest there, never more relaxed or more comfortable. Martha and I walk on the golf course with our dog, watch football or other sporting events on TV, sit in the sun, golf, have massages, enjoy our hot tub and life in general.

Martha has been very good for me. We like the same things. We suit each other.

Rarely does a man find the one right woman to marry.

I was blessed.

I found two.

CHAPTER 18

Kate

At the risk of hurting the feelings of many great ladies of the screen, I must say that of all the actresses I have worked with, Katharine Hepburn is my favorite for many reasons: her intelligence, talent, dignity, integrity, wit, and humor being just a few.

There is no one quite like her. She is unique. Her delight in life is contagious. Sparks fly when Kate's around. Her enthusiasm and vitality recharge the batteries like the wallop of a good martini.

The most down-to-earth legend I have ever met, she is laser sharp and incisive, tough as rawhide, yet as quick and sensitive as the wingbeat of a hummingbird. I admire and respect her honesty, her sense of privacy, her life-style.

The lady's beauty is ageless because her spirit is young and always will be. No energy crisis there. A generation of would-be actresses have been inspired by her, as will generations to come. She is an untapped mine of inner resources: never feels sorry for herself; never complains; never lonely; never at a loss for living. There aren't enough hours in the day for her to do all she wants to do.

Because Kate is such a private person, she won't like my writing of the good she does in her own quiet way. She takes care of people; helps them; reads and cooks for blind friends; shares her indomitable spirit with those who need it most.

In the last days of Susan Hayward's life, Kate visited her regularly, bringing courage and comfort. She never told me about it. Susan's hairdresser did.

A friend of ours had a small stroke and was forced to walk with a cane. Kate sympathized, inspired her with stories of how she herself had overcome the crippling effects of a hip operation, and gifted her with a very special cane from a store in Westwood. The manager there said that Kate had placed a standing order for canes to be given to all who needed and couldn't afford them.

She could have been a great doctor, faith healer, painter, or president. As far as I'm concerned, Katharine Hepburn's face ought to be carved into the rock of Mount Rushmore. But of course, she's already a national monument.

I first worked with her on *The Rainmaker,* in which she played Lizzie, a small-town girl who longs for the man of her dreams. She was wonderful in the part. A watercolor portrait she did of herself as Lizzie is one of my favorite possessions.

Kate is intolerant of unprofessional behavior, and with Burt Lancaster, there was trouble. He was late on the set the first day and she gave him hell. She walked into the center of the sound stage and said: "I'm here; all these people are here; and if you're not going to be here on time we can't work." He learned his lesson and was on time for the rest of the shooting.

She attributes her punctuality to a childhood experience she's never forgotten. Her family was ready for a trip to Virginia—six of them in two cars. Her father drove off because the children were late. Now she says, "I think punctuality is something you learn young. Now I'm either on time or early. I think when one is late, it shows you don't care for the person you're meeting."

My most recent picture with her was *Rooster Cogburn.* Kate was delighted when I asked her to costar with John Wayne in the film. She was in London making *Love Among the Ruins* for George Cukor and when she heard that Duke was shooting location scenes for *Brannigan* in Piccadilly Circus, she drove over, walked straight up to him, put out her hand, and announced "I'm Katharine Hepburn and I'm so happy we're going to be in a picture together!" He couldn't have been more surprised.

Rooster Cogburn was a sequel to *True Grit,* with Duke again playing the one-eyed marshal and Kate as Eula Goodnight, a religious pioneer woman not unlike the character she portrayed in *The African Queen.* Martha and I wrote the first draft of the screenplay, and as we prepared a final script, I met with Kate frequently to incorporate her ideas and changes. In her home above Sunset in West Hollywood she served English tea and home-baked cookies. Sitting in a black leather chair, pencil in hand, a legal-sized pad of paper on her knee, she listened very intently and made notes as we talked.

Because she knew that I was coming, she had her questions and comments on the script fully prepared. She wrote dialogue, even whole dramatic sequences herself, and I usually incorporated them into the script. Most of her ideas were bright and right. When I didn't agree with her, I told her frankly why. She weighed my points carefully and was always agreeable to change. She was totally open-minded, free, and clear-sighted about everything.

I had an equally happy relationship on this picture with Duke. My preproduction sessions with him were held at his home in Newport Beach. We discussed the script at a big round table in front of picture windows framing the waters of the bay and the yacht basin. Interestingly enough, Duke also made notes on a legal-sized yellow pad while we talked.

I pulled together Kate's suggestions, Duke's, Martha's, and my own, and we finally had a workable screenplay. It was a collaborative effort. Charles Portis, author of the novel *True Grit* and creator of the Cogburn character, put a polish on the script.

Kate's wardrobe for the picture was a problem at first. She and Edith Head put her costumes together while I was away scouting locations, and when we shot the wardrobe tests, I realized they had made a mistake: Kate wore a dashing-looking hat with great style and a smart Gucci-type shoulder bag which was no good at all. I insisted on a floppy, cheap-looking Western hat which Kate improved by adding a scarf drawn over the crown and tied in a knot under the chin. The smart shoulder bag was out. Kate, the complete pro, didn't argue for a minute. She and Edith went over to Western Costume and selected a wardrobe of old clothes: ancient jackets and skirts just right for a preacher's daughter living in a remote Western village.

We left for location work in Oregon in perfect weather and began shooting at Bend. We did our river work at Grant's Pass on the Rogue. The scenery was magnificent, and our crew was a very good one. It was a happy picture.

Kate was wonderfully herself. She found the house we had rented for her in Bend too fancy and suddenly turned up in Bill Gray's motel room, announcing that it was the only place she would consider staying! Fortunately, he found a house she liked better, a modest, comfortable place at Sunriver next door to Martha and me, with a marvelous view of the Three Sisters Mountains. The studio had supplied Kate with a deluxe motor home, but she seldom used it. She preferred a makeshift dressing room made of tied-together flats set out under a shade tree.

Fortunately, the insurance people were not around when Miss Hepburn went white-water-kayaking down the dangerous Rogue. The assistant director came to me one day and asked, "How much does that woman [meaning Hepburn] mean to you? She's running the rapids in a twenty-one-foot kayak." It was something she had never done. A challenge, and she was thrilled by the experience. She swam regularly in the river (in khaki pants and blouse).

A very important sequence in the picture was Rooster and Eula Goodnight's wild ride down the rapids aboard a raft. Both Duke and Kate refused to use doubles. Off they went through the churning water with only a long pole for navigation. I held my breath needlessly. It would take a lot more than the Rogue River to capsize those two.

Kate was anxious to obtain a cutting from a particular spruce tree, the weeping spruce, a rare species that grows only in Oregon. She fired up the Forestry Department, a ranger volunteered his services, and they disappeared into the mountains in his Jeep. Late that evening she returned dusty, dirty, triumphant, with a sample of the spruce and several other precivilization plants.

Duke and Kate were on the set each day at exactly the time they were called, lines letter-perfect. Old pros. In a sense, they directed themselves, and it was just as well. Director Stuart Millar was too young and inexperienced to handle a film starring such strong personalities. I told him that unless the work improved, I would have to make a change. Neither Kate, Duke, nor I wanted to hurt him professionally, so I kept him on until the end.

Aside from this problem, we had a good time on location. Phyllis, Kate's English companion, would cook dinner one night and Martha the next. We sat on the floor around a wood fire and talked and laughed and relaxed at the end of a day's work. The ladies went antiquing in the small villages nearby and bought patchwork quilts, pine furniture, and Indian artifacts.

Martha supplied Duke and Kate with burlap bags full of her famous toll-house cookies. Duke called them corn-dodgers after the saddlebag biscuits Rooster shot up in the picture. He was so fond of them that he requested some years later from his hospital bed.

One day Duke was out on the golf course at Sunriver, giving lessons to his little granddaughter. He stood behind her, holding the club in her hands, demonstrating a swing. Her follow-through was so healthy she hit him under the eye with the end of the club, leaving ugly purple bruises. When he called to me about it, he said, "It's just your luck, you son of a bitch. The eye she hit is the one with the patch on it!"

We ran the rushes in the Tower Theatre in Bend. The first night we all agreed that the film looked very dark in the opening sequences but got better later and possibly didn't need reprinting. Then the owner of the theater came out on the sidewalk to meet me. He said he was a big fan of mine and had turned up the amps on the lights in the projection machines to make my picture look better. We didn't know where we stood on the dark/light issue for days.

One morning the wardrobe girl saw Kate walking near a cliff overlooking the river. "Miss Hepburn," she called. "You don't want to walk down that steep hill."

"Leave me alone, Agnes," Kate yelled. "I am aging my shoes."

Duke and Kate loved working together. Each was fascinated by the other. Wayne told Kevin Thomas, "She is the best. She knows everything that's going on, understands the slightest move by anybody. I thought I was the only one around who watched everything." She wrote about him in *TV Guide:* "He is a very, very good actor in the most highbrow sense of the word. You don't catch him at it."

At lunch one day Kate told us, "I love working with Duke, but he tells everyone what to do, bosses everyone around, and I'm the one who usually gets to do that. Now I don't get to."

I replied, "The next time he acts as if he knows everything, remind him of *The Alamo* and *The Green Berets.*"

Duke ad-libbed too much. When the director called him on it, he said disgustedly, "I haven't said lines just as they were written in a script since I worked for Mascot Productions." Kate was just the opposite. When Millar suggested she improvise dialogue in a scene, she said, "I can't do that. I'm sorry." When she didn't agree with his direction, she told him, "It doesn't matter. I'll play me. Duke will play him. We'll do what we always do. It'll be fine." When Duke frequently overacted, she calmly advised, "You're tippin' your mitt, old boy."

On my birthday Duke gave a party for me in the hideaway house we'd rented for him at Sunriver. It belonged to the owner and had a swimming pool and private putting green. Kate's brother was visiting and we all enjoyed a marvelous meal prepared and flown in from Seattle by Duke's good friend Canlis, the famous restaurateur. Champagne flowed freely and our stars relaxed. Kate teased Duke, "I'm glad I didn't know you with two lungs. You really must have been a bastard. Losing a hip has mellowed me—but *you!*" Duke fired back with a twinkle, "I can't bully ya 'cause I promised Jack Ford I'd be nice to ya."

Kate was a delight as neighbor, star, and friend. Everyone loved her. She gathered wild flowers and arranged them in old cans; stopped the car whenever she saw a waterfall and went swimming; vowed she wouldn't eat salmon again after visiting the hatcheries and seeing the fish milked. She went to the locations even when she wasn't involved in the scenes, rode a horse like a trouper (with only one hip), and brought tears to our eyes with her work. She told a newsman on the location, "I feel time is running out on me. I want to see and do everything."

One morning I woke up and pulled back the curtains to find we were fogged in—visibility zero. There were icicles on the windows and snow on the ground. I immediately made plans for packing up and moving to Arizona, but when I called the office in Bend, they didn't know what I was talking about. The weather was beautiful there and the company had moved to the location site. We had one hundred perfect shooting days in Oregon. The day we left, it poured.

Duke got through the picture with few symptoms of the fact that he was living on one lung until the last night. At the end of the shooting in Oregon, I gave a party for the cast at Sunriver. It was Halloween and Martha made a Duke-o'-lantern. She mounted the pumpkin on a pole outside the door, put a patch over one eye, Duke's old cowboy hat on top, and wrapped his bandanna scarf around the neck. We lit the candle inside as Duke walked up the path. He loved it. But it was bitter cold that night and the altitude finally got to him. During the evening he started wheezing and gasped, "I can't breathe." We rushed oxygen to him and he rallied, but I realized for the first time the strain under which he had been working.

We chartered a Continental 727 jet to take the crew back to Hollywood. When I called Kate to invite her for a farewell drink, she said, "I know your plans. I have my spies. You are going to drive to Portland and fly from there commercial while we will take the charter and all be killed." Before I left she told me to be sure there was enough liquor on board the plane so that "we will all have a good time and the crew will be happy." They were. It was a very wet flight and every member of the unit told her how much they loved and admired and enjoyed working with her.

Critics all agreed that the combination of these two screen giants was inspired casting, but they were divided in their reaction to *Rooster Cogburn*. Maybe they expected too much. Richard Cuskelly, staff writer on the Los Angeles *Herald Examiner,* reviewed the picture in the spirit in which it was intended: "When Katharine Hepburn's sand sidles up to John Wayne's brass the chemistry is more explosive than the nitroglycerin the pair sails with down Oregon rapids. Rooster and his lady gave me the best time I've had at the movies, rooting for the good guys, hissing at the bad, since Saturday matinées. The ribald relationship between these two improbable but irresistible characters is more than enough. Indeed, memories are made of this."

Rooster won the box office blue-ribbon award given each month by the National Screen Council on the basis of outstanding merit and suitability for family entertainment. Council membership comprises motion picture editors; radio and TV film commentators; representatives of better films councils; and civic, educational, and exhibitor organizations.

It was warmly received in England and I treasure the following cable:

> Despite wettest day of year Royal Gala Première of Hal Wallis's Rooster Cogburn last night lit up Leicester Square. HM The Queen and HRH The Duke of Edinburgh attended charity performance at Empire under auspices of Variety Club. Capacity sell-out house warmly applauded movie.

Duke is gone now and the world mourns. His courage and fighting spirit made him an even greater hero in real life than he had been on screen.

Indestructible Kate looks for higher mountains to climb, sets new goals, seeks fresh fields to conquer. She is a marvel. Evergreen.

CHAPTER 19

The first question I am asked in interviews or seminars is "What is a producer?" Most people think of him as a cigar-smoking cliché who raises enough money to make a picture. Or even puts up his own money (something I have never done). But that isn't the fact at all.

To be worthy of the name, a producer must be a creator. Packagers and promoters are not producers; they make deals, not pictures. When you find a property, acquire it, work on it from beginning to end, and deliver the finished product as you conceived it, then you're producing. Producers are men who, for better or for worse, merge the diverse talents of several hundred people in the common objective of making a film. He must be diplomat, organizer, strategist, planner, businessman, psychiatrist, juggler, midwife, and manager of egos. Above all, he is the decision maker. It's in his office where the buck stops.

I like the way Ron Haver of the Los Angeles County Museum of Art puts it: "A producer has ultimate responsibility for the design of a motion picture. To be successful he must possess a rare combination of taste, intelligence, patience, and shrewdness. He must be able to maintain a constant perspective throughout the making of a film, especially when his colleagues begin to lose theirs. The producer decides if a story is worth telling, how it should be told, and eventually how it must be sold. He influences the way the script is to be written by selecting writers who are most capable of achieving the effect he wants, often working with them from the rough drafts through the final revisions. He must choose the director, performers, cameraman, music, sets, and costumes as well as determining the deadlines and budget that are adequate to the style and needs of his film. It is his responsibility to follow through on the scoring of the picture, the dubbing, and the final editing. If all these key decisions and myriad daily details that accompany them are made with the necessary style, insight, and common sense, the result, more often than not, will be a motion picture of superior quality."

But the inner workings of the film industry today make it more and more difficult for the independent producer to function effectively. As the studios become spokes on a conglomerate wheel, one has to deal with new power bases: committees, for the most part, for whom the deal comes first. They seem to want to hit a home run every time they come to the plate. I've always believed the public is also interested in singles and doubles. Those in the latter group are the films I've always made and will continue to make.

I am currently in the process of putting together a picture called *Bradleyville*. It is an adaptation of Preston Jones's *A Texas Trilogy* and we were working together on the screenplay when he died. America lost a very talented playwright and I lost a good friend.

Bradleyville will be a medium-budget film focusing on the lives of the inhabitants of one small Texas town. It is a poignant drama that will make the kind of film seldom exhibited in today's marketplace. I look forward to the challenge with great enthusiasm.

But looking back has been stimulating, too. We had no idea in the thirties and forties that we were making classics in the "golden age of the cinema." People went to movies to see their favorite actor (how many knew the name of the director?) or to forget their problems and be entertained. Entertainment was a legitimate function of the medium then, and I believe it still is. Motion pictures should entertain, instruct, and inspire.

Life is good now. I have lived long enough to be honored with retrospectives of my work at the Museum of Modern Art in New York, the National Film Theatre in London, the French Cinémathèque in Paris, the County Museum of Art in Los Angeles, and the Desert Museum in Palm Springs, California.

In 1970 the National Association of Theatre Owners named me their Producer of the Year. In 1973 Her Majesty Queen Elizabeth II bestowed upon me the order of Commander of the British Empire, the coveted C.B.E. I was given an honorary doctor's degree by Northwestern University in Evanston, Illinois, in June 1979.

I'm grateful to the motion picture industry for a lifetime of excitement, achievement, and recognition. I've wined and dined with kings, queens, and presidents; traveled the globe; known lovely ladies; lived in good health with treasures and fond friends.

If I had to play it again, Sam, I'd play it exactly the same way.

A man couldn't ask for much more.

The following pages contain inter-office memos taken from Warner Bros. files which are now in the Archives of the University of Southern California in Los Angeles. They represent my involvement in all phases of production, as well as memoranda of significant meetings.

INTER-OFFICE COMMUNICATION

TO Mr. ___Paul Muni___ Date ___April 1, 1937___

FROM Mr. _Wallis___ Subject _"ZOLA"___

Dear Paul:

The dailies on the picture have been really
wonderful, but the scenes yesterday in the courtroom
and your big speech were magnificent.
Congratulations.

                    Sincerely,

                    HAL WALLIS

INTER-OFFICE COMMUNICATION

TO Mr. ___Henry Blanke___ Date ___April 8, 1937___

FROM Mr. _Wallis___ Subject _"ZOLA"___

After seeing the dailies, I was really quite
surprised that you and Mr. Dieterle even considered
re-casting and re-shooting the scenes with Cézanne.

I think the scenes are excellent, particularly the
long scene with Cézanne and Zola in the doorway
where he says goodbye to him. I don't know whom
you can get that could do it any better or more
naturally than he does. The man looked like the
part, and I think he gets it very well. It is
probably because you know the man in real life and
you cannot get the real personality out of your
minds, and it therefore affects your judgment of
the characterization and the scene.

There were several people in the projection room
while I was running, none of whom knew about the
discussion we had had about re-casting, and every
one of them commented on how fine and how natural
the man was in the scene.

                              HAL WALLIS

HW:ab

cc - Mr. Dieterle

INTER-OFFICE COMMUNICATION

TO Mr. _____Jack Warner_____ Date _____September 9, 1937_____

FROM Mr. _Wallis_ · _____ Subject _Première of ZOLA_

I hope that you are still sticking to the routine
that we discussed the other day for the opening
tonight; namely, to have only an overture and then
go into the picture.

I think it would be entirely out of keeping with
the nature of this picture to show a cartoon or a
short of any kind. If we are to run anything, I
hope it will be a newsreel with perhaps the war
stuff cut out of it, but please let's don't have
any cartoons on tonight, as it is just the type of
thing that would start the evening off in a bad way.
Somehow or other for a picture of this kind, the
people come keyed up to see a certain type of
picture, and I think we should keep them in that
mood and let them see only the picture.

                              HAL WALLIS

HW:ab

INTER-OFFICE COMMUNICATION

TO Mr. __Blanke__   Date __October 28, 1937__

FROM Mr. __Wallis__   Subject __"JEZEBEL"__

Wyler came up to talk to me and explain that he wanted John Huston to sort of represent him in preparing the last half of the script in collaboration with the writers and yourself. In other words, he apparently knows Huston personally, spends a great deal of time with him, and will see him at night, and he maintains that Huston knows exactly his feelings and thoughts about the script, and his views on the last half of it. He explains that he himself cannot devote the time to consult with the writers, and Huston apparently will be a sort of go-between operating between the writers, and you, and himself. In view of this, and in order to keep Wyler* happy on the picture, and to get a script out as quickly as possible, I have agreed to put Huston on the picture, and told Wyler we would try it out. In other words, I told Wyler that I did not want him to come in and start writing a new story, and that I would put Huston on on a trial basis to see if it did work out. Will you, therefore, get together with Huston and the writers, and let's see if we can't knock the thing out in another week or ten days, and get out a last half of the script so that we can let Huston go ahead on what he was originally hired for--a story with Bob Lord.

When you come in in the morning, come in and see me, and I will talk to you about the discussion I had with Wyler about the finish of the picture. You should know about this.

HAL WALLIS

HW:ab
cc - Tenny Wright

---

* William Wyler, director of *Jezebel*.

191

INTER-OFFICE COMMUNICATION

TO Mr. ____Blanke____ Date ___January 8, 1938___

FROM Mr. _Wallis_____ Subject _"JEZEBEL"_____

In spite of hell and high water and everything else,
Wyler is still up to his old tricks. In last
night's dailies, he had two takes printed of the
scene where DONALD CRISP leaves the house and DAVIS*
comes down the stairs and finds out that Pres is
coming. The first one was excellent, yet he took
it sixteen times.

Doesn't this man know that we have closeups to
break up a scene of this kind, and with all of the
care he used in making the closeups, certainly he
must expect that we would use the greater portion
of the scene in closeup. Yet, he takes the time
to make sixteen takes of a long shot. What the
hell is the matter with him anyhow--is he
absolutely daffy? Is he on the level when he says
he is going to speed up and try to get through?
If he is, this is a poor indication of it. Will
you please tell him I said so.

                                    HAL WALLIS

HW:ab

cc - Tenny Wright

---

* Bette Davis, star of *Jezebel*.

INTER-OFFICE COMMUNICATION

TO Mr. _____Henry Blanke_____ Date _____December 3, 1937_____

FROM Mr. _____Wallis_____ Subject _____"THE ADVENTURES OF ROBIN HOOD"_____

There is one thing that we will have to watch with Mike.* In his enthusiasm to make great shots and composition and utilize the great production values in this picture, he is, of course, more likely to go overboard than anyone else, because he just naturally loves to work with mobs and props of this kind.

I dropped in on him last night, and he was shooting a closeup of one of the knights who was answering Prince John, and the knight had one line to speak which probably took ten seconds and which will probably run about six feet on the screen. Instead of shooting a closeup of this man, as he should have done with a couple of squires in back of him or perhaps a piece of wild wall, he shot it at an angle, with the man in the foreground and shooting across the entire room, so that the entire room had to be lighted and approximately one hundred people were in the scene backing up this knight for his one line. These, of course, are the things that cost fortunes, and by the same token these are the same things where, if a little judgment was used, we could save fortunes.

Had he moved in and taken a closeup of this man, it would have taken a fraction of the time and we could have utilized the couple of hours last night for more important shots, getting into the fight, etc. As it is, Polito was running around having lights changed to get a proper highlight on one of the bow men in the extreme rear of the set, which, so far as I am concerned, is a lot of hooey.

Can't we make these people realize that a little judgment can save the Company a fortune, and when they have this sort of a shot, they should do it as a closeup and not as a production shot. After all, the man speaking the line is an extra man, and instead of cutting to him in a closeup as we should have done and getting back to Prince John immediately, we go into this huge production shot which took all of an hour or two to get, and used up valuable time.

* Michael Curtiz, director of *The Adventures of Robin Hood.*

I don't have to tell you again that the cost on this picture is mounting at a tremendous rate, and it is up to us to see that we economize where economy is possible. I did not try to stop Mike yesterday when he was on the crane and making beautiful production shots, because they were establishing shots and because they moved up to our principals and we immediately got into the story, but I do object to wasting time and money on unimportant characters and unimportant action.

I talked to Mike about this when I was on the set, and I wish you would follow through and see that he carries through accordingly. I need your help on this, because I know that you see Mike several times during the day and you are at all times in touch with what he is doing, but you must be in accord with my ideas and must be thinking the same way, not along the lines that Mike is thinking, and that is how big can he make every shot.

Also, when he gets into the fight stuff, please be sure that Mike doesn't over-shoot and get a thousand daffy shots of impossible gags, which as you know are liable to boomerang and make our scenes ridiculous. We must be very careful not to make the thing too wild with Robin escaping from a hundred men, so the quicker he gets out of the room and up on the balcony the better, and don't let him have Robin holding off a hundred men with a bow and arrow, or the audience will scream, and from that point on you won't ever get them back into the story again. This must be handled very carefully and worked out very carefully.

HAL WALLIS

HW:ab

cc - Tenny Wright

"THE ADVENTURES OF ROBIN HOOD"   February 10, 1938

Cutting Notes By Hal B. Wallis:

Shorten the last two credit cards.

After Much the Miller shoots the arrow at the deer,
cut right to Gisbourne saying "Come on men, follow
me." Take out the cuts getting him out of the
tree.

Fade a little quicker after the line "Fetch the
deer then," don't wait until they exit from the
shot.

When Flynn* runs across the banquet room, let him
run right up the stairs and climb up over the
balcony. Take out the business of grabbing the
shield and catching the arrows on it and throwing
the torch at the men--all those cuts that go with
it.

There's a little trimming that can be done on all
of Flynn's cuts firing the arrows at the men in the
chase, after he runs up on the parapet--the
beginning and the end of each cut--of Flynn's and
the other people. It may be just a few frames here
and there, but keep it moving from one to the other
in action.

Trim on the outside shot where the door finally
opens and Rathbone says "You infernal idiot." Pick
that up a foot or so later so that the door opens
right up on the cut.

Trim a little on the men chasing, two cuts before
the bridge cut. Cut a little on that chase shot
just before Flynn and Knowles.†

Take out the four cuts in the chase where Flynn
shoots the knight.

Have Rathbone†† come right in with the line "The
ransom, your Highness," after Rains§ hesitates the
first time.

* Errol Flynn.
† Patric Knowles.
‡ Basil Rathbone.
§ Claude Rains.

After the cut of Will strumming, come right back to Flynn on the line "You need a merrier tune, etc."

When Flynn exits from the scene, take out the man saying "The Black Arrow." End the scene with Flynn riding out and go to the next cruelty--the hanging, and pick that up a couple of feet later with the noose already around his neck reading the line.

The long shot of the caravan under the bough of the tree is too long--a couple of feet off anyhow.

After the line "Look, the Guards, quick," on the next cut, trim the last part of it.

After the line "They'll think they fell into a hornets' nest," cut to a long shot of the caravan, then back to the two in the bushes, "There they come."

Trim on the long shot just before Flynn says "May I serve you, M'Lady?"

Trim a little off the trumpeters at the beginning of the archery sequence, so that by the time that we're full in, they have the thing up. Have their trumpets right up to their mouths and we're faded in.

When we cut to the herald, the announcer, don't have him blow the trumpet. When we cut to him, the trumpet is already down. Go right to him on the dialogue.

Trim on the long shot where you're on the backs of Hale and Pallette.

There's one close cut of a trumpeter in that series of fast montage cuts, take him out.

Dissolve quicker on the men turning the targets round.

When Harry Carding gives the signal for the men to close in, cut. Don't have him ride out of the shot. Take out the second cut of Carding, not the first. Come right to Claude Rains' line "You're a very rash, young man." Take out Flynn laughing and kicking the men in the stomach, and all of that.

Trim at the beginning of the line "With Locksley
out of the way, we'll soon get rid of the rest."
Also, on that long, dolly-up shot at the opening
of the sequence, take a couple of feet off that,
where you cut to the group in the box.

When DeHavilland* looks off and sees Flynn in the
wagon, put in a cut of the wagon stopping, cut to
him seeing her, then change angles and have the
wagon pull out again.

Trim just a little-a few frames, a half a foot, a
foot, or whatever is necessary on all the cuts
from the shooting of the first arrow in the gallows
sequence.

After the escape through the city gates, we'll fade
out. We will fade in on Flynn climbing the wall,
and then cut to the two women sitting at their
embroidery work, and pick it up on the line as
discussed.

Dissolve from the Kent Road Tavern to the longer
shot of the group in front of the fire.

When you cut back from Best, have Rathbone already
with the door open, and he says "Guard," right on
the cut.

Start on the line "You've got it all in your stupid
head," take out "My lady's been condemned to death,"
in the tavern.

Take out that couple of cuts of Robin Hood's men
when they surround King Richard.

* Olivia DeHavilland.

197

INTER-OFFICE COMMUNICATION

TO Mr. _____ Michael Curtiz _____ Date _____ March 9, 1940 _____

FROM Mr. Wallis _____ Subject "THE SEA HAWK" _____

I am writing you separately about the boat shots
that were made yesterday, the breaking up of the
Spanish ship.

In connection with the action, we will have to get
a punchier, faster tempo with these shots on board
the ship. Here is the ship, supposedly sinking,
and Flynn and the other principals walking around
speaking their lines as though they were in a
drawing room and have all the time in the world,
and Flynn particularly has no drive in his
performance and in his delivery of lines. I don't
know whether or not he knows his lines, but if he
doesn't, we had better stop the picture until he
learns them, because the stuff as it is is not good.

We are putting a fortune into this picture, as
everyone knows, and if the actors are not prepared
to do their scenes properly, then I am not going
to start any more pictures of this kind with Flynn,
or with anyone else, who won't cooperate. Certainly,
their responsibility is a lot greater in view of
the tremendous difficulties under which we are
operating, and it seems little enough to ask an
actor to come prepared so that he can do his job
properly.

I want you to have a talk with Flynn and tell him
of my complaint, and that I expect him to do better.
The scenes on the boat where they are getting ready
to board the Albatross, are not good, and the
reason they are not good, is because the actors are
fumbling with their lines, and there is no drive
or no certainty in their performances. Instead of
thinking of the action, apparently they are
thinking of what they are going to say, and the
camera photographs this.

                    HAL WALLIS

HW:ab

INTER-OFFICE COMMUNICATION

TO Mr. _____Michael Curtiz_____ Date _____March 10, 1940_____

FROM Mr. _____Wallis_____ Subject _____"THE SEA HAWK"_____

Dear Mike:

The long shots for the big crowd, yesterday's dailies, were on the whole very good. There are some very effective shots, and they will undoubtedly help a great deal when cut into the picture.

There are two or three things which I want to comment on, however:

The first is, that the crowd was too big. The people looked like they were packed in like sardines, there was no room for anybody to move around and no feeling of the conflict, because they were packed in so solidly, that when they swang from one boat to the other, they landed right in the middle of a group of swordsmen, which in every case could have made mincemeat out of them. However, in the action, the people just land and go on about their business, while the Spaniards are busy waving their swords in the air all through the scene. The swords themselves looked very proppy and fakey. They looked like painted, wooden knives, and looked very bad in the scene, and there were so many of them waving in front of the camera, that it looked like a forest. It really killed the illusion. I hate to criticize this stuff in any way after you worked so hard and got such fine long shots, for on the whole, they will work out well when we cut in our close action, and I am only calling this to your attention so that you can correct it when you move in for your medium and closer shots, and don't have this same fakey action going on with those wooden swords waving around in the air in the closer shots. In other words, we can use the long shots up to a point, and then when we get to our closer action, let's shave it a little more realistic.

It also bothered me that in every shot, the Spanish ship was rolling while the Albatross was stationary. You got the definite feeling that the camera ship was motionless, while the other was rolling with the sea, and it seems to me that it would have been much better had we had both ships rolling. I don't understand why you didn't have. It would have been so much more effective and so much more realistic.

There's another thing in the dailies that bothered, and that bothered me the other day in a similar scene--I noticed when the sailors cheer for any reason, that a great many of them use a clenched fist in what is really the Communist salute. This is very noticeable, and I don't understand why you allow the people to do it. In every case where a shot of this kind occurs, we are going to have to cut away from it, and we have so many other reasons for cutting from shot to shot, that I would like to bring them to a minimum and eliminate some of the faults on the set. In any future action, will you please instruct the extras not to clench their fists when they wave and cheer, and see that someone on the set watches to see that they don't do it.

The principal thing that bothered me was the mass of people, that thick, milling mass that prevented you from getting any action into the scene and those fakey wooden swords waving around in the air in front of the camera. Please do your best to get more effective action in your closer shots so that we can cut away from the fakey stuff. Somehow or other, the extras in these sets didn't seem to work very well. The swinging from one ship to another--they were hesitant, they fell all over themselves, stumbled over the rails, and it didn't have the swift, adventuresome feeling that it should have had. They looked like a lot of old men who were scared to death of what they were doing.

I don't mean to be so critical, Mike, but I know that you would want me to be, as there can be no fault found when striving for perfection, which is what we all want.

As I said at the beginning, the long shots themselves, the setups and all, the boats coming together, are very effective, and I am sure that we can get as much film out of the stuff as we will need to make the sequence effective, but the

details are glaring, and we may as well correct
them in the closer action.

HAL WALLIS

HW:ab

cc - Henry Blanke
     Tenny Wright

INTER-OFFICE COMMUNICATION

TO Mr. ___Michael Curtiz___ Date ___March 27, 1940___

FROM Mr. ___Wallis___ Subject ___"THE SEA HAWK"___

Dear Mike:

I am quite concerned over the great amount of
whipping you are doing in the scenes in the galley.
In almost every scene you have these men going up
and down in long shots, medium shots, and closeups,
with the whips coming in and hitting the men as
they are rowing. As you know, we have been
cautioned by the Hays office against too much
brutality, and the way you have been shooting the
stuff, we won't be able to cut it out. You have
far too much of it, and it's going to become
offensive and repulsive. If you have any more
stuff still remaining in the galleys, please don't
do any more whipping or hold it down to a minimum
of action necessary. Also, I hope you are protected
on the individual cuts of the whippers and of the
men, so that we can play around with the film and
won't have to have all of these tie-up shots, where
you see the man whipping and the slaves in the same
shot. Not only does it become offensive, and not
only will the Hays office object, but I am afraid that
it will lose its effect if there is too much of it.

HAL WALLIS

HW:ab

cc - Henry Blanke
     Tenny Wright

INTER-OFFICE COMMUNICATION

TO Mr. ___Michael Curtiz___ Date ___April 1, 1940___

FROM Mr. _Wallis_____ Subject _"THE SEA HAWK"_____

I just want to be sure that when you shoot the exterior of the boats again, the capture of the Madre de Dios by the slaves, that you do not have any battle or any battle scenes--but rather do this all in a sinister, mysterious fashion, with just shadowy figures coming over the rail, dropping down on the deck, crawling around corners of hatches, and stealing up on individuals and Spanish sailors. I'm sure this will be much more effective than if we again go into one of those battles with everybody wielding wooden swords around.

Be sure that this is all done in sketchy lighting, as in the cabin scene where they burst in on the four Spanish soldiers around the table, they are all too brightly lighted, and those white, naked bodies, and those fat stomachs bouncing around, look anything but romantic, adventuresome men. Therefore, the less light you put on them, the better.

HAL WALLIS

HW:ab

cc - Henry Blanke
     Tenny Wright

INTER-OFFICE COMMUNICATION

TO Mr. ___Bacon_____ Date ___April 30, 1940___

FROM Mr. _Wallis_____ Subject _"KNUTE ROCKNE"_____

Dear Lloyd:

I saw most of the dailies I had missed the past few days, and on the whole everything is coming along very nicely.

However, there are one or two things that I wanted to discuss with you, but because of the fact that you are taking advantage of the good weather and working outside, I am writing.

First, I still feel that Pat* is overdoing it and you will still have to hold him down a little more.

The scene that I have reference to in this instance is in the locker room when he comes in and gives the boys the pep talk and walks up and down giving them the locker room talk, and again with that constant repetition of lines such as "down that field-right down that old field," etc., etc. Added to this he has now started a peculiar drawl which is undoubtedly characteristic to Rockne, but which, added to the other things he is doing, is putting it on a little too thick. This is the drawing out of certain words-for example, when he says we will get them in the second "haaalf" . . . He draws the word out and he did this three or four times in the speech. The last part of the scene was excellent-that is, where the man comes in and says-only two minutes to go, Rock-and where he went into the last bit of fight talk and where the boys all jumped up and ran out through the door yelling--that was great and was a hell of a kick in the scene but in the first part he again overdid the drawling and the new thing now of drawing out these words, so please watch this very carefully from here on.

Another thing I wanted to go over with you was the number--that is, the chorus girls singing where Rock gets the idea for the Four Horsemen and the shift. In the first place, I don't particularly like the angles and I thought it was rather uninterestingly photographed. You had the long shot and the medium long shot and then there were two or three close shots that panned up and down the line of girls but didn't mean anything in particular because no particular portion of the number in any of these shots was photographed . . . rather it was just a rambling camera that didn't do anything in particular. I thought we would have it shooting down the line-low camera shots and setups at the kicking shots, and while I realize the number as a number means nothing in the picture, at the same time it would have given

* Pat O'Brien, who played Knute Rockne.

us a little variety and gotten us away from shots
of football players all through the picture.

Another thing that bothers me even more than the
angles is the fact that the particular portion of
the number which impressed Rockne and was the
inspiration for the new shift was not dramatized.
Possibly that is because the number itself was not
cleverly enough designed so that it would bring
out a similarity in the girls' routine and that of
the actual shift. In any event, it doesn't quite
come off and I would like to shoot over a portion
of it, possibly having Matty King redesign a
section of the number so as to make the shift
clear-cut enough to actually give Rockne the idea.

Lastly, I don't particularly like the work of Owen
Davis. He doesn't seem to be a very good actor,
so watch him closely and try and get some of the
peculiar way he reads his lines out of him. He
seems to be on the amateurish side.

                         HAL WALLIS

HW:ca
cc - Mr. Fellows
     Mr. Wright

INTER-OFFICE COMMUNICATION

TO Mr. Lloyd Bacon   Date   May 1, 1940

FROM Mr. Wallis   Subject "KNUTE ROCKNE"

Dear Lloyd:

Last night's dailies were very nice. All of the
football stuff looked good and the low camera
setups were effective. I hope we get some more days
with these white clouds, as they certainly help to
dress the scenes.

The action was good and I liked the scene with
O'Brien and Reagan,* particularly the way O'Brien

* Ronald Reagan.

204

spoke his lines in that scene. He was more natural, and there was less acting and less effort to be the character, and really when he plays the scene more naturally, the stuff looks so much more effective than when he forces the characterization.

The one scene that I did not particularly like for this reason, was the one where he addresses the boys and tells them this is a beginning of a new season, and so on. In that one again, he went overboard just a little, particularly in the closer shot, and I thought he did too much of this bending-over business--he looked like he had a bad case of the cramps. He kept walking up and down bending over from the hips, had a pained expression on his face, and these are the things you will have to watch with Pat. Just don't let him overdo it. Everything else is coming along in fine shape.

There are a couple of cuts I would like you to pick up--one, a closeup of Reagan where he asks O'Brien, where O'Brien says "Just get in there and carry the ball," and a closeup of Reagan where he says "How far?" and then a closeup of Pat where he gives him a double take and says "Don't worry about it," or whatever his line is. I think pointing this up will be good for a laugh.

The scene with the kids, where he asks them what play they would call, and Isabel calls the forward pass play, is very cute.

HAL WALLIS

HW:ab
cc - Bob Fellow
     Tenny Wright

INTER-OFFICE COMMUNICATION

TO Mr. _____Henry Blanke_____ Date _____June 12, 1941_____

FROM Mr. _Wallis_____ Subject _"MALTESE FALCON"_

Huston's* second day's dailies are better than the
first, but I still feel that they are too leisurely
in tempo. I think my criticism is principally with
Bogart,** who has adopted a leisurely, suave form of
delivery. I don't think we can stand this all
through a picture, as it is going to have a tendency
to drag down the scene and slow them up too much.
Bogart must have his usual brisk, staccato manner
and delivery, and if he doesn't have it, I'm afraid
we are going to be in trouble. All of the action
seems a. little too slow and deliberate, a little
labored and we must quicken the tempo and the manner
of speaking the lines. Even the little scene where
Bogart answers the telephone at two in the morning,
his partner has been shot. The delivery of the
lines was a little too slow where he speaks off
stage and says, "where" etc. etc., and then before
he finally picks up the phone and dials it again
to tell somebody else about it, his secretary,
there is a long pause and this does not make for
the punchy, driving kind of tempo that this picture
requires. We must get away from this method of
delivering the dialogue, particularly on the part
of Bogart and whenever we have pieces of business,
it must be fast, there must be action in the
picture.

I know that this second day's work was almost all
shot before we told John about the slowness of
tempo on the first day, but now that he is familiar
with this fact the dailies from this point on
should show a marked change. The actual scene,
the setups etc. are fine. It is primarily a matter
of tempo and delivery.

                              HAL WALLIS

HW/b

cc - Mr. Huston.

  * John Huston.
 ** Humphrey Bogart.

INTER-OFFICE COMMUNICATION

TO Mr. _____Sam Wood_____ Date _____June 27, 1941_____

FROM Mr. _Wallis_____ Subject _"KING'S ROW"_____

I saw the wardrobe and makeup tests of ANN SHERIDAN,
and for the most part, I think they are okay. I
would definitely have SHERIDAN wear eyelashes
throughout the picture.

Most of the hairdresses are good. There are a few,
however, that are just a little too windblown, so
much so that the hairdress looks sloppy. I wouldn't
go quite to this extreme with her. The center parts,
the little hair ribbons and all of that, are good,
but don't have her hair too messy and unkempt.

The railroad station outfit, I think should be worn
with the coat, and in order to give a little life
to the costume, I think she could wear a scarf or
give her a brighter hair ribbon, not quite so gaudy
as the first check outfit that Kelly made for the
railroad station, but something along those lines.
The outfits now, are sufficiently simple for a girl
living on the wrong side of the tracks, but I think
we can color them up a little by accessories, a
bright ribbon, white collar on her dress etc., so
that we will be keeping our principal as attractive
as possible.

                              HAL WALLIS

HW/b

cc Messrs. WESTMORE
          KELLY

INTER-OFFICE COMMUNICATION

TO Mr. ___All Departments___ Date ___December 31, 1941___

FROM Mr. ___Wallis___ Subject ___TITLE CHANGE___

The story that we recently purchased entitled
"EVERYBODY COMES TO RICK'S" will hereafter be known
as . . . .

"CASABLANCA"

HAL WALLIS

INTER-OFFICE COMMUNICATION

TO Mr. ___Michael Curtiz___ Date ___June 4, 1942___

FROM Mr. ___Wallis___ Subject ___"CASABLANCA"___

Dear Mike:

Again I want to say that I don't think the Café is
dark enough. I think there is too much general
lighting and somehow or other the place doesn't seem
to have the character to me that it should have.
Either we should have something on the walls, some
matting or some decorations of some kind, or we
should have less general illumination. Everything
is much too generally lighted.

HAL WALLIS

INTER-OFFICE COMMUNICATION

TO Mr. _____Michael Curtiz_____ Date _____July 22, 1942_____

FROM Mr. _Wallis_____ Subject _"CASABLANCA"_____

Dear Mike:

I saw the dailies again last night after talking to you, and I feel the stuff will cut up all right, with the additional shots and retakes for which I asked you.

We cannot use Bogart's line "All right, Major, you're asking for it," because of censorship reasons which I explained to you. This would make Strasser's shot one of self-defense.

Therefore, we will want to pick up the line as it was in the script--"I was willing to shoot Renault, and I am willing to shoot you," and we will also want to retake Rick's speeches where he says "What are you talking about--anyway, thanks for helping me out--as soon as the plane goes," etc. This should be delivered with a little more guts, a little more of the curt hard way of speaking we have associated with Rick. Now that the girl is gone, I would like to see Rick revert to this manner of speaking.

                              H.W.

INTER-OFFICE COMMUNICATION

TO Mr. _____Owen Marks_____ · Date _July 23, 1942_____

FROM Mr. _Wallis_____ Subject _"CASABLANCA"_____

Will you please check the miniature shots of the
plane taking off from the Casablanca Airport in the
fog and see if the direction is right to match it
with the direction in which Rick and Rains look off
as they are walking out of the Airport near the end
of the picture?

Let me know, as the Miniature Department wants to
strike the set and I don't want to do this until
I am sure that what we have will cut properly.

                        HAL WALLIS

INTER-OFFICE COMMUNICATION

TO Mr. ___Don Siegel_____ Date ___August 1, 1942_____

FROM Mr. _Wallis_____ Subject _"CASABLANCA"_____

For the opening of the picture, immediately
preceding the montage of the refugees, we would like
to have a spinning globe-an unusual, interesting
shot, sketchily lighted. As the globe's spinning
slackens and stops, the camera zooms up to the
general vicinity of our locale, and at that point
you can dissolve to your montage.

Will you please discuss this with Mike Curtiz before
you shoot it?

                        HAL WALLIS

HW:og

cc - Mike Curtiz
     Tenny Wright

INTER-OFFICE COMMUNICATION

TO Mr. __Owen Marks__ Date __August 3, 1942__

FROM Mr. __Wallis__ Subject __"CASABLANCA"__

Dear Owen:

The following is the continuity that we would like you to follow in assembling the opening of the Black Market. If this works, it will eliminate the retake.

Start with the atmospheric long shots of the Black Market, and use Scene 135--with the American asking about the bus, the Englishwoman talking to the rug dealer, and the native saying "That is a job for Señor Ferrari." This latter shot was made today, and Mike added to this speech the line "You will find him at the Blue Parrot," and he points off. From this you will cut to the entrance to the Blue Parrot, which Mike shot today. From this you will cut immediately to the office with Ferrari, Annina, and Jan, and pick it up on the line "Of course I'm not saying I can get you exit visas or not, but incidentally, how much money have you got?"

From there on follow the cutting as you had it before, with Rick coming through the Blue Parrot and meeting Jan and Annina.

                              HAL WALLIS

HW: og

INTER-OFFICE COMMUNICATION

TO Mr. _____Leo Forbstein_____ Date _____August 4, 1942_____

FROM Mr. _____Wallis_____ Subject _____"CASABLANCA"_____

Dear Leo:

I want to use the song "Perfidia," a great deal in the scoring of "Casablanca," particularly through the retrospect.

HAL WALLIS

INTER-OFFICE COMMUNICATION

TO Mr. _____Owen Marks_____ Date _____August 7, 1942_____

FROM Mr. _____Wallis_____ Subject _____"CASABLANCA"_____

Attached is copy of the new narration for the opening of the picture.

There are also to be two wild lines made by Bogart. Mike is trying to get Bogart today, but if he does not succeed, will you get Bogart in within the next couple of days?

The two lines to be shot with Bogart, in the event that Mike does not get them, are:

> RICK:
> Luis, I might have known you'd mix
> your patriotism with a little larceny.

****

(Alternate line)

Luis, I think this is the beginning
of a beautiful friendship.

****

HAL WALLIS

INTER-OFFICE COMMUNICATION

TO Mr. _____Irving Rapper_____ Date _____

FROM Mr. _Wallis_____ Subject _"NOW, VOYAGER"_____

Dear Irving:

I saw the dock scenes and it didn't quite come off
to me. That is, the reaction of Davis'* appearance
and gaiety on Lisa and June. Perhaps it will cut
better than it looked, but the amazement at
Charlotte's transformation was not apparent enough.
I know that you have a couple of two shots of Lisa
and June that we can cut in while some of the ad
lib chatter is going on, but even so, they didn't
seem to make enough of Charlotte's appearance.
Possibly this is a fault in the writing of the
scene, but it seemed most matter of fact on Lisa's
part, after the farewells between Charlotte and her
boat companions, to say "Well, come on. We had
better get you through the Customs."

I think it would help the whole scene a great deal
if you were to pick up a two shot of Lisa and June
looking in Charlotte's direction as she is
descending the gangplank, with both of them wide-
eyed and open-mouthed with amazement. There you
could have the first interchange of looks between
them which would heighten the value of the two
shots later on. You might even have a line or two
of dialogue between June and Lisa. I think this
is very necessary as the whole purpose of the dock
scene is to get over Charlotte's amazing
transformation, and this does not quite come off.

                        HAL WALLIS

HW:og

cc - Al Alleborn

* Bette Davis.

INTER-OFFICE COMMUNICATION

TO Mr. ___Irving Rapper___ Date ___April 11, 1942___

FROM Mr. ___Wallis___ Subject ___"NOW, VOYAGER"___

Dear Irving:

The shots at Laguna were very lovely, and I thought the scene very well played. It is unfortunate, however, that the dialogue was partially obliterated by the surf noise. Undoubtedly a good deal of this will be overcome by the closeups, and then, if the noise in the remaining shots is still too great, we will dupe new sound track to the picture on Stage 9 after the sequence is cut.

                              HAL WALLIS

HW:og

cc - Messrs. Warren Low
             Tenny Wright
             Al Alleborn
             Sherry Shourds

Memorandum of a talk held with Jerry Lewis at the Arizona Biltmore Hotel in Phoenix about 5:30 P.M. on February 2, 1952.

I told Jerry that I wanted to have a talk with him, not to influence him in any way or to get him to make any decisions, but merely to be sure that he was fully acquainted with the negotiations and the conversations that had been taking place between his agents, Lew Wasserman and Taft Schreiber and Mr. Hazen. Jerry claimed to know nothing about the details of these talks and knew only that certain meetings were being held.

I told him that we had started negotiations with MCA early in 1951 with a view to our purchasing a one-third interest in the stock of York Corp. for approximately $1,000,000 and that there had also been talk the same time of spreading the remaining pictures under our contract so that in effect we would be making one picture a year for our own account and York Corp. would be making one a year and it was presumed that inasmuch as we had a one-third interest in York Corp. that we would be making their so-called outside pictures.

I told Jerry that because of the Screen Associates' lawsuit, all of these negotiations at the suggestion of MCA were put off until the lawsuit could be concluded one way or another and that we have the assurance of MCA that everything would be worked out as soon as the lawsuit was out of the way.

I explained to Jerry that about a week or ten days ago at the request of Taft Schreiber and Lew Wasserman, Mr. Hazen journeyed to California to continue the negotiations, only to be told in the first meeting after his arrival here that the proposed sale of York Corp. stock to us was out, and that the spreading of the pictures could be accomplished only if we agreed to the following:

1. That we reduce our commitments from eight pictures to seven pictures.

2. That we postpone the April picture 1952 and that we make a picture (one picture) with Martin and Lewis prior to the end of 1952.

215

3. That in the year 1953 Martin and Lewis would make two consecutive pictures in the York Corp. or for their own account, and that during this calendar year we would not be permitted to make a picture. Consequently, we would be without a Martin and Lewis picture from the Fall of 1952 until the early part of 1954 and I explained we could not stop our operations to this extent.

4. That for the first three years of the seven-year arrangement we would make one picture a year and that Martin and Lewis would make one picture a year, but that in the last four years Martin and Lewis would have the right to do two outside pictures for their own account, which would negate the very purpose that the spreading of the pictures was supposed to accomplish; namely, to make not more than two a year.

5. That there were other contract clauses, that is, clauses existing in the present agreement that Mr. Wasserman wanted removed.

I also told Jerry that this was put to us on a definite take it or leave it basis and that we were told that if we failed to take it, we would have considerable trouble in getting the balance of the pictures under our existing contract in and produced.

I also told Jerry that we did not like this sort of ultimatum and that we had advised Wasserman and Schreiber that we would continue to operate under our existing contract and we would forget the matter of trying to spread the pictures.

I also told Jerry that during the course of the talks between Mr. Hazen and Mr. Schreiber that Mr. Schreiber pointed out that they had to meet a payment of $160,000 to Screen Associates sometime in April and requested that we loan them the money to make this payment. I also told Jerry that after Mr. Hazen and myself had discussed the matter we decided that we could not meet the severe terms and conditions as laid out by Wasserman and that Mr. Hazen so advised Mr. Schreiber, and told him at the same time that regardless of our inability to get together on the over-all terms of the buy-out of the stock and the spreading of the pictures that we nevertheless would agree to loan them the $160,000 and that we also agreed that beginning with the next Martin and Lewis picture in April we would be ready and willing to pay the boys the compensation of $150,000 per picture. I also told Jerry that the morning following the conversations held between Mr. Hazen and Mr. Schreiber concerning the foregoing that Mr. Wasserman telephoned Mr. Hazen and told him that they did not want the $160,000 loan and they did not want the $150,000 per picture for the boys, and that unless we agreed to the terms and conditions of the spreading of the pictures as laid out by Wasserman they did not want anything else apart from that.

I told Jerry that that was the way the matter stood at present and that we stood ready and willing to proceed with the loan and with the increased compensation to $150,000 per picture.

Jerry professed ignorance of all of the foregoing and seemed particularly put out by the fact that Schreiber had asked for an increase in the boys' salary because he had previously repeatedly told Mr. Hazen and myself that they were very grateful to us and that they would never ask for an adjustment in the contract. He was quite put out about the fact that Schreiber had discussed an increase without first talking to Jerry and Dean about it.

Jerry further stated that he had a meeting with MCA officials next Tuesday, that he assumed that the foregoing matters would be discussed with him at that time. He said he would be very interested in hearing just what they had in mind when they laid out the severe conditions with us, and that he would further discuss the matter with me after his meeting on Tuesday.

I told him that regardless of his expressions to Mr. Hazen and myself about his willingness to work out the contract at the present rate of compensation, we nevertheless were ready and willing to make the increase as outlined to MCA and to him.

I also pointed out to Jerry the fact that because of the Screen Associates' lawsuit they had lost their outside picture in 1951 and that we had

217

gratuitously given them our picture JUMPING JACKS in which they now had a substantial interest and which we were under absolutely no obligation to turn over to them. I also pointed out that by doing this we were taking ten weeks out of the current year, which made it that much more difficult for us to get in our own two pictures this year. Jerry said he understood and appreciated all of this.

MEMORANDUM

On Monday, July 20, 1953, Mr. Wallis and I went to Las Vegas to keep an appointment with Howard Hughes which had been set up by Loyd Wright. We arrived in Las Vegas by plane at noon and were met by Robert Adler, Mr. Hughes' representative, who informed us that Mr. Hughes had made a reservation for us at the Flamingo Hotel. We informed him that we had made our own reservation at the Sands and we felt we would have to keep those reservations.

Mr. Adler took us to the Sands and informed us that he would phone back later in the day and fix the exact time when we would meet with Mr. Hughes. Mr. Adler told us that Mr. Hughes had requested Mr. Tevlin, who is the head of the studio in Hollywood, to come to Las Vegas to attend the meeting, and that Mr. Tevlin would be arriving about 7:30 that evening. We discussed a tentative meeting after dinner.

Mr. Tevlin phoned us shortly before 10:00 o'clock, to meet him at the Flamingo, which we did. Shortly thereafter Mr. Hughes joined Mr. Tevlin, Mr. Wallis, and myself in Mr. Tevlin's room at the Flamingo where the discussions took place.

Mr. Wallis stated to Mr. Hughes that our company had completed its contract with Paramount but we had been approached to renew it. Mr. Hughes asked what we were going to do with the assets of the company (actors' commitments, properties, etc.). Mr. Wallis told him that we wished to sell them, and that was one of the things we wanted to discuss with him.

Hughes then said to Mr. Wallis that he wanted Mr. Wallis to come into his organization, that he needed him badly, and that he would give him any kind of a deal that he wanted. Mr. Wallis said that we were principally interested in selling some of our assets, and that after we had sold the assets, it might be possible that Mr. Wallis would work out some basis of producing pictures based on the story material that would be sold to RKO. Mr. Hughes then asked what the assets were, and I enumerated them to him. Mr. Hughes then said that RKO could not pay cash, but would give its notes for the purchase price. I told him that this would not be satisfactory and he asked why it was that we wanted cash, that certainly we did not need the cash, and that he would make the notes payable as the assets were consumed. He said that he thought we would make a better deal with him since he needed the assets and Mr. Wallis, but that the payment would have to be by way of notes. With regard to the players' contracts, he made the point that the uncertainty of survival, or the possibility of injury or disfigurement would have been a factor to be taken into account in the matter of value; also the matter of performance by the artists. I told him those were all factors which could be taken into account.

He then said that he had some other people waiting for him, and that he could dispose of them in twenty minutes, and asked to be excused for that length of time. He asked that in the meanwhile I enumerate to Mr. Tevlin the assets that we wished to sell and the value we placed on them.

I then told Mr. Tevlin that I did not want to wait until Mr. Hughes returned and discuss the matter of payment in the form of notes as I did not want to argue with him about the credit or financial soundness of RKO; that speaking for myself and for my own interests, I was not interested in taking notes, but wanted cash. I asked Mr. Wallis how he felt about this, and he stated to Mr. Tevlin that he felt the same way, that he would only want cash for his interest.

Mr. Wallis and I returned to Los Angeles on the 1:15 P.M. plane the following day. Mr. Tevlin had called Mr. Wallis prior to our departure to advise us that Mr. Hughes wanted to speak to Mr. Wallis and would phone him before we left. However, Mr. Hughes did not reach Mr. Wallis before we left Las Vegas.

Mr. Tevlin was on the same plane as we were, but
we did not get into any discussion about the matter.
Mr. Tevlin's only comment was that he thought
Mr. Hughes had some idea that he thought he wanted
to discuss with Mr. Wallis. That was the only
comment made.

                              JOSEPH H. HAZEN

JHH:O

INTER-OFFICE COMMUNICATION

TO Mr. _____ Peter Glenville _____ Date _____ June 14, 1963 _____

FROM Mr. _Hal Wallis_____ Subject _"BECKET"_____

The dailies yesterday from the high shot were very
effective. I assume you also made Becket's
entrance from this angle this morning.

I also saw the dailies from the day before yesterday-
the Cloisters with Becket and the Monks-and they,
too, were excellent.

There is only one request I would like to make and
I have asked for this before, and that is not to
cut quite so closely in the camera. For example,
the shot at the end of the Cloisters with the 3
Barons in the foreground was started with all of
the Monks already there. I should like to have
seen them approaching with Becket starting down the
steps and the Monks walking towards us. It would
be very helpful if you would overlap your action,
particularly for entrances and exits, so that we
are not wedded exactly to almost cutting on the
frame from one shot to the other. It would have
been very effective after your pan shot of the Monks
and Becket going past the camera, to cut back to
the extreme long shot to see the Monks approaching,
but we do not have the footage to do it. It is only
a few feet more of film here and there that will
give us a little bit of flexibility and I would
appreciate it if you will do this in the future.

INTER-OFFICE COMMUNICATION

TO Mr. __Peter Glenville__ Date __July 3, 1963__

FROM Mr. __Hal Wallis__ Subject __"BECKET"__

Dear Peter,

When you do the extreme high shot of the
excommunication and the exit of the King, I would
like to suggest that we make the shots-particularly
the exit of the King for the finish of the picture-
in front of as well as in back of the Crucifix.
In other words, we will just lift the Crucifix out
and do the shot again of the King's exit. I think
it might be all right to have it in for the shot
of the excommunication, but we may want to end the
picture on the solitary figure of the King without
the Crucifix in the foreground.

Also, while you are up there, what would you think
of having a shot from that angle of the 4 Barons
approaching and with BECKET and JOHN on the steps?

                              HAL WALLIS

INTER-OFFICE COMMUNICATION

TO Mr. _Peter Glenville_ Date _July 29, 1963_

FROM Mr. _Hal Wallis_ Subject _"BECKET"_

Dear Peter,

When we shoot Scene 45, the two men walking their
horses at the hunt, I feel we should open the scene
with them walking along-they hear the sound of the
hunting horn, which is a straight cut from Scene
44. They look back to the direction of the sound
and the King should start the scene with the line-
"We've lost them"-then continue on with the scene.

I feel there should be some reaction to the horn
as Scene 45 is a straight cut from 44.

                    HAL WALLIS

INTER-OFFICE COMMUNICATION

TO Mr. _Peter Glenville_ Date _July 30, 1963_

FROM Mr. _Hal Wallis_ Subject _"BECKET"_

Dear Peter,

I know that you are doing everything possible to
make progress but I do hope we will be able to do
better for the balance of the picture than you did
yesterday, as evidenced by the attached Floor Diary.

This was not a particularly large set yesterday but
you will note that we did not get a shot until 2:35
P.M. Some minor delays were incurred in waiting
for Miss Hunt, and again waiting while she put on
some black stockings. I think you should tell Miss
Hunt that we expect a little more professional
behaviour from her.

In all, we got just four shots yesterday and I hope you will make every effort to complete this set within the scheduled time by Wednesday night, and on the remaining sets to be shot, as every day that we lose adds greatly to the cost of the picture.

We are already 7 or 8 days behind schedule and I do not want it to increase any more.

I will appreciate whatever you can do to help.

HAL WALLIS

INTER-OFFICE COMMUNICATION

TO Mr. _____Henry Hathaway_____ Date _____September 4, 1964_____

FROM Mr. _____Hal Wallis_____ Subject _____"SONS OF KATIE ELDER"_____

Dear Henry:

Please give some thought to the following and then we can discuss the various points in person.

1. I feel the fight sequence in the Interior Lupon Ranch should be planned for the studio. To do it on location would require building and dressing the interior, lighting, which would mean additional lights, electricians, and added time of location expense.

2. Interior of Bank. I feel we should do the establishing shot, shooting over the banker at the boys approaching the bank, on the location and do the whole interior of the scene on a set at the studio. This for the same reasons outlined above. The bank scene is 2½ pages, lighting and operation will be much more difficult on location and it will require added time for the whole company on the location to do the interior there.

3. I would like to do the scene with Mr. Peevey and the boys on the front porch, Exterior General Store, on the location, which again would eliminate dressing and lighting and interior on the location.

4. Blacksmith Shop. Would like to do all interiors here at the studio and possibly some of the exterior close action on the front with Harry Evers and Old Charlie, Tom bringing Dave in, Hastings shooting through the window, etc. It is possible, of course, when you are shooting up there that you can work some of these into better advantage than saving certain cuts for the studio and I will, of course, go along with you whenever it is feasible to do it there.

5. Heislman's. I would like only entrances and exits on the location and do all scenes with Heislman here at the studio.

6. Interior Sheriff's office, Jail. (Except for shots over the boys in the cell towards the street, at the studio. Of course, shots such as Harry and Old Charlie in the doorway, seeing Billy's horse coming back, calling Ben, etc., would be done on location.)

I know you are going to make as good time as possible, but in two areas at least I feel we could now cut a day each out of the Interior Sheriff's Office and Interior Lupon Ranch where I think we have scheduled too much time for the number of pages involved.

When we originally budgeted the picture, I believe there was an allowance of 10 or 11 days on location. This has now been expanded to approximately five weeks and I need not tell you the cost of keeping 125 or 150 people on location with living expenses, traveling time, etc. We plan a booster crew of electricians for the location, but to bring added electricians to rig and light interiors that we could just as well do here would mean great savings in many directions.

Added to the foregoing cost, of course, would be the duplication of the same sets on exterior and interior which is a considerable item.

We are going considerably higher in cost than
originally planned as well and I will appreciate
your help which I will need in reducing unnecessary
expenditures wherever possible.

HAL WALLIS

HW:in

INTER-OFFICE COMMUNICATION

TO Mr. __Charles Jarrott__ Date __June 28, 1971__

FROM Mr. __Hal Wallis__ Subject __"MARY QUEEN OF SCOTS"__

Dear Charles,

I have been thinking again about Sc.87 - Ext.
Courtyard. I really think all we need is the shot
from up high on RICCIO's body being hurled from the
window and landing on the cobbles, and then a
closer shot of him. I don't think we need ANDREW
coming in, or BALLARD.

In Sc.89 MARY says: "Find Andrew. If he has gone
it will mean he has fled to get Bothwell." This
pretty well takes care of him. Father BALLARD
coming in, picking up RICCIO was all right if we
had kept Sc.92, where BALLARD says: "There lies
David-I buried him."

I don't think we need spell out any of these things
and after Riccio crashes to the cobbles, it is a
very good cut to MARY in the next scene saying:
"You Judas."

H.W.

INTER-OFFICE COMMUNICATION

TO Mr. __Charles Jarrott__ Date __June 25, 1971__

FROM Mr. __Hal Wallis__ Subject __"MARY QUEEN OF SCOTS"__

Script changes

Dear Charles,

I have a cut that I think we should make both in the interests of saving footage, which we badly need, and because it does nothing to advance our story.

On Page 82, Mary, instead of saying "Then find Father Ballard and tell him to wait in the burial vaults for us." would say: "Then find Father Ballard and tell him to wait at the back gates of the Castle."

Then we would lose Scenes 91, 92, and cut to Scene 93, which could be the Ext. Gates which we used in ANNE. Two of the Borderers could be opening the gates, disclosing our group, and then carry on with the rest of the dialogue and have them ride out of shot.

I went over all of this on the back lot with Terry this morning, as well as a means of shooting Riccio's body falling into the Courtyard, Andrew riding through, and Ballard coming to pick up Riccio's body, all of which I think you will like. Terry can explain it in detail.

I would also like to lose Bothwell's first speech at the bottom of Page 86 (Sc.93). He could be helping her onto the horse with his preceding line, and then have him say: "Are you comfortable, Madam?" I think the situation is too tense for Bothwell to get "cute" at this point. I would just as soon lose the entire speech, except that we will probably need some dialogue to get Mary mounted.

H.W.

FILMOGRAPHY

For Warner Brothers:

1930

Sally
The Dawn Patrol
Little Caesar

1931

Five Star Final

1932

I Am a Fugitive from a Chain
  Gang
Dr. X
Cabin in the Cotton
One Way Passage
The Match King

1933

Mystery of the Wax Museum
Gold Diggers of 1933
Footlight Parade
The World Changes

1935

Sweet Adeline
G-Men

A Midsummer Night's Dream
The Story of Louis Pasteur
Captain Blood

1936

Anthony Adverse
Green Pastures
The Charge of the Light Brigade
God's Country and the Woman
Stolen Holiday

1937

Green Light
Marked Woman
Call It a Day
The Prince and the Pauper
The Go Getter
Kid Gallahad
Slim
The Life of Emile Zola
Marry the Girl
Confession
It's Love I'm After
Back in Circulation
That Certain Woman
First Lady
The Perfect Specimen

1956

Hollywood or Bust
The Rainmaker

1957

Gunfight at the O.K. Corral
Loving You
The Sad Sack
Wild Is the Wind

1958

Hot Spell
King Creole

1959

Last Train from Gun Hill
Don't Give up the Ship
Career

1960

Visit to a Small Planet
G.I. Blues

1961

All in a Night's Work
Summer and Smoke

1962

Blue Hawaii
Girls! Girls! Girls!
A Girl Named Tamiko

1963

Wives and Lovers
Fun in Acapulco

1964

Becket
Roustabout

1965

The Sons of Katie Elder
Boeing Boeing

1966

Paradise, Hawaiian Style

1967

Barefoot in the Park
Easy Come, Easy Go

1968

Five Card Stud

1969

True Grit

1970

Norwood

For Universal Pictures:
1969

Anne of the Thousand Days

1970

Red Sky at Morning

1971

Shootout
Mary, Queen of Scots

1972

The Nelson Affair
The Public Eye

1974

The Don Is Dead

1975

Rooster Cogburn

INDEX